EVERYMAN, I will go with thee,

and be thy guide,

In thy most need to go by thy side

GEORGE BERKELEY

Born at Dysert Castle, near Thomastown, Co. Kilkenny, Ireland, 12th March 1685. Educated at the Duke of Ormond School, Kilkenny (1696–1700), and Trinity College, Dublin (1700–7). Came to England, 1713, and later that year went as chaplain to Lord Peterborough to Leghorn. Returned to England, 1714. Travelled in France and Italy, 1716–20, returning to London in 1721. Dean of Derry, 1724. Married Anne Forster, daughter of a former Irish judge, 1728. Spent three years in America, 1728–31; Bishop of Cloyne, 1734. Resigned the bishopric, 1752, and retired to Oxford, where he died on 14th January 1753.

The present text of *A New Theory of Vision* is from J. Stocks's edition of the Collected Works (2 vols., 1784). The passages in square brackets were added by Berkeley in his 1734 edition. The other writings included in this volume are: *A Treatise Concerning Human Knowledge*; and *The Three Dialogues between Hylas and Philonous in Opposition to Sceptics and Atheists.*

BERKELEY

A New Theory
of Vision

AND OTHER WRITINGS

INTRODUCTION BY
A. D. LINDSAY
(afterwards 1st Baron Lindsay of Birker)

DENT: LONDON
EVERYMAN'S LIBRARY
DUTTON: NEW YORK

All rights reserved
Made in Great Britain
at the
Aldine Press · Letchworth · Herts
for
J. M. DENT & SONS LTD
Aldine House · Bedford Street · London
First published in Everyman's Library 1910
Last reprinted 1963

NO. 483

INTRODUCTION

GEORGE BERKELEY was born near Thomastown, in County Kilkenny, on the 12th of March 1685. He entered Trinity College, Dublin, at the age of fifteen, and was elected to a Fellowship there in 1707. Trinity at the time was feeling the influence of the discoveries of Newton and Boyle, and Locke's *Essay on the Human Understanding*, the philosophical exposition of the new empiricism, was already well known. In 1705, Berkeley had formed a society to discuss the New Philosophy, as it was called. The Essay had more influence upon his thought than any other philosophical writing. Berkeley is Locke's direct successor, and his main philosophical doctrines are suggested by problems which Locke had left unsolved or had solved unsatisfactorily. His one great philosophical principle—the impossibility of anything existing independently of perception—occurred to his mind during this early study of Locke. We know from his *Commonplace Book* that already in 1706 he was convinced that he had found here the key to the difficulties and inconsistencies which he found in the Essay. However much in later works he enlarges his exposition of this principle and defends it against new objections, there are certain assumptions of Locke's philosophy which he never questions, and which essentially determine his statement of philosophical problems.

Berkeley's first publications were two small treatises, entitled *Arithmetica* and *Miscellanea Mathematica*, published in 1707. His first important work, the *Essay towards a New Theory of Vision*, appeared in 1709. In the next year, when he was only twenty-five, he published his *Treatise concerning the Principles of Human Knowledge*. In 1713 appeared the *Dialogues between Hylas and Philonous*.

Berkeley spent the years between 1713–1721 in England or abroad. Shortly after his return he was made Dean of Dromore, which office, along with his position at Trinity College, he resigned on being made Dean of Derry in 1724. The next years of his life were devoted to the furtherance of a proposal for establishing a great missionary college in Bermuda, from which America was to be evangelised. Berkeley was ready to give up his Deanery to become Principal of the new college. His extraordinary powers of persuasion were applied with such effect to the House of Commons that Walpole promised a Government grant of £20,000. In 1728, having made all preparations, he sailed for America, going first to Rhode Island to interest New England in his scheme. But when the persuasive author of the scheme was no longer there to trouble them, the Government cooled, and Berkeley, after waiting in vain for the promised support, was forced to give up his scheme and return home disappointed. During his stay at Rhode Island he composed *Alciphron, or the Minute Philosopher*—the largest of his works. It was published shortly after his return to England in 1732. In it Berkeley applies his philosophical doctrines to Christian Apologetic. In 1734 he was made Bishop of Cloyne. In the same year appeared his *Analyst*, a treatise in which he applies his principles, not very successfully, to Newtonian mathematics. Ten years afterwards he published his last work, *Siris*, or *A Chain of Philosophical Reflexions and Enquiries concerning the Virtues of Tar-Water and divers other subjects connected together and arising one from another*, an extraordinary miscellany of reflections on medicine, vital spirits, and metaphysical principles. *Siris* is striking as showing the influence of Plato in Berkeley's thought. It is far removed from the empiricism of Locke. At the same time it lacks the vigour and consistency of his earlier writings, and is more noteworthy for occasional interesting suggestions and admissions than as a serious philosophical treatise.

In 1752 Berkeley left Cloyne for Oxford, where he died in the next year.

The works included in this volume, the *Essay towards a New Theory of Vision*, the *Treatise concerning the Principles of Human Knowledge*, and the *Dialogues between Hylas and Philonous*, were all published before Berkeley was thirty years of age, and yet they contain the main exposition of his philosophy. Berkeley's thought matured early, but developed little. His philosophical writings are a reiteration, an application to new problems, and a defence against new objections, of the one central principle, which, as his *Commonplace Book* has shown us, struck upon his mind with convincing force when he was only twenty-one. It was a principle which he again and again declares to be intuitively obvious, to be but the plainest common sense if only understood rightly. He appeals with confidence from "minds debauched with learning" to the sober judgment of the plain man. "I wish," Philonous says, in the *Third Dialogue*, p. 274, "both our opinions were fairly stated and submitted to the judgment of men who had plain common sense, without the prejudices of a learned education." The man in the street, to whom so many philosophers make impotent appeal, responded cruelly. Few philosophers have been so persistently misunderstood. What Berkeley proclaimed as manifest common sense was taken for a subtle metaphysical paradox. Whiston, the successor of Newton at Cambridge, said of the *Principles*, "I being not a metaphysician, was not able to answer Mr. Berkeley's subtle premises, though I did not believe his absurd conclusion. I therefore desired Dr. Clarke that he who was deep in such subtleties, but did not appear to believe Mr. Berkeley's conclusion, would answer him. Which task he declined." Other answers were less academically worded, but equally unappreciative. Few were really better than the "coxcombs," who "vanquish Berkeley with a grin." The man of plain common sense has always answered as Dr. Johnson did. "After we came out of church," says Boswell, "we stood talking for some time together of Bishop Berkeley's ingenious sophistry to prove the non-existence of matter, and that everything in the universe is merely ideal. I observed, that though we are satisfied his doctrine is not true, it is impossible to refute it. I never shall forget the alacrity with which Johnson answered, striking his foot with mighty force against a large stone, till he rebounded from it, 'I refute it *thus!*'" This

unfavourable reception had unfortunate consequences for
Berkeley's thought. For it forced him to throw all his
energies into explaining what he really meant and defending
himself against gross misunderstandings. Had this not
absorbed his energies, had his main contention been understood, it is possible that Berkeley might have been led to
examine more closely the assumptions (taken from Locke)
on which some of his arguments rested, and been led to
carry his criticism of Locke rather further. There are hints
of some such criticism in his doctrine of notions, but he was
diverted from a possible elaboration of that doctrine by the
necessity of explaining his main position, and the doctrine
of notions remained a mere sketch.

Any attempt to understand and answer Berkeley must
fail unless it is first realised why Berkeley thought he was
expounding a doctrine which had only to be understood to
win assent. His continual protest against learned subtleties,
his attacks against philosophers for raising a dust and then
complaining that they cannot see, are not hypocritical or
paradoxical. His main doctrine is really a simplification ;
an appeal to immediate experience. If it is paradoxical, it
is because this simplification brings to light contradictions
concealed in the original position, not from any paradox or
subtlety in the argument itself. He brings all philosophical
arguments to the test of experience. That does not mean
that he appeals to what empirically happens—to facts obtained by any scientific process of induction ; but that he
insists that a philosophic argument shall have meaning, that
we are to bring it to the test of what on reflection we really
perceive. In this lies the force of his continual attacks on
the doctrine of abstract ideas. He perceived in that doctrine
a confusion which he felt to be at the root of all philosophical
difficulties. Get rid of that confusion and all would become
plain. Any account of Berkeley's philosophy, therefore,
should start with an examination of his criticism of abstract
ideas.

That criticism will be found in the *New Theory of Vision*,
§§ 122–126, in the *Principles*, Introduction §§ 10–12, and in
the *First Dialogue between Hylas and Philonous*, and is
always a criticism of Locke. At the same time, it must be

clearly understood that it is not a criticism of Locke's main position. Far from it. Berkeley is rather attacking a doctrine which seemed to him, and rightly, inconsistent with the account of the contents of knowledge with which Locke started, and which Berkeley entirely accepted. In his criticism he is only insisting that Locke shall be consistent and not desert his original assumptions to suit what he conceived to be the facts. It was because Berkeley accepted so whole-heartedly Locke's doctrine of ideas that he objected to the doctrine of abstract ideas.

For Locke and Berkeley idea meant whatever was the object or content of the mind in thinking. As Berkeley says in the *Dialogues*, "idea is now commonly used by philosophers to denote the immediate objects of the understanding." They further held that all contents of the mind might on analysis be resolved into combinations of simple ideas, these being either ideas of sensation or of reflection, the latter constituted by the mind's operating on the data supplied by ideas of sensation. In receiving ideas of sensation, the data for all our knowledge of the outside world, the mind was conceived of as entirely passive. Ideas were given to the senses, and then the mind operated upon them in various ways : they were first received without any work of the mind. Thus in § 1 of the *Principles*, Berkeley classifies the objects of human knowledge as "*ideas* actually imprinted on the senses : or else such as are perceived by attending to the passions and operations of the mind ; or lastly, ideas formed by the help of memory and imagination—either compounding, dividing, or barely representing those originally perceived in the aforesaid ways." Then after giving examples of the first kind, ideas of light and colour, hard and soft, heat and cold, motion and resistance, he goes on : "And as several of these are observed to accompany each other, they come to be marked by one name, and so to be reputed as one *thing*." Here we have the chief implication of Locke's and Berkeley's doctrine of ideas, that all such contents of thinking as we call things or objects are analysable into combinations or collections of simple ideas : that these simple ideas are *given* by the senses, and there can be no other objects of thought than such simple

ideas and operations of the mind upon them. From this
it follows that all ideas are particular, for they are given
as individual sense-images, and comparison, contrast, perception of agreement or disagreement, are operations of
the mind upon these particular data. Neither Locke nor
Berkeley have any insight into the truth of Kant's dictum,
"Although all our knowledge begins *with* experience, it
does not therefore all spring *from* experience." For them
all knowledge goes back to simple analysable sense data
and the mind's reflections on such data. They never see the
implications of these facts which led Plato to assert as
fundamental a distinction between the objects of sense and
the objects of thought : for thought according to them can
only be concerned with the ideas independently given by
sense. For example, in the *First Dialogue*, there is an interesting argument in which Berkeley calls attention to the
contradictions of sense perception which seem to involve
us in saying that the same thing is hot and cold, exactly
as Plato does in *Republic*, Book vii. But whereas Plato's
conclusion is that this involves a distinction between the
objects of the senses and of thought, if we are to say that the
same thing is hot and cold, and to contrast the reality which
thought apprehends by reflecting on the sense data with the
unreal and confused character of the sense data themselves, Berkeley asserts the absolute independence of the
different sense data, and makes the confusion come from
our ever thinking that they were the same. When we say
that we feel the same thing to be hot and cold, we really
mean that we feel an idea of heat that is one object and an
idea of cold that is another. For him ideas of sense are
the only objects, and if the senses distinguish, the objects
are different, and there is no more to be said.

Locke's doctrine of abstract ideas arises from reflection on
certain difficulties involved in this fundamental position. It
all ideas are individual sensations, possibly given in combination, but always given as distinct, how are we to account
for general terms, which seem to imply a real community of
nature between different ideas. This is the problem which
led Plato to his distinction between the intelligible and the
sensible, on the ground that the general term refers to

something common to, or manifested in, the particulars, but different from any of them, and therefore not perceivable by sense as they were, but by thought. But, as for Locke, all ideas are sensible and particular, they can only become general by means of some operation which thought performs on the sense data. The operations of thought are combining and separating, and Locke tries to account for the generality of ideas by thought separating off some common element in the sense data. Let us realise what is happening here. Locke is asking : What do we mean, or of what are we thinking, when we use a general name like triangle? He is right in seeing that we do not mean a particular triangle, or even as Berkeley said, *any* particular triangle : we mean what is common to all particular triangles. He is right also in insisting that we could mean nothing by triangle unless we had had experience of particulars. But as he also holds that we start with simple sense data, and all that mind does is to combine or separate, he can really give no proper explanation of generality. For that implies that the objects of sense cannot be given as merely particular. Red can mean nothing to a man who has not seen instances of it ; nor, on the other hand, to a man who does not recognise the likeness of the different instances. The likeness so recognised is not any one of the instances, nor, strictly speaking, any part of them ; but the power of seeing the likeness is as fundamental and primary as the power of seeing the instances : the two things are, in fact, inseparable. Ideas are seen at one and the same time as individual and as instances of a common quality.

For Locke, starting with the ideas as given by sense unrelated, this solution was not possible. The universality has to be obtained by thought operating on the material given as particular. He therefore represents it as a process of abstraction. The common quality of red things, *e.g.*, is represented as something *seen* beside or among the differences in the instances. It is a simple idea seen alongside of other simple ideas, and all that the mind does is to analyse and separate the common element. Locke was clearly thinking originally of what he calls complex ideas of substances. A thing, according to him, is a collection of simple ideas. We see its colour, feel its hardness and its weight. Now we might represent this complex idea as *abcd*, another complex idea as *aefg*, another as *ahij*, &c., the letters standing for simple ideas. We might quite well abstract the different letters, and think of the *a* common to all. Locke then applies this to the problem of generality. When we see triangles, *a* might be supposed to stand for triangularity, the other letters for the differences in the proportion of the sides and angles. That this is Locke's meaning is clear from the fact that he is in some difficulty about the abstract idea of colour, because, as he says, there is nothing common between the different colours, they being simple ideas, and therefore the general idea of colour can only mean the common way in which the different colours come into the mind, a simple idea attached to each simple idea of colour and separable from it. This will not really do. For it is just as difficult to find any idea common to different shades of red as to the different colours. If in comparing the different simple ideas of crimson and pink, we take away the different simple ideas, there is *nothing* left. All instances of red are some shade, and all shades are simple ideas, which cannot be further analysed. The common quality, which red means, is not a sense datum at all, and no process of abstracting or analysing could get you any nearer it.

It is on this point that Berkeley directs his criticism. There can be no abstract idea of a triangle, which is not either scalene, isosceles, or equilateral, and the abstract idea, as Locke describes it, is not an idea at all, because it is not something of which the mind could be immediately aware : and hence it is just nothing. Berkeley attacked the doctrine so persistently because of its implications. If there were abstract ideas, then the mind had objects other than those which it immediately perceived. It implied that mind, by operating on the sense data, could get ideas which were not given in, and therefore could not be tested by the sense data. Hence the doctrine was regarded by Berkeley as the foundation of the doctrine of abstract substance and matter to which he was strenuously opposed. If there are ideas which we cannot immediately perceive, then there is some sense of talking of reality as being something unperceivable. The difficulty is that if we suppose that the primary data of the mind are particular sensibilia, universality has to be got at apart from such data; but if it is regarded as being in things and yet not an idea, it implies a mysterious power of knowing apart from ideas. Thus the doctrine of abstract ideas leads to the notion of a reality apart or different from the reality immediately perceived, and to the belief that we can somehow refer from ideas to something which is not, properly speaking, an idea, though it is called an abstract idea.

This involves the doctrine of representation, that our ideas represent or stand for something which is not itself perceived, an unknown substratum of ideas : the doctrine which makes truth consist in " the agreement of our ideas with reality," reality being something different from ideas and therefore unknowable. That implies that truth is a perception of an agreement of what we perceive with something which from its very nature cannot be perceived.

Berkeley's answer to this doctrine is simple and irrefutable. How then can the agreement be perceived? How can we possibly know whether our ideas agree with what, *ex hypothesi*, cannot be known at all? All Berkeley's denial of matter is simply an assertion of this point. The doctrine of matter is at the root of all scepticism, for it asserts that the real is something which cannot be known, and that truth is a reference to what cannot be known. Berkeley's conviction that he is defending common sense against the paradoxes of a sophisticated intellect springs from his clear recognition that in attacking the doctrine of substance, as held by Locke, he was attacking a doctrine that meant nothing. "Whenever," he says, at the conclusion of the *Dialogues*, " any difficulty occurs, try if you can find a solution for it on the hypothesis of the *materialists*. Be not deceived by words : but sound your own thoughts, and in case you cannot conceive it easier by the help of Materialism, it is plain it can be no objection against Immaterialism. Had you proceeded all along by this rule, you would probably have spared yourself abundance of trouble in objecting : since of all your difficulties I challenge you to show one that is explained by matter: nay, which is not more unintelligible with than without that supposition, and consequently makes rather *against* than *for* it." "You often talked," he proceeds, "as if you thought I maintained the non-existence of Sensible Things; whereas in truth no one can be more thoroughly assured of their existence than I am : and it is you who doubt: I should have said, positively deny it. Everything that is seen, felt, heard, or any way perceived, is on the principles I embrace, a real being, not on yours. Remember the matter you contend for is an unknown somewhat (if indeed it may be termed *somewhat*), which is quite stripped of all sensible qualities, and can neither be perceived by sense nor apprehended by the mind. Remember, I say, that it is not any object which is hard or soft, hot or cold, blue or white, round or square, &c.;—for all these things I affirm do exist." Berkeley, in fact, is contending that you cannot know reality without knowing it. In so far as he says more than this, he says it because he thought that his own doctrine, which we shall consider later, was the only alternative to one which denied this obvious truth. This is the self-evident principle at the base of his statement that all reality is in the mind. "Look you, Hylas," Philonous says, in the *Third Dialogue*, "when I speak of objects as existing in the mind, or imprinted on the senses, I would not be understood in the gross literal sense as when bodies are said to exist in a place, or a seal to make an impression on wax. My meaning is only that the mind comprehends or perceives them ; and that it is affected from without, or by some being distinct from itself."

Compare the following passage in the *Principles*, § 68 : "Let us examine a little the description that is here given of matter. It neither acts, nor perceives, nor is perceived; for this is all that is meant by saying it is an inert, senseless, unknown substance : which is a definition entirely made up of negatives, excepting only the relative notion of its standing under or supporting. But then it must be observed that it supports nothing at all, and how near this comes to the description of a *nonentity* I desire may be considered." Berkeley has been constantly misunderstood because of a failure to understand the view he is attacking.

But if Locke's doctrine of abstract ideas with all that it implied did not solve the difficulties of universality, so much the more reason for finding some other which did. The difficulties Berkeley acknowledged. " It is," he says, *Principles*, Introduction, § 15, "a point much insisted on, that all knowledge and demonstration are about universal notions, to which I fully agree ; but then it does not appear to me that these notions are formed by abstraction in the manner premised ; *universality*, so far as I can comprehend, not consisting in the absolute, positive nature or conception of anything, but in the relation it bears to the particulars signified or represented by it ; by virtue whereof it is that things, names, or notions, being in their own nature *particular*, are rendered *universal*." That is, he explains, the general term does not mean any common quality of the particulars but means any of the particulars. " There is," he says, " no such thing as one precise and definite signification annexed to any general name, they all signifying indifferently a great number of particular ideas." These particular ideas are associated ; any one of them reminds us of another ; and thus we can explain general terms, which really refer to this association, without destroying the particularity of the ideas. This is all very well, but it gives no explanation of why certain particular ideas are associated, and none could be given which did not refer to the common character of the associated ideas. Berkeley really uses association to do all the work of his positive theory without analysing the notion itself and seeing whether it could work on his principles. For inasmuch as association cannot for him be due to any thing in the ideas, for that would imply a common quality in different simple ideas, it must be, as he himself calls it, arbitrary. We are made to think the ideas together, because they have been presented to us together, that is for a reason outside their own nature. Berkeley carries as far as he can the theory that the only objects of knowledge are particular sensible ideas, which because they are simple are not further analysable and therefore cannot be compared, which cannot be ideas of the same object, for they themselves are the only objects. Their association is a relation imposed upon them, for in themselves, if they are distinguishable, they are just different entities. The ideas come together because we have them together, or, if they seem to be imposed on us, because some other mind thinks them. This arbitrariness of association led Berkeley straight to his proof of the existence of God.

Now if we talk of ideas being "together" or associated, we imply space, and the more Berkeley denies a real common nature to ideas, the more he implies their community in space, and the more important it becomes for him to explain our perception of space. This he considered he had done in the *Essay towards a New Theory of Vision*. The Essay is remarkable in not asserting all that Berkeley held. While insisting that visible qualities are in the mind and dependent on their being perceived, he retains the ordinary view in regard to tangible qualities, taking for granted that we do perceive distance by touch, and even allowing that we can have different tangible ideas of the same object. The result of this method is unfortunate. For Berkeley first reduces all visual space to visual signs of tangible space, on the ground that visual ideas are within the mind, and assuming that tangible space needs no explanation. Then in his other writings he asserts that tangible ideas also are within the mind, but does not re-examine the account of the perception of tangible space which this new position involves. If Berkeley had stated his ideal theory in the *Essay* in the thoroughgoing fashion of the *Principles*, he would have seen the difficulty of explaining any perception of space on his theory. For the objections which he brings forward to visual apply equally to tangible space. The main argument of the Essay that visual ideas and tangible ideas are different would remain the same, but it would be seen that in Berkeley's principles the perception of space must be different from either, and yet it must be perceived through both.

Berkeley's argument rests on the particularity of ideas or on the impossibility of ideas which are different being also in any way the same. § 103, "That which I see is only variety of light and colours. That which I feel is hard or soft, hot or cold, rough or smooth. What similitude, what connection have those ideas with these? Or how is it possible that any one should see reason to give one and the same name to combinations of ideas so very different, before he had experienced their coexistence?" Hence Berkeley argues, " If we take a close and accurate view of the matter, it must be acknowledged that we never see and feel one and the same object. That which is seen is one thing, and that which is felt is another." We infer from visible ideas to tangible through association. The reference therefore requires practice and experience. Visible ideas are arbitrary signs of tangible ideas. When we think we see distance, we are really arguing from visual ideas to tangible ideas of distance which we have previously found to be associated with them. The association comes from the ideas being found together, not from any inherent connection. Just because the objects of sight and of touch are different, there can be no inherent connection, unless we are to believe in an abstract idea of extension, abstracted alike from sight and touch, and that Berkeley has shown to be impossible.

In reviewing this theory, discrimination is important. It is true that we do continually argue from size as we see it to size as we feel it, and that we may argue wrongly. Hence come mistakes in arguing from " apparent" to " real" size, and hence the need of experience. But it is quite another thing to say that the relation between visual and tactual ideas is only arbitrary, that the objects of sight and of touch are different, and that there are no other objects.

In the first place, to recur to our previous argument, the same considerations which are urged against visual extension will apply to tactual extension, and we must see that if the fundamental data of perception are isolated sensible ideas, the perception of space cannot be explained at all. We can no more derive space from tangible than from visual ideas ; both imply space to begin with, space or extension is as distinct from " hard or soft, hot or cold, rough or smooth," as it is from " variety of light and colours."

Secondly, even if this objection be waived, Berkeley is unable to maintain the entire arbitrariness of the connection. For supposing that the general connection between visual and tangible ideas were the work of experience, can the same be said of the connection between a particular visual idea and a particular tangible idea ? In a noteworthy paragraph near the end of the *Essay*, § 142, Berkeley makes an admission which really destroys his position. "I answer, it must be acknowledged the visible square is fitter than the visible circle to represent the tangible square, but then it is not because it is liker or more of a species with it, but, because the visible square contains in it several distinct parts, whereby to ¦mark the several distinct corresponding parts of a tangible square, whereas the visible circle doth not," &c. But this is to acknowledge that ideas which are wholly distinct in species may yet have a quantitative correspondence, and contradicts what Berkeley has said before, § 109, that number "is entirely a creature of the mind." The point itself is obvious. The same system of longs and shorts, *e.g.*, may be represented in sounds, in visible ideas, or in tangible ideas. Since therefore sounds, colours, and touch sensations are absolutely different, the long and short system is not given by abstracting from them, but is somehow given in and through them. The difference of colour and hardness is no reason for concluding a difference in the extension which may be perceived through them. The shape of an object is no more constituted by tangible ideas than by visual. Its shape is not hard any more than it is, say, yellow. But from the tangible ideas, *e.g.* from passing our fingers over the object, or from visual ideas, we conclude what its shape must be if it feels or looks in that way, and if we know its real shape we can on reflection say what tangible and visual ideas we shall get from it in different conditions. Hence there is a perfectly real meaning in saying that we have visual and tangible ideas of the same object. That does not mean that the object is a mysterious unknown something. It is perceived or understood through the visual or tangible ideas, but does not simply consist of them. Berkeley's position which insists that what may be called bare sensibilia are the only objects of perception, and that difference in sensibilia means difference in objects, makes our perception of space inexplicable, and that inexplicability marks the breakdown of "the doctrine of ideas."

Now when we come to the statement of Berkeley's main position, that the essence of all reality is its being perceived, we find that it gets much of its force from his view that the objects of perception are isolable independent ideas of

sense and nothing more.   He begins the *Principles* by insisting that all objects of knowledge are ideas, describing
"the *ideas* actually imprinted on the senses" in separate
groups of colours, hard and soft, &c., and insisting that a
thing is simply a collection of these which "have been
observed to accompany each other." A few paragraphs
later, after stating his own doctrine, he explains that the
main objections to it come from the belief in abstract ideas.
"For can there be a nicer strain of abstraction than to distinguish the existence of sensible objects from their being
perceived, so as to conceive them existing unperceived.
Light and colours, heat and cold, extension and figures—in
a word, the things we see and feel—what are they but so
many sensations, notions, ideas, or impressions on the sense?
and is it possible to separate, even in thought, any of these
from perception?" From which it is but a simple step to
the famous statement, § 6, "Some truths there are so near
and obvious that a man need only open his eyes to see them.
Such I take this important one to be, viz., that all the choir
of heaven and furniture of the earth, in a word all those
bodies which compose the mighty frame of the world, have
not any subsistence without a mind—that their *being* is to be
perceived or *known*."

Berkeley begins by assuming that no one will assert that
pain or pleasure exist apart from their being felt, and much
of his argument, as, *e.g.*, in the *First Dialogue*, is devoted
to showing that there is no real distinction between ideas of
sense and pleasure or pain.   The mere fact that a sensation
sufficiently intense becomes painful, or that some sensations
are pleasurable, is enough to show that, once you grant that
the object of sense perception is the simple sensation.   For
you can only distinguish between the pleasure which you feel
and the sensation which gives you the pleasure, if you make
distinctions in what is one immediate act of perceiving.
Such a distinction is for Berkeley impossible.   We can
understand from this point of view why he is impervious to
the argument that it is one thing to say that you can only
know things by perceiving them, quite another to say that
they only exist when you perceive them.   For that argument
ultimately implies a distinction between the object and the

content of sensation, or implies that you can have different
sensations of the same thing. But that, as we have seen, is
in Berkeley's view impossible.

We shall find the same assumption, that the objects of
perception are indivisible, isolated sensibilia behind Berkeley's treatment of objectivity. It is perhaps the most important part of his work. He was very far from denying the
distinction between objective and subjective, or between real
and illusory ideas. As he says in the *Second Dialogue*, " It
is evident that the things I perceive are my own ideas, and
that no idea can exist unless it be in a mind. Nor is it less
plain that these ideas or things by me perceived, exist independently of my mind ; since I know myself not to be their
author, it being out of my power to determine at pleasure
what particular ideas I shall be affected with upon opening
my eyes or ears. They must therefore exist in some other
mind, whose will it is they should be exhibited to me. The
things, I say, immediately perceived are ideas or sensations.
Call them what you will. But how can any idea or sensation exist in, or be produced by any thing but a mind or
spirit ? "

Berkeley seems sometimes to come to his conclusion from
an analysis of the bare relation of knowing, as though you
could not think of knowing without thinking of the object as
dependent on the mind. The difficulty of this argument
is that knowing seems equally to involve that the object
is independent of the act of knowing it. It is the essence
of knowledge that we are aware of something which is
not our knowing. From mere analysis of the relation of
knowing we can only conclude that we cannot know a thing
without its being in some relation to us, but that that relation
must be compatible with the object being distinguished from
the act of knowing. Now in so far as Berkeley's argument
is based on an analysis of the relation of knowing, it is
fallacious. For while asserting that to be known means to
be dependent on a mind, he admits that some ideas are
independent of *our* mind, and may exist while *we* do not
perceive them. We cannot from this conclude that they
must be known by some one else or be in God's mind ;
because the reason for putting them in God's mind rather

than our own is that the analysis of our knowing reveals the fact that some objects of knowledge at least are necessarily conceived of as existing without our knowing them, while the reason for putting them in God's *mind* rather than in matter is that it is supposed to be self-evident that nothing can exist without being known.

Berkeley's real argument is different and dependent on his view of the nature of ideas. For it is the case that sensations do involve some one to have them, in the sense that as acts of knowing they only get unity and intelligibility as being acts of one knowing mind. But obviously all the unity and intelligibility there is cannot be produced by our mind. Therefore, Berkeley argues, the world, consisting as it does of ideas, must get its unity from God's mind. If we say, why any mind at all? Berkeley's answer is that it is intelligible to say that a mind has or thinks ideas. We know what that means. But it means nothing to say that matter is the substratum of ideas ; that is only abstract nonsense. We can mean something when we talk of God conceiving ideas, for we ourselves conceive ideas : we can mean nothing when we talk of substance upholding ideas. Mental activity is the only intelligible cause.

This leads us to Berkeley's doctrine of notions. If the only intelligible cause is a mind thinking ideas, how do we know that mind? Is it an idea itself? This is the argument Hume brought against Berkeley, criticising Berkeley's doctrine of self with all the arguments he had brought against Locke's abstract ideas. " I can never," Hume says, " find this idea of myself : I only observe myself wishing or acting or feeling something." But Berkeley explains that we have no idea of the self : we have a notion of it. " What I am myself—that which I denote by the term I—is the same with what is meant by *soul* or *spiritual substance*. But if I should say that I was nothing, or that I was an idea, nothing could be more evidently absurd than either of these propositions" (*Principles*, § 139). He continues, § 140 : " In a large sense indeed, we may be said to have an idea or rather a notion of *spirit* : that is, we understand the meaning of the word, otherwise we could not affirm or deny anything of it." Here Berkeley is admitting that something can be known without being an idea. It can be an inference from ideas. But his whole theory, that ideas are the only objects of knowledge, has been based on the supposition that nothing else can be known. But if we can infer from ideas to something not idea in the case of mind, why not in other cases? Ought we not to be said to have a notion of extension and space? In an interesting passage (*Principles*, § 143) Berkeley says that not only have we a notion of the self and of God, but also "of the relations and habitudes between things." Were this developed, the main argument for Berkeley's idealism would go. Berkeley never developed his doctrine of notions. If we discard it as an inconsistent accretion to his system, we must regard him mainly as preparing the way for that complete working out of the implications of Locke's empiricism afterwards accomplished by Hume. If we lay stress on it, Berkeley must be regarded as showing the impossibilities of that empiricism, and pointing, however hesitatingly, to the more thorough analysis of the elements of experience made by Kant.

A. D. LINDSAY.

SELECT BIBLIOGRAPHY

SEPARATE WORKS. *Arithmetica absque Algebrae aut Euclide demonstrata* and *Miscellanea Mathematica*, 1707; *Essay towards a New Theory of Vision*, 1709, 1734; *Treatise concerning the Principles of Human Knowledge*, Pt. I, 1710, 1734 (with Dialogues); later editions: C. Simon, 1878, and in Lubbock's Hundred Best Books and New Universal Library, 1907; *Passive Obedience*, etc., 1712; 3rd ed., 1713; *Three Dialogues between Hylas and Philonous*, 1713, 1725 (see above *Principles*); *Advice to the Tories who have taken the Oaths*, 1715; *Three Letters to Thomas Prior, and a Letter to the Rev. Dr Hales on the Virtues of Tar-Water*, 1720, 1744, 1746, 1747; *De Motu*, 1721; *An Essay towards Preventing the Ruin of Great Britain*, 1721; *A Proposal for the better Supplying of Churches in our Foreign Plantations*, etc., 1725, 1731; *Sermon before the Society for the Propagation of the Gospel*, 1732; *A Discourse addressed to Magistrates and Men in Authority*, 1732, 1736, 1738; *Alciphron, or the Minute Philosopher*, 1732; 3rd ed., 1752; *Theory of Vision, or Visual Language, Vindicated and Explained*, 1733; *The Analyst, or a Discourse addressed to an Infidel Mathematician*, etc., 1734; 2nd ed., 1754; *A Defence of Free Thinking in Mathematics*, 1735; *Reasons for not Replying to Mr Walton's Full Answer*, 1735; *The Querist*, 1735-7; 2nd ed., 1750; republished, 1829; *A Chain of Philosophical Reflections and Enquiries concerning the Virtues of Tar-Water*, etc., 1744, 1746, 1747, 1748; *A Letter to the Roman Catholics of the Diocese of Cloyne*, 1745; *A Word to the Wise*, 1749; *Maxims concerning Patriotism*, 1750; *Further Thoughts on Tar-Water* in the *Miscellany*, 1752; contributions to the *Guardian*, March to August 1713; *The Irish Patriot* (ed. J. M. Hone) (*The Times Literary Supplement*), 13th March, 3rd April 1930; *Berkeley's Commonplace Book* (ed. G. A. Johnston), 1930 (first printed in Fraser's edition of the Works, 1871); An unpublished Sermon (ed. J. Wild), *Philosophical Review*, XL, 1931.

COLLECTED WORKS. Ed. J. Stock, 2 vols., 1784; 3 vols., 1820, 1837; ed. A. C. Fraser, 4 vols., 1871, 1901; ed. G. Sampson, with biographical introduction by A. J. Balfour, 3 vols., 1897-8.

SELECTIONS. A. C. Fraser, 1874; 5th ed., 1899.

BIOGRAPHY AND CRITICISM. J. Stock: *Life of Bishop Berkeley*, 1766; J. N. Norton: *Life of Bishop Berkeley*, 1861; A. C. Fraser: *Berkeley*, 1881; *Berkeley and Spiritual Realism*, 1908; M. C. Tyler: *Three Men of Letters*, 1895; B. Rand: *Berkeley and Percival*, 1914; *Berkeley's American Sojourn*, 1932; G. A. Johnston: *The Development of Berkeley's Philosophy*, 1923; J. M. Hone and M. M. Rossi: *Berkeley: his Life, Writings and Philosophy*, 1931; G. D. Hicks: *Berkeley*, 1933; A. A. Luce: *Berkeley and Malebranche*, 1934; J. Wild: *George Berkeley: A Study of his Life and Philosophy*, 1936.

CONTENTS

AN ESSAY TOWARDS A NEW
THEORY OF VISION

TO THE RIGHT HONOURABLE

SIR JOHN PERCIVALE, Bart.,

ONE OF HER MAJESTY'S MOST HONOURABLE PRIVY COUNCIL IN
THE KINGDOM OF IRELAND.

Sir,—I could not, without doing violence to myself,
forbear upon this occasion to give some public testimony
of the great and well-grounded esteem I have conceived
for you, ever since I had the honour and happiness of
your acquaintance. The outward advantages of fortune,
and the early honours with which you are adorned,
together with the reputation you are known to have,
amongst the best and most considerable men, may well
imprint veneration and esteem on the minds of those
who behold you from a distance. But these are not
the chief motives that inspire me with the respect I
bear you. A nearer approach has given me the view
of something in your person, infinitely beyond the external ornaments of honour and estate. I mean, an
intrinsic stock of virtue and good sense, a true concern
for religion, and disinterested love of your country.
Add to these an uncommon proficiency in the best and
most useful parts of knowledge; together with (what
in my mind is a perfection of the first rank) a surpassing
goodness of nature. All which I have collected, not
from the uncertain reports of fame, but from my own
experience. Within these few months, that I have the
honour to be known unto you, the many delightful
hours I have passed in your agreeable and improving
conversation, have afforded me the opportunity of discovering in you many excellent qualities, which at once
fill me with admiration and esteem. That one at those
years, and in those circumstances of wealth and great-

3

ness, should continue proof against the charms of luxury, and those criminal pleasures, so fashionable and predominant in the age we live in. That he should preserve a sweet and modest behaviour, free from that insolent and assuming air, so familiar to those who are placed above the ordinary rank of men. That he should manage a great fortune with that prudence and inspection, and at the same time expend it with that generosity and nobleness of mind, as to show himself equally remote from a sordid parsimony, and a lavish inconsiderate profusion of the good things he is entrusted with. This, surely, were admirable and praiseworthy. But that he should moreover, by an impartial exercise of his reason, and constant perusal of the sacred scriptures, endeavour to attain a right notion of the principles of natural and revealed religion. That he should with the concern of a true patriot have the interest of the public at heart, and omit no means of informing himself what may be prejudicial or advantageous to his country, in order to prevent the one, and promote the other. In fine, that by a constant application to the most severe and useful studies, by a strict observation of the rules of honour and virtue, by frequent and serious reflections on the mistaken measures of the world, and the true end and happiness of mankind, he should in all respects qualify himself bravely to run the race that is set before him, to deserve the character of *great* and *good* in this life, and be ever happy hereafter. This were amazing, and almost incredible. Yet all this, and more than this, Sir, might I justly say of you ; did either your modesty permit, or your character stand in need of it. I know it might deservedly be thought a vanity in me, to imagine that any thing coming from so obscure a hand as mine, could add a lustre to your reputation. But I am withal sensible how far I advance the interest of my own, by laying hold on this opportunity to make it known that I am admitted into some degree of intimacy with a person of your exquisite judgment. And with that view, I have ventured to make you an address of this nature, which the goodness I have ever experienced in you inclines me to hope, will meet with a favourable reception at your hands. Though I must own, I have your pardon to ask, for touching on what may, possibly, be offensive to a virtue you are possessed of in a very distinguishing degree. Excuse me, Sir, if it was out of my power to mention the name of Sir John Percivale without paying some tribute to that extraordinary and surprising merit, whereof I have so lively and affecting an idea, and which, I am sure, cannot be exposed in too full a light for the imitation of others. Of late, I have been agreeably employed in considering the most noble, pleasant, and comprehensive of all the senses. The fruit of that (labour shall I call it or) diversion is what I now present you with, in hopes it may give some entertainment to one who, in the midst of business and vulgar enjoyments, preserves a relish for the more re-fined pleasures of thought and reflection. My thoughts concerning vision have led me into some notions, so far out of the common road, that it had been improper to address them to one of a narrow and contracted genius. But you, Sir, being master of a large and free under-standing, raised above the power of those prejudices that enslave the far greater part of mankind, may deservedly be thought a proper patron for an attempt of this kind. Add to this, that you are no less disposed to forgive, than qualified to discern, whatever faults may occur in it. Nor do I think you defective in any one point necessary to form an exact judgment on the most abstract and difficult things, so much as in a just confi-dence of your own abilities. And in this one instance, give me leave to say, you show a manifest weakness of judgment. With relation to the following essay, I shall only add, that I beg your pardon for laying a trifle of that nature in your way, at a time when you are engaged in the important affairs of the nation, and desire you to think, that I am with all sincerity and respect,—SIR, your most faithful and most humble servant,

GEORGE BERKELEY.

CONTENTS

Contents

Contents

AN ESSAY TOWARDS A NEW THEORY OF VISION

I. My design is to show the manner wherein we perceive by sight, the distance, magnitude, and situation of *objects*. Also to consider the difference there is betwixt the *ideas* of sight and touch, and whether there be any *idea* common to both senses. In treating of all which, it seems to me, the writers of optics have proceeded on wrong principles.

II. It is, I think, agreed by all, that *distance* of itself, and immediately, cannot be seen. For *distance* being a line directed end-wise to the eye, it projects only one point in the fund of the eye. Which point remains invariably the same, whether the distance be longer or shorter.

III. I find it also acknowledged, that the estimate we make of the distance of *objects* considerably remote, is rather an act of judgment grounded on *experience* than of *sense*. For example, when I perceive a great number of intermediate *objects*, such as houses, fields, rivers, and the like, which I have experienced to take up a considerable space; I thence form a judgment or conclusion, that the *object* I see beyond them is at a great distance. Again, when an *object* appears faint and small, which, at a near distance, I have experienced to make a vigorous and large appearance; I instantly conclude it to be far off. And this, it is evident, is the result of *experience*; without which, from the faintness and littleness, I should not have inferred any thing concerning the distance of *objects*.

IV. But when an *object* is placed at so near a distance,

as that the interval between the eyes bears any sensible proportion to it, it is the received opinion that the two *optic axes* (the fancy that we see only with one eye at once being exploded) concurring at the *object*, do there make an *angle*, by means of which, according as it is greater or lesser, the *object* is perceived to be nearer or further off.

V. Betwixt which, and the foregoing manner of estimating distance, there is this remarkable difference. That whereas there was no apparent, necessary connexion between small distance and a large and strong appearance, or between great distance, and a little and faint appearance. Yet there appears a very necessary connexion between an obtuse angle and near distance, and an acute angle and further distance. It does not in the least depend upon experience, but may be evidently known by any one before he had experienced it, that the nearer the concurrence of the *optic axes*, the greater the *angle*, and the remoter their concurrence is, the lesser will be the *angle* comprehended by them.

VI. There is another way, mentioned by the optic writers, whereby they will have us judge of those distances, in respect of which, the breadth of the *pupil* hath any sensible bigness. And that is the greater or lesser divergency of the rays, which, issuing from the visible point, do fall on the *pupil :* that point being judged nearest, which is seen by most diverging rays ; and that remoter, which is seen by less diverging rays. And so on, the apparent distance still increasing, as the divergency of the rays decreases, till at length it becomes infinite, when the rays that fall on the *pupil* are to sense parallel. And after this manner it is said we perceive distances when we look only with one eye.

VII. In this case also, it is plain we are not beholding to experience : it being a certain, necessary truth, that the nearer the direct rays falling on the eye approach to a *parallelism*, the further off is the point of their intersection, or the visible point from whence they flow.

VIII. I have here set down the common, current accounts that are given of our perceiving near distances by sight, which, though they are unquestionably received for true by *mathematicians*, and accordingly made use of by them in determining the apparent places of *objects*, do, nevertheless, seem to me very unsatisfactory : and that for these following reasons :—

IX. *First*, It is evident that when the mind perceives any *idea*, not immediately and of itself, it must be by the means of some other *idea*. Thus, for instance, the passions which are in the mind of another, are of themselves to me invisible. I may nevertheless perceive them by sight, though not immediately, yet by means of the colours they produce in the countenance. We do often see shame or fear in the looks of a man, by perceiving the changes of his countenance to red or pale.

X. Moreover it is evident, that no *idea* which is not itself perceived, can be to me the means of perceiving any other *idea*. If I do not perceive the redness or paleness of a man's face themselves, it is impossible I should perceive by them the passions which are in his mind.

XI. Now from Sect. ii., it is plain that distance is in its own nature imperceivable, and yet it is perceived by sight. It remains, therefore, that it be brought into view by means of some other *idea* that is itself immediately perceived in the act of *vision*.

XII. But those *lines* and *angles*, by means whereof *mathematicians* pretend to explain the perception of distance, are themselves not at all perceived, nor are they, in truth, ever thought of by those unskilful in optics. I appeal to any one's experience, whether, upon sight of an *object*, he compute its distance by the bigness of the *angle* made by the meeting of the two *optic axes*? Or whether he ever think of the greater or lesser divergency of the rays, which arrive from any point to his *pupil*? Nay, whether it be not perfectly impossible for him to perceive by sense the various angles wherewith the rays, according to their greater or lesser divergence, do fall on his eye. Every one is himself the best judge of what he perceives, and what not. In vain shall all the *mathematicians* in the world tell me, that I perceive certain *lines* and *angles* which introduce into my mind the various *ideas* of *distance;* so long as I myself am conscious of no such thing.

XIII. Since, therefore, those *angles* and *lines* are not themselves perceived by sight, it follows from Sect. x., that the mind does not by them judge of the distance of *objects.*

XIV. Secondly, the truth of this assertion will be yet further evident to any one that considers those *lines* and *angles* have no real existence in nature, being only an *hypothesis* framed by *mathematicians,* and by them introduced into *optics,* that they might treat of that science in a *geometrical* way.

XV. The third and last reason I shall give for my rejecting that doctrine is, that though we should grant the real existence of those *optic angles,* &c., and that it was possible for the mind to perceive them; yet these principles would not be found sufficient to explain the phenomena of *distance.* As shall be shown hereafter.

XVI. Now, it being already shown that distance is suggested to the mind by the mediation of some other *idea* which is itself perceived in the act of seeing. It remains that we inquire what *ideas* or *sensations* there be that attend *vision,* unto which we may suppose the *ideas* of distance are connected, and by which they are introduced into the mind. And first, it is certain by experience, that when we look at a near *object* with both eyes, according as it approaches or recedes from us, we alter the disposition of our eyes, by lessening or widening the interval between the *pupils.* This disposition or turn of the eyes is attended with a sensation, which seems to me, to be that which in this case brings the *idea* of greater or lesser distance into the mind.

XVII. Not that there is any natural or necessary connexion between the sensation we perceive by the turn of the eyes, and greater or lesser distance. But because the mind has by constant *experience* found the different sensations corresponding to the different dispositions of the eyes, to be attended each with a different degree of distance in the *object:* there has grown an habitual or customary connexion, between those two sorts of *ideas*. So that the mind no sooner perceives the sensation arising from the different turn it gives the eyes, in order to bring the *pupils* nearer or further asunder, but it withal perceives the different *idea* of distance which was wont to be connected with that sensation. Just as upon hearing a certain sound, the *idea* is immediately suggested to the understanding, which custom had united with it.

XVIII. Nor do I see, how I can easily be mistaken in this matter. I know evidently that distance is not perceived of itself. That by consequence, it must be perceived by means of some other *idea* which is immediately perceived, and varies with the different degrees of distance. I know also that the sensation arising from the turn of the eyes is of itself immediately perceived, and various degrees thereof are connected with different distances: which never fail to accompany them into my mind, when I view an *object* distinctly with both eyes, whose distance is so small, that in respect of it the interval between the eyes has any considerable magnitude.

XIX. I know it is a received opinion, that by altering the disposition of the eyes, the mind perceives whether the angle of the *optic axes* is made greater or lesser. And that accordingly by a kind of *natural geometry*, it judges the point of their intersection to be nearer, or further off. But that this is not true, I am convinced by my own experience. Since I am not conscious that I make any such use of the perception I have by the turn of my eyes. And for me to make those judgments, and draw those conclusions from it, without knowing that I do so, seems altogether incomprehensible.

XX. From all which it plainly follows, that the judgment we make of the distance of an *object*, viewed with both eyes, is entirely the *result of experience*. If we had not constantly found certain sensations arising from the various disposition of the eyes, attended with certain degrees of distance, we should never make those sudden judgments from them, concerning the distance of *objects ;*

no more than we would pretend to judge of a man's thoughts, by his pronouncing words we had never heard before.

XXI. Secondly, an *object* placed at a certain distance from the eye, to which the breadth of the *pupil* bears a considerable proportion, being made to approach, is seen more confusedly. And the nearer it is brought, the more confused appearance it makes. And this being found constantly to be so, there arises in the mind an *habitual* connexion between the several degrees of confusion and distance. The greater confusion still implying the lesser distance, and the lesser confusion, the greater distance of the *object*.

XXII. This confused appearance of the *object*, doth therefore seem to me to be the *medium*, whereby the mind judges of distance in those cases, wherein the most approved writers of optics will have it judge, by the different divergency with which the rays flowing from the radiating point fall on the *pupil*. No man, I believe, will pretend to see or feel those imaginary angles, that the rays are supposed to form according to their various inclinations on his eye. But he cannot choose seeing whether the *object* appear more or less confused. It is therefore a manifest consequence from what has been demonstrated, that instead of the greater or less divergency of the rays, the mind makes use of the greater or less confusedness of the appearance, thereby to determine the apparent place of an *object*.

XXIII. Nor doth it avail to say, there is not any necessary connexion between confused *vision*, and distance, great or small. For I ask any man, what necessary connexion he sees between the redness of a blush and shame? and yet no sooner shall he behold that colour to arise in the face of another, but it brings into his mind the *idea* of that passion which has been observed to accompany it.

XXIV. What seems to have misled the writers of optics in this matter is, that they imagine men judge of distance, as they do of a conclusion in mathematics: betwixt which and the premises, it is indeed absolutely requisite there be an apparent, necessary connexion. But it is far otherwise, in the sudden judgments men make of distance. We are not to think that brutes and children, or even grown reasonable men, whenever they perceive an *object* to approach, or depart from them, do it by virtue of *geometry* and *demonstration*.

XXV. That one *idea* may suggest another to the mind, it will suffice that they have been observed to go together : without any demonstration of the necessity of their coexistence, or without so much as knowing what it is that makes them so to coexist. Of this there are innumerable instances, of which no one can be ignorant.

XXVI. Thus greater confusion having been constantly attended with nearer distance, no sooner is the former *idea* perceived, but it suggests the latter to our thoughts. And if it had been the ordinary course of nature, that the further off an *object* were placed, the more confused it should appear; it is certain, the very same perception that now makes us think an *object* approaches, would then have made us imagine it went further off. That perception, abstracting from *custom* and *experience*, being equally fitted to produce the *idea* of great distance, or small distance, or no distance at all.

XXVII. Thirdly, an *object* being placed at the distance above specified, and brought nearer to the eye, we may nevertheless prevent, at least for some time, the appearance's growing more confused, by straining the eye. In which case, that sensation supplies the place of confused *vision*, in aiding the mind to judge of the distance of the *object*. It being esteemed so much the nearer, by how much the effort, or straining of the eye in order to distinct *vision*, is greater.

XXVIII. I have here set down those sensations or *ideas* that seem to me to be the constant and general occasions of introducing into the mind the different *ideas* of near distance. It is true in most cases, that divers other circumstances contribute to frame our *idea* of distance, viz., the particular number, size, kind, &c., of the things seen. Concerning which, as well as all other the forementioned occasions which suggest distance, I

shall only observe, they have none of them, in their own
nature, any relation or connexion with it: nor is it
possible they should ever signify the various degrees
thereof, otherwise than as by *experience* they have been
found to be connected with them.

XXIX. I shall proceed upon these principles to
account for a phenomenon, which has hitherto strangely
puzzled the writers of optics, and is so far from being
accounted for by any of their *theories of vision*, that it is,
by their own confession, plainly repugnant to them; and
of consequence, if nothing else could be objected, were
alone sufficient to bring their credit in question. The
whole difficulty I shall lay before you in the words of
the learned Doctor Barrow, with which he concludes
his optic lectures:—

"Hæc sunt, quæ circa partem opticæ præcipuè mathe-
maticam dicenda mihi suggessit meditatio. Circa
reliquas (quæ φυσικώτεραι sunt, adeoque sæpiusculè pro
certis principiis plausibiles conjecturas venditare necessum
habent), nihil ferè quicquam admodum verisimile suc-
currit, à pervulgatis (ab iis, inquam, quæ Keplerus,
Scheinerus, Cartesius, et post illos alii tradiderunt)
alienum aut diversum. Atqui tacere malo, quàm toties
oblatam cramben reponere. Proinde receptui cano;
nec ita tamen ut prorsus discedam, anteaquàm improbam
quandam difficultatem (pro sinceritate quam et vobis et
veritati debeo minimè dissimulandam) in medium pro-
tulero, quæ doctrinæ nostræ, hactenus inculcatæ, se
objicit adversam, ab eâ saltem nullam admittit solutionem.
Illa, breviter, talis est: Lenti vel speculo cavo E B F
exponatur punctum visibile A, ita distans, ut radii ex
A manantes ex inflectione versus axem A B cogantur.
Sitque radiationis limes (seu puncti A imago, qualem
supra passim statuimus) punctum Z. Inter hoc autem
et inflectentis verticem B uspiam positus concipiatur
oculus. Quæri jam potest, ubi loci debeat punctum A
apparere? Retrorsùm ad punctum Z videri non fert
natura (cùm omnis impressio sensum afficiens proveniat
a partibus A) ac experientia reclamat. Nostris autem

è placitis consequi videtur, ipsum ad partes anticas apparens, ab intervallo longissimè dissito, (quod et maximum sensibile quodvis intervallum quodammodo exsuperet) apparere. Cùm enim quò radiis minùs divergentibus attingitur objectum, eò (seclusis utique prænotionibus et præjudiciis) longiùs abesse sentiatur, et quod parallelos ad oculum radios projicit, remotissimè positum æstimetur: exigere ratio videtur, ut quod convergentibus radiis apprehenditur, adhuc magis, si fieri posset, quoad apparentiam elongetur. Quin et circa casum hunc generatim inquiri possit, quidnam omnino sit, quod apparentem puncti A locum determinet, faciatque quòd constanti ratione nunc propius, nunc remotius appareat? Cui itidem dubio nihil quicquam ex hactenus dictorum *analogiâ* responderi posse videtur, nisi debere punctum A perpetuò longissimè semotum videri. Verùm experientia secùs attestatur, illud pro diversâ oculi inter puncta B, Z, positione variè distans, nunquam ferè (si unquam) longinquius ipso A liberè spectato, subindè verò multò propinquius apparere ; quinimo, quò oculum appellentes radii magis convergunt, eò speciem objecti propiùs accedere. Nempe, si puncto B

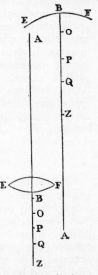

admoveatur oculus, suo (ad lentem) ferè nativo in loco conspicitur punctum A (vel æquè distans, ad speculum) ; ad O reductus oculus ejusce speciem appropinquantem cernit ; ad P adhuc vicinius ipsum existimat ; ac itâ sensim, donec alicubi tandem, velut ad Q, constituto oculo objectum summè propinquum apparens, in meram confusionem incipiat evanescere. Quæ sanè cuncta rationibus atque decretis nostris repugnare videntur, aut cum iis saltem parum amicè conspirant. Neque nostram tantùm sententiam pulsat hoc experimentum, at ex æquo

cæteras quas nôrim omnes: veterem imprimis ac vul-
gatam, nostræ præ reliquis affinem, ità convellere videtur,
ut ejus vi coactus doctissimus A. Tacquetus isti prin-
cipio (cui penè soli totam inædificaverat Captoptricam
suam) ceu infido ac inconstanti renunciârit, adeoque
suam ipse doctrinam labefactârit; id tamen, opinor,
minimè facturus, si rem totam inspexisset penitiùs, atque
difficultatis fundum attigisset. Apud me verò non ita
pollet hæc, nec eousque præpollebit ulla difficultas, ut ab
iis quæ manifestè rationi consentanea video, discedam;
præsertim quum, ut hîc accidit, ejusmodi difficultas in
singularis cujuspiam casûs disparitate fundetur. Nimirum
in præsente casu peculiare quiddam, naturæ subtilitati
involutum, delitescit, ægrè fortassis, nisi perfectiùs ex-
plorato, videndi modo, detegendum. Circa quod nil,
fateor, hactenus excogitare potui quod adblandiretur
animo meo, nedum plane satisfaceret. Vobis itaque
nodum hunc, utinam feliciore conatu, resolvendum
committo."

IN ENGLISH AS FOLLOWS:

"I have here delivered what my thoughts have suggested to me, concerning that part of optics which is
more properly mathematical. As for the other parts of
that science (which being rather physical, do consequently abound with plausible conjectures, instead of
certain principles) there has in them scarce anything
occurred to my observation, different from what has been
already said by Kepler, Scheinerus, Descartes, &c. And,
methinks, I had better say nothing at all, than repeat
that which has been so often said by others; I think it
therefore high time to take my leave of this subject.
But before I quit it for good and all, the fair and
ingenuous dealing that I owe both to you and to truth,
obliges me to acquaint you with a certain untoward
difficulty, which seems directly opposite to the doctrine
I have been hitherto inculcating, at least, admits of no
solution from it. In short it is this. Before the double
convex glass or concave speculum E B F, let the point
A be placed, at such a distance that the rays proceeding

from A, after refraction or reflection, be brought to unite
somewhere in the ax A B.   And suppose the point of
union (*i.e.* the image of the point A, as hath been
already set forth) to be Z; between which and B, the
vertex of the glass or speculum, conceive the eye to be
any where placed.   The question now is, where the point
A ought to appear.   Experience shows, that it doth not
appear behind at the point Z, and
it were contrary to nature that it
should ; since all the impression
which affects the sense comes from
towards A.   But from our tenets it
should seem to follow, that it would
appear before the eye at a vast distance off, so great as should in
some sort surpass all sensible distance.   For since, if we exclude all
anticipations and prejudices, every
object appears by so much the further
off, by how much the rays it sends
to the eye are less diverging ; and
that *object* is thought to be most
remote, from which parallel rays
proceed unto the eye ; reason would
make one think, that *object* should
appear at yet a greater distance,
which is seen by converging rays.
Moreover it may in general be asked
concerning this case, what it is that

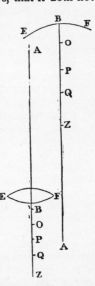

determines the apparent place of the point A, and maketh
it to appear after a constant manner, sometimes nearer, at
other times further off?   To which doubt I see nothing
that can be answered agreeable to the principles we
have laid down, except only that the point A ought
always to appear extremely remote.   But on the contrary, we are assured by experience, that the point A
appears variously distant, according to the different
situations of the eye between the points B and Z.   And
that it doth almost never (if at all) seem further off,
than it would if it were beheld by the naked eye ; but
on the contrary, it doth sometimes appear much nearer.

Nay, it is even certain, that by how much the rays falling on the eye do more converge, by so much the nearer does the *object* seem to approach. For the eye being placed close to the point B, the *object* A appears nearly in its own natural place, if the point B is taken in the glass, or at the same distance, if in the speculum. The eye being brought back to O, the *object* seems to draw near; and being come to P, it beholds it still nearer: and so on by little and little, till at length the eye being placed somewhere, suppose at Q, the *object* appearing extremely near, begins to vanish into mere confusion. All which doth seem repugnant to our principles; at least, not rightly to agree with them. Nor is our tenet alone struck at by this experiment, but likewise all others that ever came to my knowledge are every whit as much endangered by it. The ancient one especially (which is most commonly received, and comes nearest to mine) seems to be so effectually overthrown thereby, that the most learned Tacquet has been forced to reject that principle, as false and uncertain, on which alone he had built almost his whole Catoptrics, and consequently by taking away the foundation, hath himself pulled down the superstructure he had raised on it. Which nevertheless I do not believe he would have done, had he but considered the whole matter more thoroughly, and examined the difficulty to the bottom. But as for me, neither this, nor any other difficulty shall have so great an influence on me, as to make me renounce that which I know to be manifestly agreeable to reason. Especially when, as it here falls out, the difficulty is founded in the peculiar nature of a certain odd and particular case. For in the present case something peculiar lies hid, which being involved in the subtilty of nature, will perhaps hardly be discovered till such time as the manner of vision is more perfectly made known. Concerning which, I must own, I have hitherto been able to find out nothing, that has the least show of *probability*, not to mention *certainty*. I shall therefore leave this knot to be untied by you, wishing you may have better success in it than I have had."

XXX. The ancient and received principle, which

Dr. Barrow here mentions as the main foundation of Tacquet's Catoptrics, is, that 'every visible point seen by reflection from a speculum, shall appear placed at the intersection of the reflected ray and the perpendicular of incidence:' which intersection in the present case happening to be behind the eye, it greatly shakes the authority of that principle, whereon the aforementioned author proceeds throughout his whole catoptrics, in determining the apparent place of *objects* seen by reflection from any kind of speculum.

XXXI. Let us now see how this phenomenon agrees with our tenets. The eye the nearer it is placed to the point B in the above figures, the more distinct is the appearance of the *object:* but as it recedes to O, the appearance grows more confused; and at P it sees the *object* yet more confused; and so on, till the eye being brought back to Z, sees the *object* in the greatest confusion of all. Wherefore by Sect. xxi. the *object* should seem to approach the eye gradually, as it recedes from the point B, viz. at O it should (in consequence of the principle I have laid down in the aforesaid section) seem nearer than it did at B, and at P nearer than O, and at Q nearer than at P; and so on, till it quite vanishes at Z. Which is the very matter of fact, as any one that pleases may easily satisfy himself by experiment.

XXXII. This case is much the same, as if we should suppose an Englishman to meet a foreigner, who used the same words with the English, but in a direct contrary signification. The Englishman would not fail to make a wrong judgment of the *ideas* annexed to those sounds, in the mind of him that used them. Just so in the present case, the *object* speaks (if I may so say) with words that the eye is well acquainted with, viz. confusions of appearance; but whereas heretofore the greatest confusions were always wont to signify nearer distances, they have in this case a direct contrary signification, being connected with the greater distances. Whence it follows, that the eye must unavoidably be mistaken, since it will take the confusions in the sense it has been used to, which is directly opposed to the true.

XXXIII. This phenomenon, as it entirely subverts the opinion of those who will have us judge of distance by lines and angles, on which supposition it is altogether inexplicable, so it seems to me no small confirmation of the truth of that principle whereby it is explained. But in order to a more full explication of this point, and to show how far the hypothesis of the mind's judging by the various divergency of rays may be of use in determining the apparent place of an *object*, it will be necessary to premise some few things, which are already well known to those who have any skill in dioptrics.

XXXIV. First, any radiating point is then distinctly seen, when the rays proceeding from it are, by the refractive power of the crystalline, accurately reunited in the retina, or fund of the eye. But if they are reunited, either before they are at retina, or after they have passed it, then there is confused vision.

XXXV. Secondly, suppose in the adjacent figures N P represent an eye duly framed, and retaining its natural figure. In fig. 1, the rays falling nearly parallel on the eye, are by the crystalline A B refracted, so as their focus, or point of union F, falls exactly on the retina. But if the rays fall sensibly diverging on the eye, as in fig. 2, then their focus falls beyond the retina : or if the rays are made to converge by the lens Q S, before they come at the eye, as in fig. 3, their focus F will fall before the retina. In which two last cases, it is evident from the foregoing section, that the appearance of the point Z is confused. And by how much the greater is the convergency or divergency of the rays falling on the pupil, by so much the further will the point of their reunion be from the retina, either before or behind it, and consequently the point Z will appear by so much the more confused. And this, by the bye, may show us the difference between confused and faint vision. Confused vision is, when the rays proceeding from each distinct point of the *object*, are not accurately re-collected in one corresponding point of the retina, but take up some space thereon. So that rays from different points become mixed and confused together.

This is opposed to distinct vision, and attends near objects. Faint vision is, when by reason of the distance of the object, or grossness of the interjacent medium, few rays arrive from the object to the eye. This is opposed to vigorous, or clear vision, and attends remote objects. But to return.

XXXVI. The eye, or (to speak truly), the mind per-

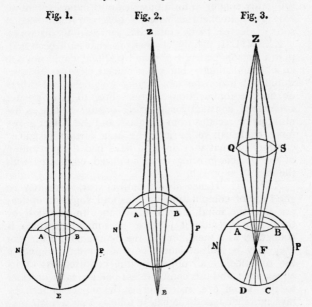

Fig. 1.   Fig. 2.   Fig. 3.

ceiving only the confusion itself, without ever considering the cause from which it proceeds, doth constantly annex the same degree of distance to the same degree of confusion. Whether that confusion be occasioned by converging or by diverging rays, it matters not. Whence it follows, that the eye following the object Z through the glass Q S (which by refraction causeth the rays Z Q, Z S, &c., to converge), should judge it to be at such a nearness, at which if it were placed, it would radiate on the eye with rays diverging to that degree, as would produce the same confusion which is now produced by converging rays, *i.e.* would cover a portion of the retina equal to D C: vide fig. 3, supra. But then this must be understood (to use Dr. Barrow's phrase) *seclusis prænotionibus et præjudiciis*, in case we abstract from all other circumstances of vision, such as the figure, size, faintness, &c., of the visible objects; all which do ordinarily concur to form our idea of distance, the mind having by frequent experience observed their several sorts or degrees to be connected with various distances.

XXXVII. It plainly follows from what hath been said, that a person perfectly purblind (*i.e.* that could not see an object distinctly, but when placed close to his eye) would not make the same wrong judgment that others do, in the forementioned case. For, to him, greater confusions constantly suggesting greater distances, he must, as he recedes from the glass, and the object grows more confused, judge it to be at a further distance; contrary to what they do, who have had the perception of the objects growing more confused, connected with the idea of approach.

XXXVIII. Hence also it doth appear, there may be good use of computation by lines and angles in optics; not that the mind judgeth of distance immediately by them, but because it judgeth by somewhat which is connected with them, and to the determination whereof they may be subservient. Thus the mind judging of the distance of an object by the confusedness of its appearance, and this confusedness being greater or lesser to the naked eye, according as the object is seen by rays more or less diverging, it follows that a man may make use of the divergency of the rays in computing the apparent distance, though not for its own sake, yet on account of the confusion with which it is connected. But, so it is, the confusion itself is entirely neglected by mathematicians, as having no necessary relation with distance, such as the greater or lesser angles of divergency are conceived to have. And these (especially for that they fall under mathematical computation) are alone regarded, in determining the apparent places of objects, as though they were the sole and immediate cause of the judgments the mind makes of distance. Whereas, in truth, they should not at all be regarded in themselves, or any otherwise, than as they are supposed to be the cause of confused vision.

XXXIX. The not considering of this has been a fundamental and perplexing oversight. For proof whereof, we need go no further than the case before us. It having been observed, that the most diverging rays brought into the mind the idea of nearest distance, and that still, as the divergency decreased, the distance increased ; and it being thought, the connexion between the various degrees of divergency and distance was immediate, this naturally leads one to conclude, from an ill grounded analogy, that converging rays shall make an object appear at an immense distance : and that, as the convergency increases, the distance (if it were possible) should do so likewise. That this was the cause of Dr. Barrow's mistake, is evident from his own words which we have quoted. Whereas had the learned Doctor observed, that diverging and converging rays, how opposite soever they may seem, do nevertheless agree in producing the same effect, to wit, confusedness of vision, greater degrees whereof are produced indifferently, either as the divergency or convergency of the rays increaseth ; and that it is by this effect, which is the same in both, that either the divergency or convergency is perceived by the eye ;—I say had he but considered this, it is certain he would have made a quite contrary judgment, and rightly concluded, that those rays which fall on the eye with greater degrees of convergency should make the object from whence they proceed appear by so much the nearer. But it was plain, it was impossible for any man to attain to a right notion of this matter, so long as he had regard only to lines and angles, and did not apprehend the true nature of vision, and how far it was of mathematical consideration.

XL. Before we dismiss this subject, it is fit we take notice of a query relating thereto, proposed by the ingenious Mr. Molyneux in his treatise of Dioptrics,[1] where, speaking of this difficulty, he has these words:

[1] Par. I. Prop. xxxi. Sect. 9.

"And so he (*i.e.* Dr. Barrow) leaves this difficulty to the solution of others, which I (after so great an example) shall do likewise ; but with the resolution of the same admirable author of not quitting the evident doctrine which we have before laid down, for determining the *locus objecti*, on account of being pressed by one difficulty, which seems inexplicable till a more intimate knowledge of the visive faculty be obtained by mortals. In the mean time, I propose it to the consideration of the ingenious, whether the *locus apparens* of an object placed as in this 9th Section, be not as much before the eye, as the distinct base is behind the eye." To which query we may venture to answer in the negative. For in the present case, the rule for determining the distance of the distinct base or respective focus from the glass is this : As the difference between the distance of the object and focus is to the focus of focal length, so the distance of the object from the glass is to the distance of the respective focus or distinct base from the glass.[1] Let us now suppose the object to be placed at the distance of the focal length, and one half of the focal length from the glass, and the eye close to the glass, hence it will follow by the rule, that the distance of the distinct base behind the eye is double the true distance of the object before the eye. If therefore Mr. Molyneux's conjecture held good, it would follow that the eye should see the object twice as far off as it really is ; and in other cases at three or four times its due distance, or more. But this manifestly contradicts experience, the object never appearing, at furthest, beyond its due distance. Whatever therefore is built on this supposition (vid. Corol. 1. Prop. lvii. ibid.) comes to the ground along with it.

XLI. From what hath been premised, it is a manifest consequence that a man born blind, being made to see, would, at first, have no idea of distance by sight ; the sun and stars, the remotest objects as well as the nearer, would all seem to be in his eye, or rather in his mind. The objects intromitted by sight, would seem to him (as in truth they are) no other than a new set of thoughts

[1] Molyneux Diopt. Par. I. Prop. **v.**

or sensations, each whereof is as near to him, as the perceptions of pain or pleasure, or the most inward passions of his soul. For our judging objects perceived by sight to be at any distance, or without the mind, is (vide Sect. XXVIII.) entirely the effect of experience, which one in those circumstances could not yet have attained to.

XLII. It is indeed otherwise upon the common supposition, that men judge of distance by the angle of the optic axes, just as one in the dark, or a blind man by the angle comprehended by two sticks, one whereof he held in each hand. For if this were true, it would follow that one blind from his birth being made to see, should stand in need of no new experience, in order to perceive distance by sight. But that this is false, has, I think, been sufficiently demonstrated.

XLIII. And perhaps upon a strict inquiry, we shall not find that even those, who from their birth have grown up in a continued habit of seeing, are irrecoverably prejudiced on the other side, to wit, in thinking what they see to be at a distance from them. For at this time it seems agreed on all hands, by those who have had any thoughts of that matter, that colours, which are the proper and immediate object of sight. are not without the mind. But then it will be said, by sight we have also the ideas of extension, and figure, and motion; all which may well be thought without, and at some distance from the mind, though colour should not. In answer to this, I appeal to any man's experience whether the visible extension of any object doth not appear as near to him, as the colour of that object; nay, whether they do not both seem to be in the very same place. Is not the extension we see coloured, and is it possible for us, so much as in thought, to separate and abstract colour from extension? Now, where the extension is, there surely is the figure, and there the motion too. I speak of those which are perceived by sight.

XLIV. But for a fuller explication of this point, and to show that the immediate objects of sight are not so much as the ideas or resemblances of things placed at a distance, it is requisite that we look nearer into the matter, and carefully observe what is meant in common discourse, when one says, that which he sees is at a distance from him. Suppose, for example, that looking at the moon I should say it were fifty or sixty semidiameters of the earth distant from me. Let us see what moon this is spoken of: it is plain it cannot be the visible moon, or any thing like the visible moon, or that which I see, which is only a round, luminous plain, of about thirty visible points in diameter. For in case I am carried from the place where I stand directly towards the moon, it is manifest the object varies, still as I go on; and by the time that I am advanced fifty or sixty semidiameters of the earth, I shall be so far from being near a small, round, luminous flat, that I shall perceive nothing like it; this object having long since disappeared, and if I would recover it, it must be by going back to the earth from whence I set out. Again, suppose I perceive by sight the faint and obscure idea of something, which I doubt whether it be a man, or a tree, or a tower, but judge it to be at the distance of about a mile: it is plain I cannot mean, that what I see is a mile off, or that it is the image or likeness of any thing which is a mile off, since that every step I take towards it, the appearance alters, and from being obscure, small, and faint, grows clear, large, and vigorous. And when I come to the mile's end, that which I saw first is quite lost, neither do I find any thing in the likeness of it.

XLV. In these and the like instances, the truth of the matter stands thus: having of a long time experienced certain ideas, perceivable by touch, as distance, tangible figure, and solidity, to have been connected with certain ideas of sight, I do, upon perceiving these ideas of sight, forthwith conclude what tangible ideas are, by the wonted ordinary course of nature, like to follow. Looking at an object, I perceive a certain visible figure and colour, with some degree of faintness and other circumstances, which from what I have formerly observed, determine me to think, that if I advance forward so many paces or miles, I shall be affected with such and such ideas of touch : so that in truth and strictness of speech, I neither see distance itself nor any thing that I take to be at a distance. I say, neither distance nor things placed at a distance are themselves, or their ideas, truly perceived by sight. This I am persuaded of, as to what concerns myself; and I believe whoever will look narrowly into his own thoughts, and examine what he means by saying, he sees this or that thing at a distance, will agree with me, that what he sees only suggests to his understanding, that after having passed a certain distance, to be measured by the motion of his body, which is perceivable by touch, he shall come to perceive such and such tangible ideas which have been usually connected with such and such visible ideas. But that one might be deceived by these suggestions of sense, and that there is no necessary connexion between visible and tangible ideas suggested by them, we need go no further than the next looking-glass or picture to be convinced. Note, that when I speak of tangible ideas, I take the word idea for any the immediate object of sense, or understanding, in which large signification it is commonly used by the moderns.

XLVI. From what we have shown it is a manifest consequence, that the ideas of space, outness, and things placed at a distance, are not, strictly speaking, the object of sight; they are not otherwise perceived by the eye than by the ear. Sitting in my study I hear a coach drive along the street ; I look through the casement and see it ; I walk out and enter into it ; thus, common speech would incline one to think, I heard, saw, and touched the same thing, to wit, the coach. It is nevertheless certain, the ideas intromitted by each sense are widely different, and distinct from each other ; but having been observed constantly to go together, they are spoken of as one and the same thing. By the variation of the noise I perceive the different distances of the coach, and know that it approaches before I look out. Thus by the ear I perceive distance, just after the same manner as I do by the eye.

XLVII. I do not nevertheless say, I hear distance in like manner as I say that I see it, the ideas perceived by hearing not being so apt to be confounded with the ideas of touch, as those of sight are; so likewise a man is easily convinced that bodies and external things are not properly the object of hearing, but only sounds, by the mediation whereof the idea of this or that body or distance is suggested to his thoughts. But then one is with more difficulty brought to discern the difference there is betwixt the ideas of sight and touch : though it be certain, a man no more sees or feels the same thing, than he hears and feels the same thing.

XLVIII. One reason of which seems to be this : It is thought a great absurdity to imagine, that one and the same thing should have any more than one extension, and one figure. But the extension and figure of a body, being let into the mind two ways, and that indifferently, either by sight or touch, it seems to follow that we see the same extension, and the same figure which we feel.

XLIX. But if we take a close and accurate view of things, it must be acknowledged that we never see and feel one and the same object. That which is seen is one thing, and that which is felt is another; if the visible figure and extension be not the same with the tangible figure and extension, we are not to infer that one and the same thing has divers extensions. The true consequence is, that the objects of sight and touch are two distinct things. It may perhaps require some thought rightly to conceive this distinction. And the difficulty seems not a little increased, because the combination of visible ideas hath constantly the same name as the combination of tangible ideas wherewith it is connected : which doth of necessity arise from the use and end of language.

L. In order therefore to treat accurately and unconfusedly of vision, we must bear in mind that there are two sorts of objects apprehended by the eye, the one primarily and immediately, the other secondarily and by intervention of the former. Those of the first sort neither are, nor appear to be, without the mind, or at any distance off; they may indeed grow greater or smaller, more confused, or more clear, or more faint, but they do not, cannot approach or recede from us. Whenever we say an object is at a distance, whenever we say it draws near, or goes further off, we must always mean it of the latter sort, which properly belong to the touch, and are not so truly perceived, as suggested by the eye in like manner as thoughts by the ear.

LI. No sooner do we hear the words of a familiar language pronounced in our ears, but the ideas corre· sponding thereto present themselves to our minds; in the very same instant the sound and the meaning enter the understanding: so closely are they united, that it is not in our power to keep out the one, except we exclude the other also. We even act in all respects as if we heard the very thoughts themselves. So likewise the secondary objects, or those which are only suggested by sight, do often more strongly affect us, and are more regarded than the proper objects of that sense, along with which they enter into the mind, and with which they have a far more strict connexion, than ideas have with words. Hence it is, we find it so difficult to discriminate between the immediate and mediate objects of sight, and are so prone to attribute to the former, what belongs only to the latter. They are, as it were, most closely twisted, blended, and incorporated together. And the prejudice is confirmed and riveted in our thoughts by a long tract of time, by the use of language and want of reflection. However, I believe any one that shall attentively consider what we have already said, and shall say upon this subject before we have done (especially if he pursue it in his own thoughts) may be able to deliver himself from that prejudice. Sure I am, it is worth some attention to whoever would understand the true nature of vision.

LII. I have now done with distance, and proceed to show how it is, that we perceive by sight the magnitude of objects. It is the opinion of some that we do it by angles, or by angles in conjunction with distance. But neither angles nor distance being perceivable by sight, and the things we see being in truth at no distance from us, it follows, that as we have shown lines and angles not to be the medium the mind makes use of in apprehending the apparent place, so neither are they the medium whereby it apprehends the apparent magnitude of objects.

LIII. It is well known, that the same extension at a near distance shall subtend a greater angle, and at a further distance a lesser angle. And by this principle, we are told, the mind estimates the magnitude of an object, comparing the angle under which it is seen with its distance, and thence inferring the magnitude thereof. What inclines men to this mistake (beside the humour of making one see by geometry) is, that the same perceptions or ideas which suggest distance, do also suggest magnitude. But if we examine it, we shall find they suggest the latter, as immediately as the former. I say they do not first suggest distance, and then leave it to the judgment to use that as a medium, whereby to collect the magnitude; but they have as close and immediate a connexion with the magnitude, as with the distance; and suggest magnitude as independently of distance, as they do distance independently of magnitude. All which will be evident to whoever considers what hath been already said, and what follows.

LIV. It hath been shown, there are two sorts of objects apprehended by sight; each whereof hath its distinct magnitude, or extension. The one properly tangible, *i.e.* to be perceived and measured by touch, and not immediately falling under the sense of seeing: the other, properly and immediately visible, by mediation of which the former is brought in view. Each of these magnitudes are greater or lesser, according as they contain in them more or fewer points; they being made up of points or minimums. For, whatever may be said of extension in abstract, it is certain, sensible extension is not infinitely divisible. There is a *minimum tangibile*, and a *minimum visibile*, beyond which sense cannot perceive. This every one's experience will inform him.

LV. The magnitude of the object which exists without the mind, and is at a distance, continues always invariably the same : but the visible object still changing as you approach to, or recede from the tangible object, it hath no fixed and determinate greatness. Whenever therefore we speak of the magnitude of any thing, for instance a tree or a house, we must mean the tangible magnitude; otherwise there can be nothing steady and free from ambiguity spoken of it. But though the tangible and visible magnitude in truth belong to two distinct objects, I shall nevertheless (especially since those objects are called by the same name and are observed to coexist) to avoid tediousness and singularity of speech, sometimes speak of them as belonging to one and the same thing.

LVI. Now in order to discover by what means the magnitude of tangible objects is perceived by sight, I need only reflect on what passes in my own mind, and observe what those things be which introduce the ideas of greater or lesser into my thoughts, when I look on any object. And these I find to be, first, the magnitude or extension of the visible object, which being immediately perceived by sight, is connected with that other which is tangible, and placed at a distance; secondly, the confusion or distinctness : and thirdly, the vigorousness or faintness of the aforesaid visible appearance. *Cæteris paribus*, by how much the greater or lesser the visible object is, by so much the greater or lesser do I conclude the tangible object to be. But be the idea immediately perceived by sight never so large, yet if it be withal confused, I judge the magnitude of the thing to be but small : if it be distinct and clear, I judge it greater : and if it be faint, I apprehend it to be yet greater. What is here meant by confusion and faintness, hath been explained in Sect. xxxv.

LVII. Moreover the judgments we make of greatness do, in like manner, as those of distance, depend on the disposition of the eye ; also on the figure, number, and situation of objects, and other circumstances that have been observed to attend great or small tangible magnitudes. Thus, for instance, the very same quantity of visible extension, which in the figure of a tower doth

suggest the idea of great magnitude, shall in the figure
of a man suggest the idea of much smaller magnitude.
That this is owing to the experience we have had of the
usual bigness of a tower and a man, no one, I suppose,
need be told.

LVIII. It is also evident, that confusion or faintness
have no more a necessary connexion with little or great
magnitude, than they have with little or great distance.
As they suggest the latter, so they suggest the former to
our mind. And by consequence, if it were not for experience, we should no more judge a faint or confused
appearance to be connected with great or little magnitude, than we should that it was connected with great or
little distance.

LIX. Nor will it be found, that great or small visible
magnitude hath any necessary relation to great or small
tangible magnitude; so that the one may certainly be
inferred from the other. But, before we come to the
proof of this, it is fit we consider the difference there is
betwixt the extension and figure which is the proper
object of touch, and that other which is termed visible;
and how the former is principally, though not immediately, taken notice of, when we look at any object.
This has been before mentioned, but we shall here inquire into the cause thereof. We regard the objects
that environ us, in proportion as they are adapted to
benefit or injure our own bodies, and thereby produce
in our minds the sensations of pleasure or pain. Now
bodies operating on our organs by an immediate application, and the hurt or advantage arising therefrom depending altogether on the tangible, and not at all on the
visible, qualities of any object; this is a plain reason
why those should be regarded by us much more than
these : and for this end the visive sense seems to have
been bestowed on animals, to wit, that by the perception of visible ideas (which in themselves are not capable
of affecting, or any wise altering the frame of their bodies)
they may be able to foresee (from the experience they
have had, what tangible ideas are connected with such
and such visible ideas) the damage or benefit which is

like to ensue, upon the application of their own bodies
to this or that body which is at a distance : which foresight how necessary it is to the preservation of an animal,
every one's experience can inform him.   Hence it is,
that when we look at an object, the tangible figure and
extension thereof are principally attended to ; whilst
there is small heed taken of the visible figure and magnitude, which, though more immediately perceived, do
less concern us, and are not fitted to produce any alteration in our bodies.

LX. That the matter of fact is true, will be evident to
any one, who considers that a man placed at ten foot
distance, is thought as great, as if he were placed at the
distance of only five foot : which is true, not with relation to the visible, but tangible greatness of the object.
The visible magnitude being far greater at one station
than it is at the other.

LXI. Inches, feet, &c., are settled, stated lengths,
whereby we measure objects, and estimate their magnitude.   We say, for example, an object appears to be six
inches or six foot long.   Now, that this cannot be meant
of visible inches, &c., is evident, because a visible inch
is itself no constant, determinate magnitude, and cannot
therefore serve to mark out and determine the magnitude of any other thing.   Take an inch marked upon a
ruler ; view it successively, at the distance of half a
foot, a foot, a foot and a half, &c., from the eye : at
each of which, and at all the intermediate distances, the
inch shall have a different visible extension, *i.e.* there
shall be more or fewer points discerned in it.   Now I
ask, which of all these various extensions is that stated,
determinate one, that is agreed on for a common measure of other magnitudes ?   No reason can be assigned,
why we should pitch on one, more than another : and
except there be some invariable, determinate extension
fixed on to be marked by the word inch, it is plain, it
can be used to little purpose ; and to say, a thing contains this or that number of inches, shall imply no more
than that it is extended, without bringing any particular
idea of that extension into the mind.   Further, an inch

and a foot, from different distances, shall both exhibit the same visible magnitude, and yet at the same time you shall say, that one seems several times greater than the other. From all which it is manifest, that the judgments we make of the magnitude of objects by sight, are altogether in reference to their tangible extension. Whenever we say an object is great or small, of this or that determinate measure, I say, it must be meant of the tangible, and not the visible extension, which, though immediately perceived, is nevertheless little taken notice of.

LXII. Now, that there is no necessary connexion between these two distinct extensions, is evident from hence ; because our eyes might have been framed in such a manner, as to be able to see nothing but what were less than the *minimum tangibile*. In which case, it is not impossible we might have perceived all the immediate objects of sight, the very same that we do now : but unto those visible appearances, there would not be connected those different tangible magnitudes, that are now. Which shows, the judgments we make of the magnitude of things placed at a distance, from the various greatness of the immediate objects of sight, do not arise from any essential or necessary, but only a customary tie, which has been observed between them.

LXIII. Moreover, it is not only certain, that any idea of sight might not have been connected with this or that idea of touch, which we now observe to accompany it ; but also, that the greater visible magnitudes might have been connected with, and introduced into our minds lesser tangible magnitudes, and the lesser visible magnitudes greater tangible magnitudes. Nay, that it actually is so, we have daily experience ; that object which makes a strong and large appearance, not seeming near so great as another, the visible magnitude whereof is much less, but more faint, and the appearance upper, or which is the same thing painted lower on the *retina*, which faintness and situation suggest both greater magnitude and greater distance.

LXIV. From which, and from Sect. LVII. LVIII., it is

manifest, that as we do not perceive the magnitude of objects immediately by sight, so neither do we perceive them by the mediation of any thing which has a necessary connexion with them. Those ideas that now suggest unto us the various magnitudes of external objects, before we touch them, might possibly have suggested no such thing : or they might have signified them, in a direct contrary manner ; so that the very same ideas, on the perception whereof we judge an object to be small, might as well have served to make us conclude it great. Those ideas being in their own nature equally fitted to bring into our minds the idea of small, or great, or no size at all of outward objects ; just as the words of any language are in their own nature indifferent to signify this or that thing, or nothing at all.

LXV. As we see distance, so we see magnitude. And we see both, in the same way that we see shame or anger in the looks of a man. Those passions are themselves invisible : they are nevertheless let in by the eye along with colours and alterations of countenance, which are the immediate object of vision, and which signify them for no other reason, than barely because they have been observed to accompany them : without which experience, we should no more have taken blushing for a sign of shame, than of gladness.

LXVI. We are nevertheless exceeding prone to imagine those things, which are perceived only by the mediation of others, to be themselves the immediate objects of sight ; or, at least, to have in their own nature a fitness to be suggested by them, before ever they had been experienced to coexist with them. From which prejudice every one, perhaps, will not find it easy to emancipate himself, by any the clearest convictions of reason. And there are some grounds to think, that if there was one only invariable and universal language in the world, and that men were born with the faculty of speaking it, it would be the opinion of many, that the ideas in other men's minds were properly perceived by the ear, or had at least a necessary and inseparable tie with the sounds that were affixed to them. All which seems to arise from a want of due application of our discerning faculty, thereby to discriminate between the ideas that are in our understandings, and consider them apart from each other; which would preserve us from confounding those that are different, and make us see what ideas do, and what do not include or imply this or that other idea.

LXVII. There is a celebrated phenomenon, the solution whereof I shall attempt to give, by the principles that have been laid down, in reference to the manner wherein we apprehend by sight the magnitude of objects. The apparent magnitude of the moon, when placed in the horizon, is much greater than when it is in the meridian; though the angle under which the diameter of the moon is seen, be not observed greater in the former case, than in the latter: and the horizontal moon doth not constantly appear of the same bigness, but at some times seemeth far greater than at others.

LXVIII. Now in order to explain the reason of the moon's appearing greater than ordinary in the horizon, it must be observed, that the particles which compose our atmosphere intercept the rays of light proceeding from any object to the eye; and by how much the greater is the portion of atmosphere interjacent between the object and the eye, by so much the more are the rays intercepted; and by consequence, the appearance of the object rendered more faint, every object appearing more vigorous or more faint, in proportion as it sendeth more or fewer rays into the eye. Now, between the eye and the moon, when situated in the horizon, there lies a far greater quantity of atmosphere, than there does when the moon is in the meridian. Whence it comes to pass, that the appearance of the horizontal moon is fainter, and therefore by Sect. LVI. it should be thought bigger in that situation, than in the meridian, or in any other elevation above the horizon.

LXIX. Further, the air being variously impregnated, sometimes more and sometimes less with vapours and exhalations fitted to retund and intercept the rays of light, it follows, that the appearance of the horizontal moon hath not always an equal faintness, and by consequence, that luminary, though in the very same situation, is at one time judged greater than at another.

LXX. That we have here given the true account of the phenomena of the horizontal moon, will, I suppose, be further evident to any one from the following considerations. First, it is plain, that which in this case suggests the idea of greater magnitude, must be something which is itself perceived; for, that which is unperceived cannot suggest to our perception any other thing. Secondly, it must be something that does not constantly remain the same, but is subject to some change or variation, since the appearance of the horizontal moon varies, being at one time greater than at another. And yet, thirdly, it cannot be the visible figure or magnitude, since that remains the same, or is rather lesser, by how much the moon is nearer to the horizon. It remains therefore, that the true cause is that affection or alteration of the visible appearance, which proceeds from the greater paucity of rays arriving at the eye, and which I term *faintness*, since this answers all the forementioned conditions, and I am not conscious of any other perception that doth.

LXXI. Add to this, that in misty weather it is a common observation, that the appearance of the horizontal moon is far larger than usual, which greatly conspires with, and strengthens our opinion. Neither would it prove, in the least, irreconcileable with what we have said, if the horizontal moon should chance sometimes to seem enlarged beyond its usual extent, even in more serene weather. For we must not only have regard to the mist which happens to be in the place where we stand; we ought also to take into our thoughts the whole sum of vapours and exhalations, which lie betwixt the eye and the moon: all which co-operating to render the appearance of the moon more faint, and thereby increase its magnitude, it may chance to appear greater than it usually does, even in the horizontal position, at a time when, though there be no extraordinary fog or haziness just in the place where we stand; yet, the air between the eye and the moon, taken altogether, may be loaded with a greater quantity of interspersed vapours and exhalations, than at other times.

LXXII. It may be objected, that in consequence of our principles, the interposition of a body in some degree opaque, which may intercept a great part of the rays of light, should render the appearance of the moon in the meridian as large, as when it is viewed in the horizon. To which I answer, it is not faintness any how applied, that suggests greater magnitude, there being no necessary, but only an experimental connexion between those two things: it follows, that the faintness, which enlarges the appearance, must be applied in such sort, and with such circumstances, as have been observed to attend the vision of great magnitudes. When from a distance we behold great objects, the particles of the intermediate air and vapours, which are themselves unperceivable, do interrupt the rays of light, and thereby render the appearance less strong and vivid; now, faintness of appearance, caused in this sort, hath been experienced to coexist with great magnitude. But when it is caused by the interposition of an opaque sensible body, this circumstance alters the case, so that a faint appearance this way caused, doth not suggest greater magnitude, because it hath not been experienced to coexist with it.

LXXIII. Faintness, as well as all other ideas of perceptions, which suggest magnitude or distance, doth it in the same way that words suggest the notions to which they are annexed. Now it is known, a word pronounced with certain circumstances, or in a certain context with other words, hath not always the same import and signification that it hath when pronounced in some other circumstances, or different context of words. The very same visible appearance as to faintness and all other respects, if placed on high, shall not suggest the same magnitude that it would if it were seen at an equal distance, on a level with the eye. The reason whereof is, that we are rarely accustomed to view objects at a great height; our concerns lie among things situated rather before than above us; and accordingly our eyes are not placed on the top of our heads, but in such a position as is most convenient for us to see distant objects standing in our way, and this situation of them being a circumstance which usually attends the vision of distant objects, we may from hence account for (what is commonly observed) an object's appearing of different magnitude, even with respect to its horizontal extension, on the top of a steeple, for example, a hundred feet high, to one standing below, from what it would if placed at a hundred feet distance on a level with his eye. For it hath been shown, that the judgment we make on the magnitude of a thing, depends not on the visible appearance alone, but also on divers other circumstances, any one of which being omitted or varied may suffice to make some alteration in our judgment. Hence, the circumstance of viewing a distant object in such a situation as is usual, and suits with the ordinary posture of the head and eyes, being omitted, and instead thereof a different situation of the object which requires a different posture of the head taking place, it is not to be wondered at, if the magnitude be judged different; but it will be demanded, why a high object should constantly appear less than an equidistant low object of the same dimensions, for so it is observed to be; it may indeed be granted that the variation of some circumstances may vary the judgment, made on the magnitude of high objects, which we are less used to look at; but it does not hence appear, why they should be judged less rather than greater? I answer, that in case the magnitude of distant objects was suggested by the extent of their visible appearance alone, and thought proportional thereto, it is certain they would then be judged much less than now they seem to be, vide Sect. LXXIX. But several circumstances concurring to form the judgment we make on the magnitude of distant objects, by means of which they appear far larger than others, whose visible appearance hath an equal or even greater extension; it follows, that upon the change or omission of any of those circumstances, which are wont to attend the vision of distant objects, and so come to influence the judgments made on their magnitude, they shall proportionably appear less than otherwise they would. For any of those things that caused an object to be thought greater, than in proportion to its visible extension, being either omitted or applied without the usual circumstances, the judgment depends more entirely on the visible extension, and consequently the object must be judged less. Thus in the present case, the situation of the thing seen being different from what it usually is in those objects we have occasion to view, and whose magnitude we observe, it follows, that the very same object, being a hundred feet high, should seem less than if it was a hundred feet off on (or nearly on) a level with the eye. What has been here set forth, seems to me to have no small share in contributing to magnify the appearance of the horizontal moon, and deserves not to be passed over in the explication of it.

LXXIV. If we attentively consider the phenomenon before us, we shall find the not discerning between the mediate and immediate objects of sight, to be the chief cause of the difficulty that occurs in the explication of it. The magnitude of the visible moon, or that which is the proper and immediate object of vision, is no greater when the moon is in the horizon, than when it is in the meridian. How comes it, therefore, to seem greater in one situation than the other? What is it can put this cheat on the understanding? It has no other perception of the moon, than what it gets by sight: and that which is seen, is of the same extent, I say the visible appearance hath the same, or rather a less magnitude, when the moon is viewed in the horizontal, than when in the meridional position: and yet it is esteemed greater in the former than in the latter. Herein consists the difficulty, which doth vanish and admit of a most easy solution, if we consider that as the visible moon is not greater in the horizon than in the meridian, so neither is it thought to be so. It hath been already shown, that in any act of vision, the visible object absolutely, or in itself, is little taken notice of, the mind still carrying its view from that to some tangible ideas, which have been observed to be connected with it, and by that means come to be suggested by it. So that when a thing is said to appear great or small, or whatever estimate be made of the magnitude of any thing, this is meant not of the visible, but of the tangible object. This duly considered, it will be no hard matter to reconcile the seeming contradiction there is, that the moon should appear of a different bigness, the visible magnitude thereof remaining still the same. For by Sect. LVI. the very same visible extension, with a different faintness, shall suggest a different tangible extension. When therefore the horizontal moon is said to appear greater than the meridional moon, this must be understood not of a greater visible extension, but of a greater tangible or real extension, which by reason of the more than ordinary faintness of the visible appearance, is suggested to the mind along with it.

LXXV. Many attempts have been made by learned men, to account for this appearance. Gassendus, Descartes, Hobbes, and several others, have employed their thoughts on that subject; but how fruitless and unsatisfactory their endeavours have been, is sufficiently shown in the Philosophical Transactions,[1] where you may see their several opinions at large set forth and confuted, not without some surprise at the gross blunders that ingenious men have been forced into, by endeavouring to reconcile this appearance with the ordinary principles of optics. Since the writing of which, there hath been published in the Transactions [2] another paper relating to the same affair, by the celebrated Dr. Wallis, wherein he attempts to account for that phenomena, which, though it seems not to contain any thing new, or different from what had been said before by others, I shall nevertheless consider in this place.

LXXVI. His opinion, in short, is this; we judge not of the magnitude of an object by the visual angle alone, but by the visual angle in conjunction with the distance. Hence, though the angle remain the same, or even

[1] Phil. Trans. Num. 187, p. 314.   [2] Num. 187, p. 323.

become less, yet if withal the distance seem to have
been increased, the object shall appear greater. Now,
one way whereby we estimate the distance of any thing,
is by the number and extent of the intermediate objects :
when therefore the moon is seen in the horizon, the
variety of fields, houses, &c., together with the large prospect of the wide, extended land or sea, that lies between
the eye and the utmost limb of the horizon, suggest
unto the mind the idea of greater distance, and consequently magnify the appearance. And this, according
to Dr. Wallis, is the true account of the extraordinary
largeness attributed by the mind to the horizontal moon,
at a time when the angle subtended by its diameter is
not one jot greater than it used to be.

LXXVII. With reference to this opinion, not to repeat
what hath already been said concerning distance, I shall
only observe, first, that if the prospect of interjacent
objects be that which suggests the idea of further distance, and this idea of further distance be the cause that
brings into the mind the idea of greater magnitude, it
should hence follow, that if one looked at the horizontal
moon from behind a wall, it would appear no bigger
than ordinary. For in that case, the wall interposing
cuts off all that prospect of sea and land, &c., which
might otherwise increase the apparent distance, and
thereby the apparent magnitude of the moon. Nor
will it suffice to say, the memory doth even then
suggest all that extent of land, &c., which lies
within the horizon; which suggestion occasions a
sudden judgment of sense, that the moon is further off
and larger than usual. For ask any man, who from
such a station beholding the horizontal moon, shall
think her greater than usual, whether he hath at that
time in his mind any idea of the intermediate objects, or
long tract of land that lies between his eye and the
extreme edge of the horizon? And whether it be that
idea which is the cause of his making the aforementioned
judgment? He will, I suppose, reply in the negative,
and declare the horizontal moon shall appear greater
than the meridional, though he never thinks of all or

any of those things that lie between him and it. Secondly, it seems impossible by this hypothesis to account for the moon's appearing in the very same situation, at one time greater than at another; which nevertheless has been shown to be very agreeable to the principles we have laid down, and receives a most easy and natural explication from them. For the further clearing up of this point, it is to be observed that what we immediately and properly see are only lights and colours in sundry situations and shades, and degrees of faintness and clearness, confusion and distinctness. All which visible objects are only in the mind; nor do they suggest aught external, whether distance or magnitude, otherwise than by habitual connexion as words do things. We are also to remark that, beside the straining of the eyes, and beside the vivid and faint, the distinct and confused appearances (which bearing some proportions to lines and angles, have been substituted instead of them, in the foregoing part of this treatise), there are other means which suggest both distance and magnitude; particularly, the situation of visible points, or objects, as upper or lower; the former suggesting a further distance, and greater magnitude, the latter a nearer distance, and lesser magnitude: all which is an effect only of custom and experience, there being really nothing intermediate in the line of distance, between the uppermost and lower-most, which are both equidistant, or rather at no distance from the eye, as there is also nothing in upper or lower, which by necessary connexion should suggest greater or lesser magnitude. Now, as these customary, experimental means of suggesting distance, do likewise suggest magnitude, so they suggest the one as immediately as the other. I say they do not (vide Sect. LIII.) first suggest distance, and then leave the mind from thence to infer or compute magnitude, but suggest magnitude as immediately and directly as they suggest distance.

LXXVIII. This phenomenon of the horizontal moon is a clear instance of the insufficiency of lines and angles, for explaining the way wherein the mind perceives and estimates the magnitude of outward objects. There is nevertheless a use of computation by them, in order to determine the apparent magnitude of things, so far as they have a connexion with, and are proportional to those other ideas or perceptions, which are the true and immediate occasions that suggest to the mind the apparent magnitude of things. But this in general may, I think, be observed concerning mathematical computation in optics; that it can never be very precise and exact, since the judgments we make of the magnitude of external things do often depend on several circumstances, which are not proportionable to, or capable of being defined by lines or angles.

LXXIX. From what has been said, we may safely deduce this consequence, to wit, that a man born blind, and made to see, would at first opening of his eyes make a far different judgment of the magnitude of objects intromitted by them, from what others do. He would not consider the ideas of sight, with reference to, or as having any connexion with the ideas of touch : his view of them being entirely terminated within themselves, he can no otherwise judge them great or small, than as they contain a greater or lesser number of visible points. Now, it being certain that any visible point can cover or exclude from view only one other visible point, it follows that whatever object intercepts the view of another, hath an equal number of visible points with it ; and consequently they shall both be thought by him to have the same magnitude. Hence it is evident, one in those circumstances would judge his thumb, with which he might hide a tower, or hinder its being seen, equal to that tower, or his hand, the interposition whereof might conceal the firmament from his view, equal to the firmament : how great an inequality soever there may, in our apprehensions, seem to be betwixt those two things, because of the customary and close connexion that has grown up in our minds between the objects of sight and touch, whereby the very different and distinct ideas of those two senses are so blended and confounded together, as to be mistaken for one and the same thing ; out of which prejudice we cannot easily extricate ourselves.

LXXX. For the better explaining the nature of vision, and setting the manner wherein we perceive magnitudes in a due light, I shall proceed to make some observations concerning matters relating thereto, whereof the want of reflection, and duly separating between tangible and visible ideas, is apt to create in us mistaken and confused notions. And first, I shall observe that the *minimum visibile* is exactly equal in all beings whatsoever, that are endowed with the visive faculty. No exquisite formation of the eye, no peculiar sharpness of sight, can make it less in one creature than in another; for it not being distinguishable into parts, nor in any wise consisting of them, it must necessarily be the same to all. For suppose it otherwise, and that the *minimum visibile* of a mite, for instance, be less than the *minimum visibile* of a man; the latter therefore may by detraction of some part be made equal to the former: it doth therefore consist of parts, which is inconsistent with the notion of a *minimum visibile*, or point.

LXXXI. It will perhaps be objected that the *minimum visibile* of a man doth really and in itself contain parts whereby it surpasses that of a mite, though they are not perceivable by the man. To which I answer, the *minimum visibile* having (in like manner as all other the proper and immediate objects of sight) been shown not to have any existence without the mind of him who sees it, it follows there cannot be any part of it that is not exactly perceived, and therefore visible. Now for any object to contain several distinct visible parts, and at the same time to be a *minimum visibile*, is a manifest contradiction.

LXXXII. Of these visible points we see at all times an equal number. It is every whit as great when our view is contracted and bounded by near objects, as when it is extended to larger and remoter. For it being impossible that one *minimum visibile* should obscure or keep out of sight more than another, it is a plain consequence, that when my view is on all sides bounded by the walls of my study, I see just as many visible points as I could, in case that by the removal of the study-walls, and all other obstructions, I had a full prospect of the circumjacent fields, mountains, sea, and open firmament; for so long as I am shut up within the walls, by their interposition, every point of the external objects is covered from my view: but each point that is seen being able to cover or exclude from sight one only other corresponding point, it follows that whilst my sight is confined to those narrow walls, I see as many points, or *minima visibilia*, as I should were those walls away, by looking on all the external objects, whose prospect is intercepted by them.   Whenever therefore we are said to have a greater prospect at one time than another, this must be understood with relation not to the proper and immediate, but the secondary and mediate objects of vision, which, as hath been shown, properly belong to the touch.

LXXXIII. The visive faculty, considered with reference to its immediate objects, may be found to labour of two defects: first, in respect of the extent or number of visible points that are at once perceivable by it, which is narrow and limited to a certain degree.   It can take in at view but a certain determinate number of *minima visibilia*, beyond which it cannot extend its prospect.   Secondly, our sight is defective in that its view is not only narrow, but also for the most part confused; of those things that we take in at one prospect, we can see but a few at once clearly and unconfusedly; and the more we fix our sight on any one object, by so much the darker and more indistinct shall the rest appear.

LXXXIV. Corresponding to these two defects of sight, we may imagine as many perfections, to wit, first, that of comprehending in one view a greater number of visible points; secondly, of being able to view them all equally and at once, with the utmost clearness and distinction.   That those perfections are not actually in some intelligences of a different order and capacity from ours, it is impossible for us to know.

LXXXV. In neither of those two ways do microscopes contribute to the improvement of sight; for when we look through a microscope, we neither see more visible points nor are the collateral points more distinct than when we look with the naked eye, at objects placed in a due distance. A microscope brings us as it were into a new world: it presents us with a new scene of visible objects, quite different from what we behold with the naked eye. But herein consists the most remarkable difference, to wit, that whereas the objects perceived by the eye alone, have a certain connexion with tangible objects, whereby we are taught to foresee what ensue upon the approach or application of distant objects to the parts of our own body, which much conduceth to its preservation; there is not the like connexion between things tangible and those visible objects that are perceived by help of a microscope.

LXXXVI. Hence it is evident, that were our eyes turned into the nature of microscopes, we should not be much benefited by the change; we should be deprived of the forementioned advantage we at present receive by the visive faculty; and have left us only the empty amusement of seeing, without any other benefit arising from it. But in that case, it will perhaps be said, our sight would be endued with a far greater sharpness and penetration than it now hath. But I would fain know wherein consists that sharpness, which is esteemed so great an excellency of sight. It is certain from what we have already shown, that the *minimum visibile* is never greater or lesser, but in all cases constantly the same: and in the case of microscopical eyes, I see only this difference, to wit, that upon the ceasing of a certain observable connexion betwixt the divers perceptions of sight and touch, which before enabled us to regulate our actions by the eye, it would now be rendered utterly unserviceable to that purpose.

LXXXVII. Upon the whole, it seems that if we consider the use and end of sight, together with the present state and circumstances of our being, we shall not find any great cause to complain of any defect or imperfection in it, or easily conceive how it could be mended. With such admirable wisdom is that faculty contrived, both for the pleasure and convenience of life.

LXXXVIII. Having finished what I intended to say, concerning the distance and magnitude of objects, I come now to treat of the manner wherein the mind perceives by sight their situation. Among the discoveries of the last age, it is reputed none of the least, that the manner of vision hath been more clearly explained than ever it had been before. There is, at this day, no one ignorant, that the pictures of external objects are painted on the *retina*, or fund of the eye. That we can see nothing which is not so painted: and that, according as the picture is more distinct or confused, so also is the perception we have of the object: but then in this explication of vision, there occurs one mighty difficulty. The objects are painted in an inverted order on the bottom of the eye: the upper part of any object being painted on the lower part of the eye, and the lower part of the object on the upper part of the eye: and so also as to right and left. Since therefore the pictures are thus inverted, it is demanded how it comes to pass, that we see the objects erect and in their natural posture?

LXXXIX. In answer to this difficulty, we are told, that the mind, perceiving an impulse of a ray of light on the upper part of the eye, considers this ray as coming in a direct line from the lower part of the object, and in like manner tracing the ray that strikes on the lower part of the eye, it is directed to the upper part of the object. Thus in the adjacent figure C the lower point of the object A B C is projected on *c* the upper part of the eye. So likewise, the highest point A is projected on *a* the lowest part of the eye, which makes the representation *c b a* inverted: but the mind, considering the stroke that is made on *c* as coming in the straight line C *c* from the lower end of the object, and the stroke or impulse on *a* as coming in the line A *a* from the upper end of the object, is directed to make a right judgment of the situation of the object A B C, notwithstanding the picture of it is inverted. This is illustrated by conceiving a blind man, who, holding in his hand two sticks that cross each other, doth with them touch the extremities of an object, placed in a perpendicular situation. It is certain, this man will judge that to be the upper part of the object, which he touches with the stick held in the

undermost hand, and that to be the lower part of the
object, which he touches with the stick in his uppermost
hand. This is the common explication of the erect

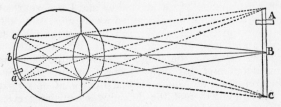

appearance of objects, which is generally received and
acquiesced in, being (as Mr. Molyneux tells us [1]) *allowed
by all men as satisfactory.*

XC. But this account to me does not seem in any
degree true. Did I perceive those impulses, decussa-
tions, and directions of the rays of light, in like manner
as hath been set forth, then, indeed, it would not at first
view be altogether void of probability. And there might
be some pretence for the comparison of the blind man
and his cross sticks. But the case is far otherwise. I
know very well that I perceive no such thing. And, of
consequence, I cannot thereby make an estimate of the
situation of objects. I appeal to any one's experience,
whether he be conscious to himself, that he thinks on the
intersection made by the radious pencils, or pursues the
impulses they give in right lines, whenever he perceives
by sight the position of any object? To me it seems
evident, that crossing and tracing of the rays, is never
thought on by children, idiots, or in truth by any other,
save only those who have applied themselves to the
study of optics. And for the mind to judge of the
situation of objects by those things, without perceiving
them, or to perceive them without knowing it, is equally
beyond my comprehension. Add to this, that the explaining the manner of vision by the example of cross
sticks, and hunting for the object along the axes of the
radious pencils, doth suppose the proper objects of sight

[1] Diopt. Par. ii. c. 7, p. 289.

to be perceived at a distance from us, contrary to what hath been demonstrated.

XCI. It remains, therefore, that we look for some other explanation of this difficulty : and I believe it not impossible to find one, provided we examine it to the bottom, and carefully distinguish between the ideas of sight and touch ; which cannot be too oft inculcated in treating of vision : but more especially throughout the consideration of this affair, we ought to carry that distinction in our thoughts : for that from want of a right understanding thereof, the difficulty of explaining erect vision seems chiefly to arise.

XCII. In order to disentangle our minds from whatever prejudices we may entertain with relation to the subject in hand, nothing seems more apposite, than the taking into our thoughts the case of one born blind, and afterwards, when grown up, made to see. And though perhaps it may not be an easy task to divest ourselves entirely of the experience received from sight, so as to be able to put our thoughts exactly in the posture of such a one's : we must nevertheless, as far as possible, endeavour to frame true conceptions of what might reasonably be supposed to pass in his mind.

XCIII. It is certain that a man actually blind, and who had continued so from his birth, would by the sense of feeling attain to have ideas of upper and lower. By the motion of his hand he might discern the situation of any tangible object placed within his reach. That part on which he felt himself supported, or towards which he perceived his body to gravitate, he would term lower, and the contrary to this upper ; and accordingly denominate whatsoever objects he touched.

XCIV. But then, whatever judgments he makes concerning the situation of objects, are confined to those only that are perceivable by touch. All those things that are intangible, and of a spiritual nature, his thoughts and desires, his passions, and in general all the modifications of his soul, to these he would never apply the terms upper and lower, except only in a metaphorical sense. He may, perhaps, by way of allusion, speak of high or low thoughts : but those terms, in their proper signification, would never be applied to any thing that was not conceived to exist without the mind. For a man born blind, and remaining in the same state, could mean nothing else by the words higher and lower, than a greater or lesser distance from the earth : which distance he would measure by the motion or application of his hand, or some other part of his body. It is, therefore, evident, that all those things which, in respect of each other, would by him be thought higher or lower, must be such as were conceived to exist without his mind, in the ambient space.

XCV. Whence it plainly follows, that such a one, if we suppose him made to see, would not at first sight think that any thing he saw was high or low, erect or inverted : for it hath been already demonstrated in Sect. XLI. that he would not think the things he perceived by sight to be at any distance from him, or without his mind. The objects to which he had hitherto been used to apply the terms up and down, high and low, were such only as affected, or were some way perceived by his touch ; but the proper objects of vision make a new set of ideas, perfectly distinct and different from the former, and which can in no sort make themselves perceived by touch. There is, therefore, nothing at all that could induce him to think those terms applicable to them : nor would he ever think it, till such time as he had observed their connexion with tangible objects, and the same prejudice began to insinuate itself into his understanding, which from their infancy had grown up in the understandings of other men.

XCVI. To set this matter in a clearer light, I shall make use of an example. Suppose the above-mentioned blind person, by his touch, perceives a man to stand erect. Let us inquire into the manner of this. By the application of his hand to the several parts of a human body, he had perceived different tangible ideas, which being collected into sundry complex ones have distinct names annexed to them. Thus one combination of a certain tangible figure, bulk, and consistency of parts is called the head, another the hand, a third the foot, and so of the rest: all which complex ideas could, in his understanding, be made up only of ideas perceivable by touch. He had also by his touch obtained an idea of earth or ground, towards which he perceives the parts of his body to have a natural tendency. Now, by erect nothing more being meant, than that perpendicular position of a man, wherein his feet are nearest to the earth: if the blind person, by moving his hand over the parts of the man who stands before him, perceives the tangible ideas that compose the head, to be furthest from, and those that compose the feet to be nearest to, that other combination of tangible ideas which he calls earth: he will denominate that man erect. But if we suppose him on a sudden to receive his sight, and that he behold a man standing before him, it is evident, in that case, he would neither judge the man he sees to be erect nor inverted; for he never having known those terms applied to any other save tangible things, or which existed in the space without him, and what he sees neither being tangible, nor perceived as existing without, he could not know that in propriety of language they were applicable to it.

XCVII. Afterwards, when upon turning his head or eyes up and down to the right and left, he shall observe the visible objects to change, and shall also attain to know, that they are called by the same names, and connected with the objects perceived by touch; then, indeed, he will come to speak of them and their situation, in the same terms that he has been used to apply to tangible things: and those that he perceives by turning up his eyes, he will call upper, and those that by turning down his eyes, he will call lower.

XCVIII. And this seems to me the true reason why he should think those objects uppermost that are painted on the lower part of his eye: for, by turning the eye up they shall be distinctly seen; as likewise those that are painted on the highest part of the eye shall be distinctly seen, by turning the eye down, and are for that reason esteemed lowest: for we have shown that to the immediate objects of sight, considered in themselves, he would not attribute the terms high and low. It must therefore be on account of some circumstances which are observed to attend them ; and these, it is plain, are the actions of turning the eye up and down, which suggest a very obvious reason, why the mind should denominate the objects of sight accordingly high or low. And without this motion of the eye, this turning it up and down in order to discern different objects, doubtless, erect, inverse, and other the like terms relating to the position of tangible objects, would never have been transferred, or in any degree apprehended to belong to the ideas of sight : the mere act of seeing including nothing in it to that purpose ; whereas the different situations of the eye naturally direct the mind to make a suitable judgment of the situation of objects intromitted by it.

XCIX. Further, when he has by experience learned the connexion there is between the several ideas of sight and touch, he will be able, by the perception he has of the situation of visible things in respect of one another, to make a sudden and true estimation of the situation of outward, tangible things corresponding to them. And thus it is, he shall perceive by sight the situation of external objects, which do not properly fall under that sense.

C. I know we are very prone to think, that if just made to see, we should judge of the situation of visible things as we do now : but, we are also as prone to think, that at first sight, we should in the same way apprehend the distance and magnitude of objects, as we do now : which hath been shown to be a false and groundless persuasion. And for the like reasons, the same censure may be passed on the positive assurance, that most men, before they have thought sufficiently of the matter, might have of their being able to determine by the eye, at first view, whether objects were erect or inverse.

CI. It will, perhaps, be objected to our opinion, that a man, for instance, being thought erect when his feet are next the earth, and inverted when his head is next the earth, it doth hence follow, that by the mere act of vision, without any experience or altering the situation of the eye, we should have determined whether he were erect or inverted: for both the earth itself, and the limbs of the man who stands thereon, being equally perceived by sight, one cannot choose seeing what part of the man is nearest the earth, and what part furthest from it, *i.e.* whether he be erect or inverted.

CII. To which I answer, the ideas which constitute the tangible earth and man, are entirely different from those which constitute the visible earth and man. Nor was it possible, by virtue of the visive faculty alone, without superadding any experience of touch, or altering the position of the eye, ever to have known, or so much as suspected, there had been any relation or connexion between them: hence a man at first view would not denominate any thing he saw, earth, or head, or foot; and consequently, he could not tell by the mere act of vision, whether the head or feet were nearest the earth: nor, indeed, would he have thereby any thought of earth or man, erect or inverse, at all: which will be made yet more evident if we nicely observe, and make a particular comparison between the ideas of both senses.

CIII. That which I see is only variety of light and colours. That which I feel is hard or soft, hot or cold, rough or smooth. What similitude, what connexion have those ideas with these? Or how is it possible, that any one should see reason to give one and the same name to combinations of ideas so very different before he had experienced their co-existence? We do not find there is any necessary connexion betwixt this or that tangible quality, and any colour whatsoever. And we may sometimes perceive colours, where there is nothing to be felt. All which doth make it manifest that no man, at first receiving of his sight, would know there was any agreement between this or that particular object of his sight, and any object of touch he had been already acquainted with: the colours therefore of the head, would to him no more suggest the idea of head, than they would the idea of foot.

CIV. Further, we have at large shown (vide Sect. LXIII. and LXIV.) there is no discoverable necessary connexion, between any given visible magnitude, and any one particular tangible magnitude; but that it is entirely the result of custom and experience, and depends on foreign and accidental circumstances, that we can by the perception of visible extension inform ourselves, what may be the extension of any tangible object connected with it. Hence it is certain that neither the visible magnitude of head or foot, would bring along with them into the mind, at first opening of the eyes, the respective tangible magnitude of these parts.

CV. By the foregoing section, it is plain the visible figure of any part of the body hath no necessary connexion with the tangible figure thereof, so as at first sight to suggest it to the mind: for figure is the termination of magnitude, whence it follows, that no visible magnitude, having in its own nature an aptness to suggest any one particular tangible magnitude, so neither can any visible figure be inseparably connected with its corresponding tangible figure: so as of itself and in a way prior to experience, it might suggest it to the understanding. This will be further evident, if we consider that what seems smooth and round to the touch, may to sight, if viewed through a microscope, seem quite otherwise.

CVI. From all which laid together and duly considered, we may clearly deduce this inference. In the first act of vision, no idea entering by the eye would have a perceivable connexion with the ideas to which the names earth, man, head, foot, &c., were annexed in the understanding of a person blind from his birth; so as in any sort to introduce them into his mind, or make themselves be called by the same names, and reputed the same things with them, as afterwards they come to be.

CVII. There doth, nevertheless, remain one difficulty, which perhaps may seem to press hard on our opinion, and deserve not to be passed over: for though it be granted that neither the colour, size, nor figure of the visible feet have any necessary connexion with the ideas that compose the tangible feet, so as to bring them at first sight into my mind, or make me in danger of confounding them before I had been used to, and for some time experienced their connexion: yet thus much seems undeniable, namely, that the number of the visible feet, being the same with that of the tangible feet, I may from hence, without any experience of sight, reasonably conclude, that they represent or are connected with the feet rather than the head. I say, it seems the idea of two visible feet will sooner suggest to the mind the idea of two tangible feet than of one head; so that the blind man, upon first reception of the visive faculty, might know which were the feet or two, and which the head or one.

CVIII. In order to get clear of this seeming difficulty, we need only observe, that diversity of visible objects doth not necessarily infer diversity of tangible objects corresponding to them. A picture painted with great variety of colours affects the touch in one uniform manner; it is therefore evident, that I do not by any necessary consecution, independent of experience, judge of the number of things tangible, from the number of things visible. I should not therefore at first opening my eyes conclude, that because I see two I shall feel two. How, therefore can I, before experience teaches me, know that the visible legs, because two, are connected with the tangible legs, or the visible head, because one, is connected with the tangible head? The truth is, the things I see are so very different and heterogeneous from the things I feel, that the perception of the one would never have suggested the other to my thoughts, or enabled me to pass the least judgment thereon, until I had experienced their connexion.

CIX. But for a fuller illustration of this matter, it ought to be considered that number (however some may reckon it amongst the primary qualities) is nothing fixed and settled, really existing in things themselves. It is entirely the creature of the mind, considering, either an idea by itself, or any combination of ideas to which it gives one name, and so makes it pass for a unit. According as the mind variously combines its ideas, the unit varies; and as the unit, so the number, which is only a collection of units, doth also vary. We call a window one, a chimney one, and yet a house in which there are many windows, and many chimneys, hath an equal right to be called one, and many houses go to the making of one city. In these and the like instances, it is evident the *unit* constantly relates to the particular draughts the mind makes of its ideas, to which it affixes names, and wherein it includes more or less, as best suits its own ends and purposes. Whatever therefore the mind considers as one, that is a unit. Every combination of ideas is considered as one thing by the mind, and in token thereof is marked by one name. Now, this naming and combining together of ideas is perfectly arbitrary, and done by the mind in such sort, as experience shows it to be most convenient: without which, our ideas had never been collected into such sundry distinct combinations as they now are.

CX. Hence it follows, that a man born blind, and afterwards, when grown up, made to see, would not, in the first act of vision, parcel out the ideas of sight into the same distinct collections that others do, who have experienced which do regularly coexist and are proper to be bundled up together under one name. He would not, for example, make into one complex idea, and thereby esteem and unite all those particular ideas, which constitute the visible head or foot. For there can be no reason assigned why he should do so, barely upon his seeing a man stand upright before him : there crowd into his mind the ideas which compose the visible man, in company with all the other ideas of sight perceived at the same time: but all these ideas offered at once to his view, he would not distribute into sundry distinct combinations, till such time as, by observing the motion of the parts of the man and other experiences, he comes to know which are to be separated, and which to be collected together.

CXI. From what hath been premised, it is plain the objects of sight and touch make, if I may so say, two sets of ideas which are widely different from each other. To objects of either kind, we indifferently attribute the terms high and low, right and left, and such like, denoting the position or situation of things: but then we must well observe that the position of any object is determined with respect only to objects of the same sense. We say any object of touch is high or low, according as it is more or less distant from the tangible earth: and in like manner we denominate any object of sight high or low, in proportion as it is more or less distant from the visible earth: but to define the situation of visible things, with relation to the distance they bear from any tangible thing, or *vice versa*, this were absurd and perfectly unintelligible. For all visible things are equally in the mind, and take up no part of the external space: and consequently are equidistant from any tangible thing, which exists without the mind.

CXII. Or rather to speak truly, the proper objects of sight are at no distance, neither near nor far from any tangible thing. For if we inquire narrowly into the matter, we shall find that those things only are compared together in respect of distance, which exist after the same manner, or appertain unto the same sense. For by the distance between any two points, nothing more is meant than the number of intermediate points: if the given points are visible, the distance between them is marked out by the number of the interjacent visible points: if they are tangible, the distance between them is a line consisting of tangible points; but if they are one tangible, and the other visible, the distance between them doth neither consist of points perceivable by sight nor by touch, *i.e.* it is utterly inconceivable. This, perhaps, will not find an easy admission into all men's understanding: however, I should gladly be informed whether it be not true, by any one who will be at the pains to reflect a little, and apply it home to his thoughts.

CXIII. The not observing what has been delivered in the two last sections, seems to have occasioned no small part of the difficulty that occurs in the business of erect appearances. The head, which is painted nearest the earth, seems to be furthest from it ; and on the other hand, the feet, which are painted furthest from the earth, are thought nearest to it. Herein lies the difficulty, which vanishes if we express the thing more clearly and free from ambiguity, thus : how comes it that, to the eye, the visible head, which is nearest the tangible earth, seems furthest from the earth, and the visible feet, which are furthest from the tangible earth, seem nearest the earth. The question being thus proposed, who sees not the difficulty is founded on a supposition, that the eye, or visive faculty, or rather the soul by means thereof, should judge of the situation of visible objects, with reference to their distance from the tangible earth ? Whereas it is evident the tangible earth is not perceived by sight: and it hath been shown in the two last preceding sections, that the location of visible objects is determined only by the distance they bear from one another ; and that it is nonsense to talk of distance, far or near, between a visible and tangible thing.

CXIV. If we confine our thoughts to the proper objects of sight, the whole is plain and easy. The head is painted furthest from, and the feet nearest to the visible earth ; and so they appear to be. What is there strange or unaccountable in this ? Let us suppose the pictures in the fund of the eye, to be the immediate objects of the sight. The consequence is, that things should appear in the same posture they are painted in ; and is it not so ? The head which is seen, seems furthest from the earth which is seen ; and the feet which are seen, seem nearest to the earth which is seen ? and just so they are painted.

CXV. But, say you, the picture of the man is inverted, and yet the appearance is erect : I ask, what mean you by the picture of the man, or, which is the same thing, the visible man's being inverted ? You tell me it is inverted, because the heels are uppermost, and the head undermost ? Explain me this. You say, that by the head's being undermost, you mean that it is nearest to the earth ; and by the heels being uppermost, that they are furthest from the earth. I ask again, what earth you mean ? You cannot mean the earth that is painted on the eye, or the visible earth : for the picture of the head is furthest from the picture of the earth, and the picture of the feet nearest to the picture of the earth; and accordingly the visible head is furthest from the visible earth, and the visible feet nearest to it. It remains, therefore, that you mean the tangible earth, and so determine the situation of visible things with respect to tangible things : contrary to what hath been demonstrated in Sect. CXI. and CXII. The two distinct provinces of sight and touch should be considered apart, and as if their objects had no intercourse, no manner of relation to one another, in point of distance or position.

CXVI. Further, what greatly contributes to make us mistake in this matter is, that when we think of the pictures in the fund of the eye, we imagine ourselves looking on the fund of another's eye, or another looking on the fund of our own eye, and beholding the pictures painted thereon. Suppose two eyes A and B : A from some distance looking on the pictures in B sees them inverted, and for that reason concludes they are inverted in B : but this is wrong. There are projected in little on the bottom of A, the images of the pictures of, suppose man, earth, &c., which are painted on B. And besides these, the eye B itself, and the objects which environ it, together with another earth, are projected in a larger size on A. Now, by the eye A, these larger images are deemed the true objects, and the lesser only pictures in miniature. And it is with respect to those greater images, that it determines the situation of the smaller images ; so that comparing the little man with the great earth, A judges him inverted, or that the feet are furthest from, and the head nearest to the great earth. Whereas, if A compare the little man with the little earth, then he will appear erect, *i.e.* his head shall seem furthest from, and his feet nearest to the little earth. But we must consider that B does not see two earths as A does ; it sees only what is represented by the little pictures in A, and consequently shall judge the man erect : for, in truth, the man in B is not inverted, for there the feet are next the earth ; but it is the representation of it in A which is inverted, for there the head of the representation of the picture of the man in B is next the earth, and the feet furthest from the earth, meaning the earth which is without the representation of the pictures in B. For if you take the little images of the pictures in B, and consider them by themselves, and with respect only to one another, they are all erect and in their natural posture.

CXVII. Further, there lies a mistake in our imagining that the pictures of external objects are painted on the bottom of the eye. It hath been shown, there is no resemblance between the ideas of sight, and things tangible. It hath likewise been demonstrated, that the proper objects of sight do not exist without the mind. Whence it clearly follows, that the pictures painted on the bottom of the eye, are not the pictures of external objects. Let any one consult his own thoughts, and then say what affinity, what likeness there is between that certain variety and disposition of colours, which constitute the visible man, or picture of a man, and that other combination of far different ideas, sensible by touch, which compose the tangible man. But if this be the case, how come they to be accounted pictures or images, since that supposes them to copy or represent some originals or other?

CXVIII. To which I answer : in the forementioned instance, the eye A takes the little images, included within the representation of the other eye B, to be pictures or copies, whereof the archetypes are not things existing without, but the larger pictures projected on its own fund : and which by A are not thought pictures, but the originals, or true things themselves. Though if we suppose a third eye C, from a due distance to behold the fund of A, then indeed the things projected thereon, shall to C seem pictures or images, in the same sense that those projected on B do to A.

CXIX. Rightly to conceive this point, we must carefully distinguish between the ideas of sight and touch, between the visible and tangible eye: for certainly on the tangible eye, nothing either is or seems to be painted. Again, the visible eye, as well as all other visible objects, hath been shown to exist only in the mind, which perceiving its own ideas, and comparing them together, calls some pictures in respect of others. What hath been said, being rightly comprehended and laid together, doth, I think, afford a full and genuine explication of the erect appearance of objects: which phenomenon, I must confess, I do not see how it can be explained by any theories of vision hitherto made public.

CXX. In treating of these things, the use of language is apt to occasion some obscurity and confusion, and create in us wrong ideas: for language being accommodated to the common notions and prejudices of men, it is scarce possible to deliver the naked and precise truth, without great circumlocution, impropriety, and (to an unwary reader) seeming contradictions: I do, therefore, once for all desire whoever shall think it worth his while to understand what I have written concerning vision, that he would not stick in this or that phrase, or manner of expression, but candidly collect my meaning from the whole sum and tenor of my discourse, and laying aside the words as much as possible, consider the bare notions themselves, and then judge whether they are agreeable to truth and his own experience, or no.

CXXI. We have shown the way wherein the mind by mediation of visible ideas doth perceive or apprehend the distance, magnitude, and situation of tangible objects. I come now to inquire more particularly concerning the difference between the ideas of sight and touch, which are called by the same names, and see whether there be any idea common to both senses. From what we have at large set forth and demonstrated in the foregoing parts of this treatise, it is plain there is no one selfsame numerical extension, perceived both by sight and touch; but that the particular figures and extensions perceived by sight, however they may be called by the same names, and reputed the same things, with those perceived by touch, are nevertheless different, and have an existence distinct and separate from them : so that the question is not now concerning the same numerical ideas, but whether there be any one and the same sort or species of ideas equally perceivable to both senses ? or, in other words, whether extension, figure, or motion perceived by sight, are not specifically distinct from extension, figure, and motion perceived by touch ?

CXXII. But before I come more particularly to discuss this matter, I find it proper to consider extension in abstract : for of this there is much talk, and I am apt to think, that when men speak of extension, as being an idea common to two senses, it is with a secret supposition, that we can single out extension from all other tangible and visible qualities, and form thereof an abstract idea, which idea they will have common both to sight and touch. We are therefore to understand by extension in abstract, an idea of extension ; for instance, a line or surface, entirely stripped of all other sensible qualities and circumstances that might determine it to any particular existence ; it is neither black, nor white, nor red, nor hath it any colour at all, or any tangible quality whatsoever, and consequently it is of no finite determinate magnitude : for that which bounds or distinguishes one extension from another, is some quality or circumstance wherein they disagree.

CXXIII. Now I do not find that I can perceive, imagine, or any wise frame in my mind such an abstract idea, as is here spoken of. A line or surface, which is neither black, nor white, nor blue, nor yellow, &c., nor long, nor short, nor rough, nor smooth, nor square, nor round, &c., is perfectly incomprehensible. This I am sure of as to myself : how far the faculties of other men may reach, they best can tell.

CXXIV. It is commonly said, that the object of geometry is abstract extension ; but geometry contemplates figures : now, figure is the termination of magnitude, but we have shown that extension in abstract hath no finite determinate magnitude, whence it clearly follows that it can have no figure, and consequently is not the object of geometry. It is indeed a tenet as well of the modern as of the ancient philosophers, that all general truths are concerning universal abstract ideas; without which, we are told, there could be no science, no demonstration of any general proposition in geometry. But it were no hard matter, did I think it necessary to my present purpose, to show that propositions and demonstrations in geometry might be universal, though they who make them never think of abstract general ideas of triangles or circles.

CXXV. After reiterated endeavours to apprehend the general idea of a triangle, I have found it altogether incomprehensible. And surely if any one were able to introduce that idea into my mind, it must be the author of the Essay concerning Human Understanding; he, who has so far distinguished himself from the generality of writers, by the clearness and significancy of what he says. Let us therefore see how this celebrated author describes the general, or abstract idea of a triangle. "It must be (says he) neither oblique, nor rectangular, neither equilateral, equicrural, nor scalenum; but all and none of these at once. In effect it is somewhat imperfect that cannot exist; an idea wherein some parts of several different and inconsistent ideas are put together." Essay on Human Understanding, b. iv. c. vii. § 9. This is the idea, which he thinks needful for the enlargement of knowledge, which is the subject of mathematical demonstration, and without which we could never come to know any general proposition concerning triangles. That author acknowledges it doth "require some pains and skill to form this general idea of a triangle," ibid. But had he called to mind what he says in another place, to wit, "that ideas of mixed modes, wherein any inconsistent ideas are put together, cannot so much as exist in the mind, *i.e.* be conceived." Vide b. iii. c. x. § 33, ibid. I say, had this occurred to his thoughts, it is not improbable he would have owned it above all the pains and skill he was master of, to form the above-mentioned idea of a triangle, which is made up of manifest, staring contradictions. That a man who thought so much, and laid so great a stress on clear and determinate ideas, should nevertheless talk at this rate, seems very surprising. But the wonder will lessen if it be considered, that the source whence this opinion flows, is the prolific womb which has brought forth innumerable errors and difficulties in all parts of philosophy, and in all the sciences. But this matter, taken in its full extent, were a subject too vast and comprehensive to be insisted on in this place. And so much for extension in abstract.

CXXVI. Some, perhaps, may think pure space, vacuum, or trine dimension to be equally the object of sight and touch: but though we have a very great propension, to think the ideas of outness and space to be the immediate object of sight; yet if I mistake not, in the foregoing parts of this essay, that hath been clearly demonstrated to be a mere delusion, arising from the quick and sudden suggestion of fancy, which so closely connects the idea of distance with those of sight, that we are apt to think it is itself a proper and immediate object of that sense, till reason corrects the mistake.

CXXVII. It having been shown, that there are no abstract ideas of figure, and that it is impossible for us, by any precision of thought, to frame an idea of extension separate from all other visible and tangible qualities, which shall be common both to sight and touch: the question now remaining is, whether the particular extensions, figures, and motions, perceived by sight be of the same kind, with the particular extensions, figures, and motions, perceived by touch. In answer to which, I shall venture to lay down the following proposition: *The extension, figures, and motions perceived by sight are specifically distinct from the ideas of touch, called by the same names, nor is there any such thing as one idea or kind of idea common to both senses.* This proposition may, without much difficulty, be collected from what hath been said in several places of this essay. But because it seems so remote from, and contrary to, the received notions and settled opinion of mankind, I shall attempt to demonstrate it more particularly, and at large, by the following arguments :—

CXXVIII. When, upon perception of an idea, I range it under this or that sort; it is because it is perceived after the same manner, or because it has a likeness or conformity with, or affects me in the same way as the ideas of the sort I rank it under. In short, it must not be entirely new, but have something in it old, and already perceived by me : it must, I say, have so much at least, in common with the ideas I have before known and named, as to make me give it the same name with them. But it has been, if I mistake not, clearly made out, that a man born blind would not, at first reception of his sight, think the things he saw were of the same nature with the objects of touch, or had anything in common with them ; but that they were a new set of ideas, perceived in a new manner, and entirely different from all he had ever perceived before : so that he would not call them by the same name, nor repute them to be of the same sort, with any thing he had hitherto known.

CXXIX. Secondly, light and colours are allowed by all to constitute a sort or species entirely different from the ideas of touch : nor will any man, I presume, say they can make themselves perceived by that sense : but there is no other immediate object of sight besides light and colours. It is therefore a direct consequence, that there is no idea common to both senses.

CXXX. It is a prevailing opinion, even amongst those who have thought and writ most accurately concerning our ideas, and the ways whereby they enter into the understanding, that something more is perceived by sight, than barely light and colours with their variations. Mr. Locke termeth sight, "The most comprehensive of all our senses, conveying to our minds the ideas of light and colours, which are peculiar only to that sense ; and also the far different ideas of space, figure, and motion." Essay on Human Understanding, b. ii. c. ix. § 9. Space or distance, we have shown, is no otherwise the object of sight than of hearing. Vide Sect. XLVI. And as for figure and extension, I leave it to any one, that shall calmly attend to his own clear and distinct ideas, to decide, whether he has any idea intromitted immediately and properly by sight, save only light and colours: or whether it be possible for him to frame in his mind a distinct abstract idea of visible extension, or figure, exclusive of all colour; and, on the other hand, whether he can conceive colour without visible extension? For my own part, I must confess, I am not able to attain so great a nicety of abstraction; in a strict sense, I see nothing but light and colours, with their several shades and variations. He who beside these doth also perceive by sight ideas far different and distinct from them, hath that faculty in a degree more perfect and comprehensive than I can pretend to. It must be owned, that by the mediation of light and colours, other far different ideas are suggested to my mind: but so they are by hearing, which, beside sounds, which are peculiar to that sense, doth by their mediation suggest not only space, figure, and motion, but also all other ideas whatsoever that can be signified by words.

CXXXI. Thirdly, it is, I think, an axiom universally received, that quantities of the same kind may be added together, and make one entire sum. Mathematicians add lines together, but they do not add a line to a solid, or conceive it as making one sum with a surface: these three kinds of quantity being thought incapable of any such mutual addition, and consequently of being compared together, in the several ways of proportion, are by them esteemed entirely disparate and heterogeneous. Now let any one try in his thoughts to add a visible line or surface to a tangible line or surface, so as to conceive them making one continued sum or whole. He that can do this, may think them homogeneous; but he that cannot must, by the foregoing axiom, think them heterogeneous: a blue and a red line I can conceive added together into one sum, and making one continued line; but to make, in my thoughts, one continued line of a visible and tangible line added together is, I find, a task far more difficult, and even insurmountable; and I leave it to the reflection and experience of every particular person to determine for himself.

CXXXII. A further confirmation of our tenet may be drawn from the solution of Mr. Molyneux's problem, published by Mr. Locke in his Essay : which I shall set down as it there lies, together with Mr. Locke's opinion of it, " Suppose a man born blind, and now adult, and taught by his touch to distinguish between a cube and a sphere of the same metal, and nighly of the same bigness, so as to tell when he felt one and the other, which is the cube and which the sphere. Suppose then the cube and sphere placed on a table, and the blind man to be made to see : Quære, Whether by his sight, before he touched them, he could now distinguish, and tell, which is the globe, which is the cube. To which the acute and judicious proposer answers : Not. For though he has obtained the experience of how a globe, how a cube affects his touch ; yet he has not yet attained the experience, that what affects his touch so or so must affect his sight so or so : or that a protuberant angle in the cube, that pressed his hand unequally, shall appear to his eye, as it doth in the cube. I agree with this thinking gentleman, whom I am proud to call my friend, in his answer to this his problem ; and am of opinion, that the blind man, at first sight, would not be able with certainty to say, which was the globe, which the cube, whilst he only saw them." Essay on Human Understanding, b. ii. c. ix. § 8.

CXXXIII. Now, if a square surface perceived by touch be of the same sort with a square surface perceived by sight ; it is certain the blind man here mentioned might know a square surface, as soon as he saw it : it is no more but introduced into his mind, by a new inlet, an idea he has been already well acquainted with. Since therefore he is supposed to have known by his touch, that a cube is a body terminated by square surfaces, and that a sphere is not terminated by square surfaces ; upon the supposition that a visible and tangible square differ only *in numero*, it follows, that he might know, by the unerring mark of the square surfaces, which was the cube, and which not, while he only saw them.

We must therefore allow, either that visible extension and figures are specifically distinct from tangible extension and figures, or else, that the solution of this problem, given by those two thoughtful and ingenious men, is wrong.

CXXXIV. Much more might be laid together in proof of the proposition I have advanced: but what has been said is, if I mistake not, sufficient to convince any one that shall yield a reasonable attention: and as for those that will not be at the pains of a little thought, no multiplication of words will ever suffice to make them understand the truth, or rightly conceive my meaning.

CXXXV. I cannot let go the above-mentioned problem without some reflection on it.   It hath been made evident, that a man blind from his birth, would not, at first sight, denominate any thing he saw, by the names he had been used to appropriate to ideas of touch, vide Sect. CVI.   Cube, sphere, table, are words he has known applied to things perceivable by touch, but to things perfectly intangible he never knew them applied.   Those words, in their wonted application, always marked out to his mind bodies, or solid things which were perceived by the resistance they gave: but there is no solidity, no resistance or protrusion perceived by sight.   In short, the ideas of sight are all new perceptions, to which there be no names annexed in his mind; he cannot therefore understand what is said to him concerning them: and to ask of the two bodies he saw placed on the table, which was the sphere, which the cube, were to him a question downright bantering and unintelligible; nothing he sees being able to suggest to his thoughts the idea of body, distance, or, in general, of any thing he had already known.

CXXXVI. It is a mistake, to think the same thing affects both sight and touch.   If the same angle or square, which is the object of touch, be also the object of vision, what should hinder the blind man, at first sight, from knowing it?   For though the manner wherein it affects the sight, be different from that wherein it affected his touch; yet, there being, beside this manner or circumstance, which is new and unknown, the angle or figure, which is old and known, he cannot choose but discern it.

CXXXVII. Visible figure and extension having been demonstrated to be of a nature entirely different and heterogeneous from tangible figure and extension, it remains that we inquire concerning motion. Now that visible motion is not of the same sort with tangible motion, seems to need no further proof, it being an evident corollary from what we have shown concerning the difference there is between visible and tangible extension : but for a more full and express proof hereof, we need only observe, that one who had not yet experienced vision, would not at first sight know motion. Whence it clearly follows, that motion perceivable by sight is of a sort distinct from motion perceivable by touch. The antecedent I prove thus : by touch he could not perceive any motion, but what was up or down, to the right or left, nearer or further from him ; besides these, and their several varieties or complications, it is impossible he should have any idea of motion. He would not therefore think any thing to be motion or give the name motion to any idea, which he could not range under some or other of those particular kinds thereof. But from Sect. xcv., it is plain that by the mere act of vision, he could not know motion upwards or downwards, to the right or left, or in any other possible direction. From which I conclude, he would not know motion at all at first sight. As for the idea of motion in abstract, I shall not waste paper about it, but leave it to my reader to make the best he can of it. To me it is perfectly unintelligible.

CXXXVIII. The consideration of motion may furnish a new field for inquiry : but since the manner wherein the mind apprehends by sight the motion of tangible objects, with the various degrees thereof, may be easily collected, from what hath been said concerning the manner wherein that sense doth suggest the various distances, magnitudes, and situations, I shall not enlarge any further on this subject, but proceed to inquire what may be alleged with greatest appearance of reason, against the proposition we have shown to be true : for where there is so much prejudice to be encountered, a bare and naked demonstration of the truth will scarce suffice. We must also satisfy the scruples that men may raise in favour of their preconceived notions, show whence the mistake arises, how it came to spread, and carefully disclose and root out those false persuasions that an early prejudice might have implanted in the mind.

CXXXIX. First, therefore, it will be demanded, how visible extension and figures come to be called by the same name with tangible extension and figures, if they are not of the same kind with them ? It must be something more than humour or accident, that could occasion a custom so constant and universal as this, which has obtained in all ages and nations of the world, and amongst all ranks of men, the learned as well as the illiterate.

CXL. To which I answer, we can no more argue a visible and tangible square to be of the same species, from their being called by the same name, than we can, that a tangible square and the monosyllable consisting of six letters, whereby it is marked, are of the same species because they are both called by the same name. It is customary to call written words, and the things they signify, by the same name : for words not being regarded in their own nature, or otherwise than as they are marks of things, it had been superfluous, and beside the design of language, to have given them names distinct from those of the things marked by them. The same reason holds here also. Visible figures are the marks of tangible figures, and from Sect. LIX. it is plain, that in themselves they are little regarded, or upon any other score than for their connexion with tangible figures, which by nature they are ordained to signify. And because this language of nature does not vary in different ages or nations, hence it is, that in all times and places, visible figures are called by the same names as the respective tangible figures suggested by them, and not because they are alike, or of the same sort with them.

*D 43

CXLI. But, say you, surely a tangible square is liker to a visible square, than to a visible circle: it has four angles, and as many sides; so also has the visible square, but the visible circle has no such thing, being bounded by one uniform curve, without right lines or angles, which makes it unfit to represent the tangible square, but very fit to represent the tangible circle. Whence it clearly follows, that visible figures are patterns of, or of the same species with the respective tangible figures represented by them; that they are like unto them, and of their own nature fitted to represent them, as being of the same sort; and that they are in no respect arbitrary signs, as words.

CXLII. I answer, it must be acknowledged, the visible square, is fitter than the visible circle, to represent the tangible square, but then it is not because it is liker, or more of a species with it; but because the visible square contains in it several distinct parts, whereby to mark the several distinct, corresponding parts of a tangible square, whereas the tangible circle doth not. The square perceived by touch, hath four distinct, equal sides, so also hath it four distinct, equal angles. It is therefore necessary, that the visible figures which shall be most proper to mark it, contain four distinct, equal parts, corresponding to the four sides of a tangible square; as likewise four other distinct and equal parts, whereby to denote the four equal angles of the tangible square. And accordingly we see the visible figures contain in them distinct visible parts, answering to the distinct tangible parts of the figures signified or suggested by them.

CXLIII. But it will not hence follow, that any visible figure is like unto, or of the same species with its corresponding tangible figure, unless it be also shown, that not only the number, but also the kind of the parts be the same in both. To illustrate this, I observe that visible figures represent tangible figures, much after the same manner that written words do sounds. Now in this respect words are not arbitrary, it being not indifferent, what written word stands for any sound: but it is requisite, that each word contain in it so many distinct characters, as there are variations in the sound it stands for. Thus the single letter *a* is proper to mark one simple uniform sound; and the word *adultery* is accommodated to represent the sound annexed to it, in the formation whereof, there being eight different collisions, or modifications of the air by the organs of speech, each of which produces a difference of sound, it was fit the word representing it should consist of as many distinct characters, thereby to mark each particular difference or part of the whole sound: and yet nobody, I presume, will say, the single letter *a*, or the word *adultery*, are like unto, or of the same species with the respective sounds by them represented. It is indeed arbitrary that, in general, letters of any language represent sound at all; but when that is once agreed, it is not arbitrary what combination of letters shall represent this or that particular sound. I leave this with the reader to pursue, and apply it in his own thoughts.

CXLIV. It must be confessed that we are not so apt to confound other signs with the things signified, or to think them of the same species, as we are visible and tangible ideas. But a little consideration will show us how this may be, without our supposing them of a like nature. These signs are constant and universal; their connexion with tangible ideas has been learnt at our first entrance into the world; and ever since, almost every moment of our lives, it has been occurring to our thoughts, and fastening and striking deeper in our minds. When we observe that signs are variable, and of human institution; when we remember, there was a time they were not connected in our minds, with those things they now so readily suggest; but that their signification was learned by the slow steps of experience; this preserves us from confounding them. But when we find the same signs suggest the same things all over the world; when we know they are not of human institution, and cannot remember that we ever learned their signification, but think that at first sight they would have suggested to us the same things they do now: all this persuades us they are of the same species as the things respectively represented by them, and that it is by a natural resemblance they suggest them to our minds.

CXLV. Add to this, that whenever we make a nice survey of any object, successively directing the optic axis to each point thereof; there are certain lines and figures described by the motion of the head or eye, which being in truth perceived by feeling, do nevertheless so mix themselves, as it were, with the ideas of sight, that we can scarce think but they appertain to that sense. Again, the ideas of sight enter into the mind, several at once, more distinct and unmingled, than is usual in the other senses beside the touch. Sounds, for example, perceived at the same instant, are apt to coalesce, if I may so say, into one sound, but we can perceive at the same time great variety of visible objects, very separate and distinct from each other. Now tangible extension being made up of several distinct co-existent parts, we may hence gather another reason, that may dispose us to imagine a likeness or analogy between the immediate objects of sight and touch. But nothing, certainly, doth more contribute to blend and confound them together, than the strict and close connexion they have with each other. We cannot open our eyes, but the ideas of distance, bodies, and tangible figures are suggested by them. So swift, and sudden, and unperceived is the transition from visible to tangible ideas, that we can scarce forbear thinking them equally the immediate object of vision.

CXLVI. The prejudice, which is grounded on these, and whatever other cause may be assigned thereof, sticks so fast, that it is impossible, without obstinate striving and labour of the mind, to get entirely clear of it. But then the reluctancy we find, in rejecting any opinion, can be no argument of its truth, to whoever considers what has been already shown, with regard to the prejudices we entertain concerning the distance, magnitude, and situation of objects; prejudices so familiar to our minds, so confirmed and inveterate, as they will hardly give way to the clearest demonstration.

CXLVII. Upon the whole, I think we may fairly conclude, that the proper objects of vision constitute a universal language of the Author of nature, whereby we are instructed how to regulate our actions, in order to attain those things that are necessary to the preservation and well-being of our bodies, as also to avoid whatever may be hurtful and destructive of them. It is by their information that we are principally guided in all the transactions and concerns of life. And the manner wherein they signify, and mark unto us the objects which are at a distance, is the same with that of languages and signs of human appointment, which do not suggest the things signified, by any likeness or identity of nature, but only by an habitual connexion, that experience has made us to observe between them.

CXLVIII. Suppose one who had always continued blind, be told by his guide, that after he has advanced so many steps, he shall come to the brink of a precipice, or be stopped by a wall; must not this to him seem very admirable and surprising? He cannot conceive how it is possible for mortals to frame such predictions as these, which to him would seem as strange and unaccountable as prophecy doth to others. Even they who are blessed with the visive faculty may (though familiarity make it less observed) find therein sufficient cause of admiration. The wonderful art and contrivance wherewith it is adjusted to those ends and purposes for which it was apparently designed, the vast extent, number, and variety of objects that are at once with so much ease, and quickness, and pleasure suggested by it: all these afford subject for much and pleasing speculation, and may, if any thing, give us some glimmering, analogous prenotion of things, which are placed beyond the certain discovery and comprehension of our present state.

CXLIX. I do not design to trouble myself with drawing corollaries from the doctrines I have hitherto laid down. If it bears the test, others may, so far as they shall think convenient, employ their thoughts in extending it further, and applying it to whatever purposes it may be subservient to : only, I cannot forbear making some inquiry concerning the object of geometry, which the subject we have been upon doth naturally lead one to. We have shown there is no such idea as that of extension in abstract, and that there are two kinds of sensible extension and figures, which are entirely distinct and heterogeneous from each other. Now, it is natural to inquire which of these is the object of geometry.

CL. Some things there are, which at first sight incline one to think geometry conversant about visible extension. The constant use of the eyes, both in the practical and speculative parts of that science, doth very much induce us thereto. It would, without doubt, seem odd to a mathematician to go about to convince him, the diagrams he saw upon paper were not the figures, or even the likeness of the figures, which make the subject of the demonstration. The contrary being held an unquestionable truth, not only by mathematicians, but also by those who apply themselves more particularly to the study of logic; I mean, who consider the nature of science, certainty, and demonstration : it being by them assigned as one reason of the extraordinary clearness and evidence of geometry, that in this science the reasonings are free from those inconveniences which attend the use of arbitrary signs, the very ideas themselves being copied out, and exposed to view upon paper. But, by the bye, how well this agrees with what they likewise assert of abstract ideas, being the object of geometrical demonstration, I leave to be considered.

CLI. To come to a resolution in this point we need only observe what hath been said in Sect. LIX., LX., LXI., where it is shown that visible extensions in themselves are little regarded, and have no settled determinate greatness, and that men measure altogether by the application of tangible extension to tangible extension. All which makes it evident, that visible extension and figures are not the object of geometry.

CLII. It is therefore plain that visible figures are of the same use in geometry, that words are ; and the one may as well be accounted the object of that science, as the other; neither of them being any otherwise concerned therein, than as they represent or suggest to the mind the particular tangible figures connected with them. There is indeed this difference between the signification of tangible figures by visible figures, and of ideas by words : that whereas the latter is variable and uncertain, depending altogether on the arbitrary appointment of men, the former is fixed and immutably the same in all times and places. A visible square, for instance, suggests to the mind the same tangible figure in Europe, that it doth in America. Hence it is that the voice of the Author of nature, which speaks to our eyes, is not liable to that misinterpretation and ambiguity, that languages of human contrivance are unavoidably subject to.

CLIII. Though what has been said may suffice to show what ought to be determined, with relation to the object of geometry; I shall nevertheless, for the fuller illustration thereof, consider the case of an intelligence, or unbodied spirit, which is supposed to see perfectly well, *i.e.* to have a clear perception of the proper and immediate objects of sight, but to have no sense of touch. Whether there be any such being in nature or no, is beside my purpose to inquire. It sufficeth, that the supposition contains no contradiction in it. Let us now examine, what proficiency such a one may be able to make in geometry. Which speculation will lead us more clearly to see, whether the ideas of sight can possibly be the object of that science.

CLIV. First, then, it is certain the aforesaid intelligence could have no idea of a solid, or quantity of three dimensions, which followeth from its not having any idea of distance. We indeed are prone to think, that we have by sight the ideas of space and solids, which ariseth from our imagining that we do, strictly speaking, see distance, and some parts of an object at a greater distance than others, which hath been demonstrated to be the effect of the experience we have had, what ideas of touch are connected with such and such ideas attending vision : but the intelligence here spoken of is supposed to have no experience of touch. He would not, therefore, judge as we do, nor have any idea of distance, outness, or profundity, nor consequently of space or body, either immediately or by suggestion. Whence it is plain, he can have no notion of those parts of geometry which relate to the mensuration of solids, and their convex or concave surfaces, and contemplate the properties of lines generated by the section of a solid; the conceiving of any part whereof, is beyond the reach of his faculties.

CLV. Further, he cannot comprehend the manner wherein geometers describe a right line or circle; the rule and compass, with their use, being things of which it is impossible he should have any notion: nor is it an easier matter for him to conceive the placing of one plane or angle on another, in order to prove their equality: since that supposeth some idea of distance, or external space. All which makes it evident, our pure intelligence could never attain to know so much as the first elements of plane geometry. And perhaps, upon a nice inquiry, it will be found, he cannot even have an idea of plane figures any more than he can of solids; since some idea of distance is necessary, to form the idea of a geometrical plane, as will appear to whoever shall reflect a little on it.

CLVI. All that is properly perceived by the visive faculty amounts to no more than colours with their variations, and different proportions of light and shade: but the perpetual mutability and fleetingness of those immediate objects of sight, render them incapable of being managed after the manner of geometrical figures; nor is it in any degree useful that they should. It is true, there are divers of them perceived at once; and more of some, and less of others: but accurately to compute their magnitude, and assign precise determinate proportions, between things so variable and inconstant, if we suppose it possible to be done, must yet be a very trifling and insignificant labour.

CLVII. I must confess, it seems to be the opinion of some ingenious men, that flat or plane figures are immediate objects of sight, though they acknowledge solids are not. And this opinion of theirs is grounded on what is observed in painting, wherein (say they) the ideas immediately imprinted on the mind are only of planes variously coloured, which by a sudden act of the judgment are changed into solids: but, with a little attention we shall find the planes here mentioned, as the immediate objects of sight, are not visible, but tangible planes. For when we say that pictures are planes, we mean thereby, that they appear to the touch smooth and uniform. But then this smoothness and uniformity, or, in other words, this planeness of the picture, is not perceived immediately by vision; for it appeareth to the eye various and multiform.

CLVIII. From all which we may conclude, that planes are no more the immediate object of sight than solids. What we strictly see are not solids, nor yet planes variously coloured; they are only diversity of colours. And some of these suggest to the mind solids, and others plane figures; just as they have been experienced to be connected with the one, or the other: so that we see planes in the same way that we see solids; both being equally suggested by the immediate objects of sight, which accordingly are themselves denominated planes and solids: but though they are called by the same names with the things marked by them, they are nevertheless of a nature entirely different, as hath been demonstrated.

CLIX. What hath been said is, if I mistake not, sufficient to decide the question we propose to examine concerning the ability of a pure spirit, such as we have described, to know geometry. It is, indeed, no easy matter for us to enter precisely into the thoughts of such an intelligence; because we cannot, without great pains, cleverly separate and disentangle in our thoughts the proper objects of sight from those of touch which are connected with them. This, indeed, in a complete degree, seems scarce possible to be performed: which will not seem strange to us, if we consider how hard it is, for any one to hear the words of his native language pronounced in his ears without understanding them.

Though he endeavour to disunite the meaning from the sound, it will nevertheless intrude into his thoughts, and he shall find it extreme difficult, if not impossible, to put himself exactly in the posture of a foreigner, that never learned the language, so as to be affected barely with the sounds themselves, and not perceive the signification annexed to them.

CLX. By this time, I suppose, it is clear that neither abstract nor visible extension makes the object of geometry; the not discerning of which may, perhaps, have created some difficulty and useless labour in mathematics. Sure I am, that somewhat relating thereto has occurred to my thoughts, which, though after the most anxious and repeated examination I am forced to think it true, doth, nevertheless, seem so far out of the common road of geometry, that I know not whether it may not be thought presumption, if I should make it public in an age, wherein that science hath received such mighty improvements by new methods; great part whereof, as well as of the ancient discoveries, may perhaps lose their reputation, and much of that ardour with which men study the abstruse and fine geometry be abated, if what to me, and those few to whom I have imparted it, seems evidently true, should really prove to be so.

A TREATISE
CONCERNING THE PRINCIPLES
OF HUMAN KNOWLEDGE,

WHEREIN THE CHIEF CAUSES OF ERROR AND DIFFI-
CULTY IN THE SCIENCES, WITH THE GROUNDS
OF SCEPTICISM, ATHEISM, AND IRRELIGION, ARE
INQUIRED INTO.

TO THE RIGHT HONOURABLE

THOMAS, EARL OF PEMBROKE, ETC.

KNIGHT OF THE MOST NOBLE ORDER OF THE GARTER, AND ONE OF
THE LORDS OF HER MAJESTY'S MOST HONOURABLE
PRIVY COUNCIL

MY LORD, — You will, perhaps, wonder that an obscure person, who has not the honour to be known to your lordship, should presume to address you in this manner. But that a man, who has written something with a design to promote useful knowledge and religion in the world, should make choice of your lordship for his patron, will not be thought strange by any one that is not altogether unacquainted with the present state of the church and learning, and consequently ignorant how great an ornament and support you are to both. Yet, nothing could have induced me to make you this present of my poor endeavours, were I not encouraged by that candour and native goodness, which is so bright a part in your lordship's character. I might add, my lord, that the extraordinary favour and bounty you have been pleased to show towards our society, gave me hopes, you would not be unwilling to countenance the studies of one of its members. These considerations determined me to lay this treatise at your lordship's feet. And the rather, because I was ambitious to have it known that I am, with the truest and most profound respect, on account of that learning and virtue which the world so justly admires in your lordship,—MY LORD, your lordship's most humble and most devoted servant,

GEORGE BERKELEY.

PREFACE

WHAT I here make public has, after a long and scrupulous inquiry, seemed to me evidently true, and not unuseful to be known, particularly to those who are tainted with scepticism, or want a demonstration of the existence and immateriality of God, or the natural immortality of the soul. Whether it be so or no, I am content the reader should impartially examine. Since I do not think myself any further concerned for the success of what I have written than as it is agreeable to truth. But to the end this may not suffer, I make it my request that the reader suspend his judgment till he has once, at least, read the whole through with that degree of attention and thought which the subject matter shall seem to deserve. For as there are some passages that, taken by themselves, are very liable (nor could it be remedied) to gross misinterpretation, and to be charged with most absurd consequences, which, nevertheless, upon an entire perusal will appear not to follow from them: so likewise, though the whole should be read over, yet if this be done transiently, it is very probable my sense may be mistaken; but to a thinking reader, I flatter myself, it will be throughout clear and obvious. As for the characters of novelty and singularity, which some of the following notions may seem to bear, it is, I hope, needless to make any apology on that account. He must surely be either very weak, or very little acquainted with the sciences, who shall reject a truth that is capable of demonstration, for no other reason but because it is newly known and contrary to the prejudices of mankind. Thus much I thought fit to premise, in order to prevent, if possible, the hasty censures of a sort of men, who are too apt to condemn an opinion before they rightly comprehend it.

INTRODUCTION

I. PHILOSOPHY being nothing else but *the study of wisdom and truth*, it may with reason be expected, that those who have spent most time and pains in it should enjoy a greater calm and serenity of mind, a greater clearness and evidence of knowledge, and be less disturbed with doubts and difficulties than other men. Yet so it is, we see the illiterate bulk of mankind, that walk the high road of plain, common sense, and are governed by the dictates of nature, for the most part easy and undisturbed. [To them nothing *that is familiar* appears unaccountable or difficult to comprehend.] They complain not of any want of evidence in their senses, and are out of all danger of becoming *sceptics*. But no sooner do we depart from sense and instinct to follow the light of a superior principle, to reason, meditate, and reflect on the nature of things, but a thousand scruples spring up in our minds, concerning those things which before we seemed fully to comprehend. Prejudices and errors of sense do from all parts discover themselves to our view; and endeavouring to correct these by reason, we are insensibly drawn into uncouth paradoxes, difficulties, and inconsistences, which multiply and grow upon us as we advance in speculation; till at length, having wandered through many intricate mazes, we find ourselves just where we were, or, which is worse, sit down in a forlorn scepticism.

II. [The cause of this is thought to be (1) the obscurity of things, or the natural weakness and imperfection of our understandings.] It is said the faculties we have are few, and those designed by nature for the *support* and comfort (pleasure) of life, and not to penetrate into the *inward essence* and constitution of things. [Besides, (2) the mind of man being finite, when it treats of things which partake of infinity, it is not to be wondered at if it run into absurdities and contradictions; out of which it is impossible it should ever extricate itself, it being of the nature of infinite not to be comprehended by that which is finite.]

III. But perhaps we may be too partial to ourselves in placing the fault originally in our faculties, and not rather in the wrong use we make of them. *It is a hard thing to suppose, that right deductions from true principles should ever end in consequences which cannot be maintained* or made consistent. We should believe that God has dealt more bountifully with the sons of men, than to give them a strong desire for that knowledge which he had placed quite out of their reach. [This were not agreeable to the wonted indulgent methods of Providence, which, whatever appetites it may have implanted in the creatures, doth usually furnish them with such means as, if rightly made use of, will not fail to satisfy them.] Upon the whole I am inclined to think that the far greater part, if not all, of those difficulties which have hitherto amused philosophers, and blocked up the way to knowledge, are entirely owing to ourselves. That we have first raised a dust, and then complain we cannot see.

IV. My purpose therefore is, to try if I can discover what those principles are, which have introduced all that doubtfulness and uncertainty, those absurdities and contradictions into the several sects of philosophy; insomuch that the wisest men have thought our ignorance incurable, conceiving it to arise from the natural dulness and limitation of our faculties. And surely it is a work well deserving our pains, to make a strict inquiry concerning the first principles of human knowledge, to sift and examine them on all sides: especially since there may be some grounds to suspect that those lets and difficulties, which stay and embarrass the mind in its search after truth, do not spring from any darkness and intricacy in the objects, or natural defect in the understanding, so much as from false principles which have been insisted on, and might have been avoided.

V. How difficult and discouraging soever this attempt may seem, when I consider how many great and extraordinary men have gone before me in the same designs : yet I am not without some hopes, upon the consideration that the largest views are not always the clearest, and that he who is short-sighted will be obliged to draw the object nearer, and may, perhaps, by a close and narrow survey, discern that which had escaped far better eyes.

VI. *A chief source of error in all parts of knowledge.*— In order to prepare the mind of the reader for the easier conceiving what follows, it is proper to premise somewhat, by way of introduction, concerning the nature and abuse of language. But the unravelling this matter leads me in some measure to anticipate my design, by taking notice of what seems to have had a chief part in rendering speculation intricate and perplexed, and to have occasioned innumerable errors and difficulties in almost all parts of knowledge. [And that is the opinion that the mind hath a power of framing *abstract ideas* or notions of things.] He who is not a perfect stranger to the writings and disputes of philosophers, must needs acknowledge that no small part of them are spent about abstract ideas. [These are, in a more especial manner, thought to be the object of those sciences which go by the name of *logic* and *metaphysics*,] and of all that which passes under the notion of the most abstracted and sublime learning, in all which one shall scarce find any question handled in such a manner, as does not suppose their existence in the mind, and that it is well acquainted with them.

VII. *Proper acceptation of abstraction.*—It is agreed, on all hands, that the qualities or modes of things do never *really exist each of them apart by itself*, and separated from all others, but are mixed, as it were, and blended together, several in the same object. But we are told, the mind being able to consider each quality singly, or abstracted from those other qualities with which it is united, does by that means frame to itself abstract ideas. For example, there is perceived by sight an object extended, coloured, and moved: this mixed or compound idea the mind resolving into its simple, constituent parts, and viewing each by itself, exclusive of the rest, does frame the abstract ideas of extension, colour, and motion. Not that it is possible for colour or motion to exist without extension: but only that the mind can frame to itself by *abstraction* the idea of colour exclusive of extension, and of motion exclusive of both colour and extension.

VIII.—*Of generalizing*[1].—Again, the mind having observed that in the particular extensions perceived by sense, there is something *common* and alike *in all*, and some other things peculiar, as this or that figure or magnitude, which distinguish them one from another; it considers apart or singles out by itself that which is common, making thereof a most abstract idea of extension, which is neither line, surface, nor solid, nor has any figure or magnitude, but is an idea entirely pre-scinded from all these. So likewise the mind, by leaving out of the particular colours perceived by sense, that which distinguishes them one from another, and retaining that only which is *common to all*, makes an idea of colour in abstract, which is neither red, nor blue, nor white, nor any other determinate colour. And in like manner, by considering motion abstractedly not only from the body moved, but likewise from the figure it describes, and all particular directions and velocities, the abstract idea of motion is framed; which equally corresponds to all particular motions whatsoever that may be perceived by sense.

IX. *Of compounding.*—And as the mind frames to itself abstract ideas of qualities or *modes*, so does it, by the same precision or mental separation, attain abstract ideas of the more compounded *beings*, which include several coexistent qualities. For example, the mind having observed that Peter, James, and John resemble

[1] Vide Reid, on the Intellectual Powers of Man, Essay V. chap. iii. sec. 1, edit. 1843.

each other, in certain common agreements of shape and other qualities, leaves out of the complex or compounded idea it has of Peter, James, and any other particular man, that which is peculiar to each, retaining only what is common to all ; and so makes an abstract idea wherein all the particulars equally partake, abstracting entirely from and cutting off all those circumstances and differences, which might determine it to any particular existence. And after this manner it is said we come by the abstract idea of *man*, or, if you please, humanity or human nature ; wherein it is true there is included colour, because there is no man but has some colour, but then it can be neither white, nor black, nor any particular colour ; because there is no one particular colour wherein all men partake. So likewise there is included stature, but then it is neither tall stature nor low stature, nor yet middle stature, but something abstracted from all these. And so of the rest. Moreover, there being a great variety of other creatures that partake in some parts, but not all, of the complex idea of *man*, the mind leaving out those parts which are peculiar to men, and retaining those only which are common to all the living creatures, frameth the idea of *animal*, which abstracts not only from all particular men, but also all birds, beasts, fishes, and insects. The constituent parts of the abstract idea of animal are body, life, sense, and spontaneous motion. By *body* is meant, body without any particular shape or figure, there being no one shape or figure common to all animals, without covering, either of hair or feathers, or scales, &c., nor yet naked : hair, feathers, scales, and nakedness being the distinguishing properties of particular animals, and for that reason left out of the *abstract idea*. Upon the same account the spontaneous motion must be neither walking, nor flying, nor creeping; it is nevertheless a motion, but what that motion is, it is not easy to conceive.[1]

X. *Two objections to the existence of abstract ideas.*— Whether others have this wonderful faculty of *abstract-*

[1] Vide Hobbes' Tripos, ch. v. sect. 6.

ing their ideas, they best can tell: for myself I find
indeed I have a faculty of imagining, or representing
to myself the ideas of those particular things I have
perceived, and of variously compounding and dividing
them. I can imagine a man with two heads, or the
upper parts of a man joined to the body of a horse. I
can consider the hand, the eye, the nose, each by itself
abstracted or separated from the rest of the body. But
then whatever hand or eye I imagine, it must have some
particular shape and colour. Likewise the idea of man
that I frame to myself, must be either of a white, or a
black, or a tawny, a straight, or a crooked, a tall, or a
low, or a middle-sized man. I cannot by any effort of
thought conceive the abstract idea above described.
And it is equally impossible for me to form the abstract
idea of motion distinct from the body moving, and
which is neither swift nor slow, curvilinear nor rectilinear; and the like may be said of all other abstract
general ideas whatsoever. To be plain, [I own myself
able to abstract *in one sense*, as when I consider some
particular parts or qualities separated from others, with
which though they are united in some object, yet it is
possible they may really exist without them. But I
deny that I can abstract one from another, or conceive
separately, those qualities which it is impossible should
exist so separated; or that I can frame a general notion
by abstracting from particulars in the manner aforesaid.
Which two last are the proper acceptations of *abstraction*.] And there are grounds to think most men will
acknowledge themselves to be in my case. The generality of men which are simple and illiterate never
pretend to *abstract notions*. [(1) It is said they are
difficult, and not to be attained without pains and study.
We may therefore reasonably conclude that, if such there
be, they are confined only to the learned.]

XI. I proceed to examine what can be alleged in
defence of the doctrine of abstraction, and try if I can
discover what it is that inclines the men of speculation
to embrace an opinion so remote from common sense
as that seems to be. There has been a late deservedly

esteemed philosopher, who, no doubt, has given it very much countenance by seeming to think the having abstract general ideas is what puts the widest difference in point of understanding betwixt man and beast. "The having of general ideas," saith he, "is that which puts a perfect distinction betwixt man and brutes, and is an excellency which the faculties of brutes do by no means attain unto. For it is evident we observe no footsteps in them of making use of general signs for universal ideas; from which we have reason to imagine that they have not the faculty of *abstracting*, or making general ideas, since they have no use of words or any other general signs." And a little after: "Therefore, I think, we may suppose that it is in this that the species of brutes are discriminated from men and it is that proper difference wherein they are wholly separated, and which at last widens to so wide a distance. For if they have any ideas at all, and are not bare machines (as some would have them), we cannot deny them to have some reason. It seems as evident to me that they do some of them in certain instances reason as that they have sense, but it is only in particular ideas, just as they receive them from their senses. They are the best of them tied up within those narrow bounds, and have not (as I think) the faculty to enlarge them by any kind of *abstraction*." Essay on Hum. Underst., b. ii. ch. xi. sect. 10, 11. I readily agree with this learned author, that the faculties of brutes can by no means attain to *abstraction*. But then if this be made the distinguishing property of that sort of animals, I fear a great many of those that pass for men must be reckoned into their number. The reason that is here assigned why we have no grounds to think brutes have abstract general ideas, is that we observe in them no use of words or any other general signs; [which is built on this supposition, to wit, that the making use of words implies the having general ideas.] From which it follows, that men who use language are able to *abstract* or *generalize* their ideas. That this is the sense and arguing of the author will further appear by his answering the question he in another place puts. "Since all things that exist are only particulars, how come we by general terms?" His answer is, "Words become general by being made the signs of general ideas." Essay on Hum. Underst., b. iii. ch. iii. sect. 6. But[1] it seems that [(2) a word becomes general by being made the sign, not of an *abstract* general idea, but of several particular ideas,[2] any one of which it indifferently suggests to the mind.] For example, when it is said *the change of motion is proportional to the impressed force*, or that *whatever has extension is divisible ;* these propositions are to be understood of motion and extension in general, and nevertheless it will not follow that they suggest to my thoughts an idea of motion without a body moved, or any determinate direction and velocity, or that I must conceive an abstract general idea of extension, which is neither line, surface, nor solid, neither great nor small, black, white, nor red, nor of any other determinate colour. It is only implied that whatever motion I consider, whether it be swift or slow, perpendicular, horizontal, or oblique, or in whatever object, the axiom concerning it holds equally true. As does the other of every particular extension, it matters not whether line, surface, or solid, whether of this or that magnitude or figure.

XII. *Existence of general ideas admitted.*—By observing how ideas become general, we may the better judge how words are made so. And here it is to be noted that I do not deny absolutely there are general ideas, but only that there are any *abstract general ideas :* for in the passages above quoted, wherein there is mention of general ideas, it is always supposed that they are formed by *abstraction*, after the manner set forth in Sects. VIII. and IX. Now if we will annex a meaning to our words, and speak only of what we can conceive, I believe we shall acknowledge, that an idea, which considered in itself is particular, becomes general, by being made to represent or stand for all other particular ideas of the *same sort.* ☞ To make this plain by an example, sup-

---

[1] " *To this I cannot assent, being of opinion*," edit. of 1710.
[2] Of the same sort.

pose a geometrician is demonstrating the method of cutting a line in two equal parts. He draws, for instance, a black line of an inch in length ; this, which in itself is a particular line, is nevertheless with regard to its signification general, since, as it is there used, it represents all particular lines whatsoever ; so that what is demonstrated of it, is demonstrated of all lines, or, in other words, of a line in general. And as that particular line becomes general, by being made a sign, so the name *line*, which taken absolutely is *particular*, by being a sign is made *general*. And as the former owes its generality, not to its being the sign of an abstract or general line, but of *all particular* right lines that may possibly exist ; so the latter must be thought to derive its generality from the same cause, namely, the *various particular* lines which it indifferently denotes.[1]

XIII. *Abstract general ideas necessary, according to Locke.*—To give the reader a yet clearer view of the nature of abstract ideas, and the uses they are thought necessary to, I shall add one more passage out of the Essay on Human Understanding, which is as follows. "*Abstract ideas* are not so obvious or easy to children or the yet unexercised mind as particular ones. If they seem so to grown men, it is only because by constant and familiar use they are made so. For when we nicely reflect upon them, we shall find that general ideas are fictions and contrivances of the mind, that carry difficulty with them, and do not so easily offer themselves as we are apt to imagine. For example, does it not require some pains and skill to form the general idea of a triangle ? (which is yet none of the most abstract, comprehensive, and difficult ;) for it must be neither oblique nor rectangle, neither equilateral, equicrural, nor scalenon, but *all and none* of these at once. In effect, it is something imperfect that cannot exist, an idea wherein some parts of several different and *inconsistent* ideas are put

---

[1] " I look upon this (doctrine) to be one of the greatest and most valuable discoveries that have been made of late years in the republic of letters."—Treatise of Human Nature, book i. part i. sect. 7. Also Stewart's Philosophy of the Mind, part i. chap. iv. sect. iii. p. 99.

together. It is true the mind in this imperfect state has need of such ideas, and makes all the haste to them it can, for the (1) *conveniency of communication and* (2) *enlargement of knowledge*, to both which it is naturally very much inclined. But yet one has reason to suspect such ideas are marks of our imperfection. At least this is enough to show that the most abstract and general ideas are not those that the mind is first and most easily acquainted with, nor such as its earliest knowledge is conversant about." Book iv. ch. vii. sect. 9. If any man has the faculty of framing in his mind such an idea of a triangle as is here described, it is in vain to pretend to dispute him out of it, nor would I go about it. All I desire is, that the reader would fully and certainly inform himself whether he has such an idea or no. And this, methinks, can be no hard task for any one to perform. What more easy than for any one to look a little into his own thoughts, and there try whether he has, or can attain to have, an idea that shall correspond with the description that is here given of the general idea of a triangle, which is, *neither oblique, nor rectangle, equilateral, equicrural, nor scalenon, but all and none of these at once?*

XIV. *But they are not necessary for communication.*— Much is here said of the difficulty that abstract ideas carry with them, and the pains and skill requisite to the forming them. And it is on all hands agreed that there is need of great toil and labour of the mind, to emancipate our thoughts from particular objects, and raise them to those sublime speculations that are conversant about abstract ideas. [From all which the natural consequence should seem to be, that so *difficult* a thing as the forming abstract ideas was not necessary for *communication*, which is so *easy* and familiar to *all sorts of men*.] But we are told, if they seem obvious and easy to grown men, *it is only because by constant and familiar use they are made so.* [Now I would fain know at what time it is men are employed in surmounting that difficulty, and furnishing themselves with those necessary helps for discourse. It cannot be when they are grown-up, for then it seems they are not conscious of any such painstaking; it remains therefore to be the business of their childhood. And surely, the great and multiplied labour of framing abstract notions will be found a hard task for that tender age.] ☞ Is it not a hard thing to imagine, that a couple of children cannot prate together of their sugar-plums, and rattles, and the rest of their little trinkets, till they have first tacked together numberless inconsistencies, and so framed in their minds *abstract general ideas*, and annexed them to every common name they make use of?

XV. *Nor for the enlargement of knowledge.*—Nor do I think them a whit more needful for the *enlargement of knowledge* than for *communication*. It is, I know, a point much insisted on, that all knowledge and demonstration are about universal notions, to which I fully agree : but then it doth not appear to me that these notions are formed by *abstraction* in the manner premised ; [*universality*, so far as I can comprehend, not consisting in the absolute, *positive* nature or conception of any thing, but in the *relation* it bears to the particulars signified or represented by it :] by virtue whereof it is that things, names, or notions, being in their own nature *particular*, are rendered *universal*. Thus when I demonstrate any propositions concerning triangles, it is to be supposed that I have in view the universal idea of a triangle ; which ought not to be understood as if I could frame an idea of a triangle which was neither equilateral, nor scalenon, nor equicrural. But only that the particular triangle I consider, whether of this or that sort it matters not, doth equally stand for and represent all rectilinear triangles whatsoever, and is, in that sense, *universal*. All which seems very plain, and not to include any difficulty in it.

XVI. *Objection.—Answer.*—But here it will be demanded, *how we can know any proposition to be true of all particular triangles, except* we have first seen it *demonstrated of the abstract idea of a triangle* which equally agrees to all ? For, because a property may be demonstrated to agree to some one particular triangle, it will not thence follow that it equally belongs to any other triangle, which in all respects is not the same with it. For example, having demonstrated that the three angles of an isosceles rectangular triangle are equal to two right ones, I cannot therefore conclude this affection agrees to all other triangles, which have neither a right angle, nor two equal sides. It seems therefore that, to be certain this proposition is universally true, we must either make a particular demonstration for every particular triangle, which is impossible, or once for all demonstrate it of the *abstract idea of a triangle*, in which all the particulars do indifferently partake, and by which they are all equally represented. To which I answer, that though the idea I have in view whilst I make the demonstration, be, for instance, that of an isosceles rectangular triangle, whose sides are of a determinate length, I may nevertheless be certain it extends to all other rectilinear triangles, of what sort or bigness soever. [And that, because neither the right angle, nor the equality, nor determinate length of the sides, are at all concerned in the demonstration.] It is true, the diagram I have in view includes all these particulars, but then there is not the least mention made of them in the proof of the proposition. It is not said, the three angles are equal to two right ones, because one of them is a right angle, or because the sides comprehending it are of the same length. Which sufficiently shows that the right angle might have been oblique, and the sides unequal, and for all that the demonstration have held good. And for this reason it is, that I conclude that to be true of any obliquangular or scalenon, which I had demonstrated of a particular right-angled, equicrural triangle; and not because I demonstrated the proposition of the abstract idea of a triangle. [[1] And here it must be acknowledged, that a man may consider a figure merely as triangular, without attending to the particular qualities of the angles, or relations of the sides. So far he may abstract : but this will never prove that he can frame an abstract general inconsistent idea of a triangle. In like manner we may

---

[1] The passage here enclosed by brackets does not appear in the edition of 1710.

consider Peter so far forth as man, or so far forth as
animal, without framing the forementioned abstract
idea, either of man or of animal, inasmuch as all that is
perceived is not considered.]

XVII. *Advantage of investigating the doctrine of
abstract general ideas.*—It were an endless, as well as a
useless thing, to trace the *schoolmen*, those great masters
of abstraction, through all the manifold, inextricable
labyrinths of error and dispute, which their doctrine of
abstract natures and notions seems to have led them
into.   What bickerings and controversies, and what a
learned dust have been raised about those matters, and
what mighty advantage hath been from thence derived
to mankind, are things at this day too clearly known to
need being insisted on.   And it had been well if the ill
effects of that doctrine were confined to those only who
make the most avowed profession of it.   When men
consider the great pains, industry, and parts, that have,
for so many ages, been laid out on the cultivation and
advancement of the sciences, and that notwithstanding
all this, the far greater part of them remain full of
darkness and uncertainty, and disputes that are like
never to have an end, and even those that are thought
to be supported by the most clear and cogent demonstrations, contain in them paradoxes which are perfectly
irreconcilable to the understandings of men, and that,
taking all together, a small portion of them doth supply
any real benefit to mankind, otherwise than by being an
innocent diversion and amusement: I say, the consideration of all this is apt to throw them into a despon-
dency, and perfect contempt of all study.   But this may
perhaps cease, upon a view of the false principles that
have obtained in the world, amongst all which there is
none, methinks, hath a more wide influence over the
thoughts of speculative men, than [1] this of abstract
general ideas.

XVIII. [I come now to consider the *source of this
prevailing notion,* and that seems to me to be *language.*
And surely nothing of less extent than reason itself

[1] "That we have been endeavouring to overthrow."—Edit. 1710.

could have been the source of an opinion so universally received.] The truth of this appears as from other reasons, so also from the plain confession of the ablest patrons of abstract ideas, [who acknowledge that they are made in order to naming; from which it is a clear consequence, that if there had been no such thing as speech or universal signs, there never had been any thought of abstraction.] See book iii. ch. vi. sect. 39, and elsewhere, of the Essay on Human Understanding. Let us therefore examine the manner wherein words have contributed to the origin of that mistake. [First,[1] then, it is thought that every name hath, or ought to have, *one only* precise and settled signification, which inclines men to think there are certain *abstract, determinate ideas*, which constitute the true and only immediate signification of each general name. And that it is by the mediation of these abstract ideas, that a general name comes to signify any particular thing.] [Whereas, in truth, there is no such thing as one precise and definite signification annexed to any general name, they all signifying indifferently a great number of particular ideas.] All which doth evidently follow from what has been already said, and will clearly appear to any one by a little reflection. [To this it will be *objected*, that every name that has a definition, is thereby restrained to one certain signification.] For example, a *triangle* is defined to be a *plain surface comprehended by three right lines;* by which that name is limited to denote one certain idea and no other. To which I answer, that in the definition it is not said whether the surface be great or small, black or white, nor whether the sides are long or short, equal or unequal, nor with what angles they are inclined to each other; in all which there may be great variety, [and consequently there is *no one settled idea* which limits the signification of the word *triangle*.] [It is one thing for to keep a name constantly to the same definition, and another to make it stand every where for the same idea: the one is necessary, the other useless and impracticable.]

[1] Vide sect. xix.

XIX. [*Secondly*, But to give a further account how *words* came to *produce the doctrine of abstract ideas*, it must be observed that it is a received opinion, that language has *no other end* but the communicating our ideas, and that every significant name stands for an idea.] This being so, and it being withal certain, that names, which yet are not thought altogether insignificant, do not always mark out *particular* conceivable ideas, it is straightway concluded that *they stand for abstract notions*. That there are many names in use amongst speculative men, which do not always suggest to others determinate particular ideas, is what nobody will deny. And a little attention will discover, that it is not necessary (even in the strictest reasonings) significant names which stand for ideas should, every time they are used, excite in the understanding the ideas they are made to stand for : [in reading and discoursing, names being, for the most part, used as letters are in *algebra*, in which, though a particular quantity be marked by each letter, yet to proceed right it is not requisite that in every step each letter suggest to your thoughts that particular quantity it was appointed to stand for.[1]]

XX. *Some of the ends of language.*—[Besides, the (1) communicating of ideas marked by words is not the chief and only end of language, as is commonly supposed. There are other ends, as the (2) raising of some passion, the exciting to, or (3) deterring from an action, the (4) putting the mind in some particular disposition]; to which the former is, in many cases, barely subservient, and sometimes entirely omitted, when these can be obtained without it, as I think doth not infrequently happen in the familiar use of language. I entreat the reader to reflect with himself, and see if it doth not often happen, either in hearing or reading a discourse, that the passions of fear, love, hatred, admiration, disdain, and the like, arise immediately in his mind upon

---

[1] Language has become the source or origin of abstract general ideas on account of a twofold error.—(1.) That every word has one only signification. (2.) That the only end of language is the communication of our ideas.—Ed.

the perception of certain words, without any ideas coming between. At first, indeed, the words might have occasioned ideas that were fit to produce those emotions; but, if I mistake not, it will be found that when language is once grown familiar, the hearing of the sounds or sight of the characters is oft immediately attended with those passions, which at first were wont to be produced by the intervention of ideas, that are now quite omitted. May we not, for example, ☞ be affected with the promise of a *good thing*, though we have not an idea of what it is? Or is not the being threatened with danger sufficient to excite a dread, though we think not of any particular evil likely to befall us, nor yet frame to ourselves an idea of danger in abstract? If any one shall join ever so little reflection of his own to what has been said, I believe it will evidently appear to him, that general names are often used in the propriety of language without the speaker's designing them for marks of ideas in his own, which he would have them raise in the mind of the hearer. Even proper names themselves do not seem always spoken with a design to bring into our view the ideas of those individuals that are supposed to be marked by them. ☞ For example, when a schoolman tells me "Aristotle hath said it," all I conceive he means by it, is to dispose me to embrace his opinion with the deference and submission which custom has annexed to that name. And this effect may be so instantly produced in the minds of those who are accustomed to resign their judgment to the authority of that philosopher, as it is impossible any idea either of his person, writings, or reputation, should go before.[1] Innumerable examples of this kind may be given, but why should I insist on those things which every one's experience will, I doubt not, plentifully suggest unto him?

XXI. *Caution in the use of language necessary.*—We have, I think, shown (1) the impossibility of *abstract*

---

[1] "So close and immediate a connexion may custom establish betwixt the very word *Aristotle*, and the motions of assent and reverence in the minds of some men."—Edit. 1710.

ideas. We have considered (2) what has been said for them by their ablest patrons; and endeavoured to show they are of no use for those ends to which they are thought necessary. And lastly, we have (3) traced them to the source from whence they flow, which appears to be language. It cannot be denied that words are of excellent use; in that, by their means, all that stock of knowledge, which has been purchased by the joint labours of inquisitive men in all ages and nations, may be drawn into the view and made the possession of one single person. But at the same time it must be owned that most parts of knowledge have been strangely perplexed ånd darkened by the abuse of words, and general ways of speech wherein they are delivered.[1] Since, therefore, words are so apt to impose on the understanding,[2] whatever ideas I consider, I shall endeavour to take them bare and naked into my view, keeping out of my thoughts, so far as I am able, those names which long and constant use hath so strictly united with them; from which I may expect to derive the following advantages :—

XXII. *First,* I shall be sure to get clear of all controversies *purely verbal;* the springing up of which weeds in almost all the sciences has been a main hindrance to the growth of true and sound knowledge. *Secondly,* this seems to be a sure way to extricate myself out of that fine and subtile net of *abstract ideas,* which has so miserably perplexed and entangled the minds of men, and that with this peculiar circumstance, that by how much the finer and more curious was the wit of any man, by so much the deeper was he like to be ensnared, and faster held therein. *Thirdly,* so long as I confine my thoughts to my own ideas divested of words, I do not see how I can be easily mistaken. The objects, I consider, I clearly and adequately know. I cannot be deceived in thinking I have an idea which I have

---

1 "That it may almost be made a question, whether language has contributed more to the hindrance or advancement of the sciences."— Edit. 1710.

2 "I am resolved in my inquiries to make as little use of them as possibly I can."—Edit. 1710.

not. It is not possible for me to imagine, that any of my own ideas are like or unlike, that are not truly so. To discern the agreements or disagreements that are between my ideas, to see what ideas are included in any compound idea, and what not, there is nothing more requisite, than an attentive perception of what passes in my own understanding.

XXIII. But the attainment of all *these advantages* doth *presuppose an entire deliverance from the deception of words*, which I dare hardly promise myself; so difficult a thing it is to dissolve a union so early begun, and confirmed by so long a habit as that betwixt words and ideas. [Which difficulty seems to have been very much increased by the doctrine of *abstraction*. For so long as men thought abstract ideas were annexed to their words, it doth not seem strange that they should use words for ideas: it being found an impracticable thing to lay aside the word, and *retain the abstract idea in the mind, which in itself was perfectly inconceivable.*] This seems to me the principal cause, why those men who have so emphatically recommended to others the laying aside all use of words in their meditations, and contemplating their bare ideas, have yet failed to perform it themselves. Of late many have been very sensible of the absurd opinions and insignificant disputes, which grow out of the abuse of words. And in order to remedy these evils they advise well, that we attend to the ideas signified, and draw off our attention from the words which signify them. [But how good soever this advice may be they have given others, it is plain they could not have a due regard to it themselves, so long as they thought (1) the only immediate use of words was to signify ideas, and that (2) the immediate signification of every general name was a *determinate, abstract idea*.]

XXIV. But *these being known to be mistakes, a man may* with greater ease *prevent his being imposed on by words*. He that knows he has no other than particular ideas, will not puzzle himself in vain to find out and conceive the abstract idea, annexed to any name. And he that knows names do not always stand for ideas, will spare himself the labour of looking for ideas, where there are none to be had. It were therefore to be wished that every one would use his utmost endeavours, to obtain a clear view of the ideas he would consider, separating from them all that dress and encumbrance of words which so much contribute to blind the judgment and divide the attention. In vain do we extend our view into the heavens, and pry into the entrails of the earth ; in vain do we consult the writings of learned men, and trace the dark footsteps of antiquity ; we need only draw the curtain of words, to behold the fairest tree of knowledge, whose fruit is excellent, and within the reach of our hand.

XXV. Unless we take care *to clear the first principles of knowledge, from the* embarrass and *delusion of words,* we may make infinite reasonings upon them to no purpose : we may draw consequences from consequences, and be never the wiser. The further we go, we shall only lose ourselves the more irrecoverably, and be the deeper entangled in difficulties and mistakes. Whoever therefore designs to read the following sheets, I entreat him to make my words the occasion of his own thinking, and endeavour to attain the same train of thoughts in reading, that I had in writing them. By this means it will be easy for him to discover the truth or falsity of what I say. He will be out of all danger of being deceived by my words, and I do not see how he can be led into an error by considering his own naked, undisguised ideas.

OF THE PRINCIPLES OF
HUMAN KNOWLEDGE

PART I

I. *Objects of human knowledge.*—[It is evident to any one who takes a survey of the objects of human knowledge, that they are either *ideas* actually (1) imprinted on the senses, or else such as are (2) perceived by attending to the passions and operations of the mind, or lastly, ideas (3) formed by help of memory and imagination, either compounding, dividing, or barely representing those originally perceived in the aforesaid ways.] By sight I have the ideas of light and colours with their several degrees and variations. By touch I perceive, for example, hard and soft, heat and cold, motion and resistance, and of all these more and less either as to quantity or degree. Smelling furnishes me with odours; the palate with tastes; and hearing conveys sounds to the mind in all their variety of tone and composition. And as several of these are observed to accompany each other, they come to be marked by one name, and so to be reputed as one thing. ☞ Thus, for example, a certain colour, taste, smell, figure, and consistence having been observed to go together, are accounted one distinct thing, signified by the name *apple*. Other collections of ideas constitute a stone, a tree, a book, and the like sensible things; which, as they are pleasing or disagreeable, excite the passions of love, hatred, joy, grief, and so forth.

II. *Mind—spirit—soul.*—But besides all that endless variety of ideas or objects of knowledge, there is likewise something which knows or perceives them, and exercises divers operations, as willing, imagining, remembering about them. This perceiving, active being is what I call *mind, spirit, soul,* or *myself.* By which words I do not denote any one of my ideas, but a thing entirely distinct from them, *wherein they exist,* or, which is the same thing, whereby they are perceived ; for the existence of an idea consists in being perceived.

III. *How far the assent of the vulgar conceded.*—[That neither our thoughts, nor passions, nor ideas formed by the imagination, exist *without* the mind, is what *every body will allow.*] And (to me) it seems no less evident that the various sensations or ideas imprinted on the sense, however blended or combined together (that is, whatever objects they compose), cannot exist otherwise than *in* a mind perceiving them. [I think an intuitive knowledge may be obtained of this, by any one that shall attend to *what is meant by the term exist,* when applied to sensible things. The table I write on, I say, exists, that is, I see and feel it ; and if I were out of my study I should say it existed, meaning thereby that if I was in my study I might perceive it, or that some other spirit actually does perceive it.][1] There was an odour, that is, it was smelled ; there was a sound, that is to say, it was heard ; a colour or figure, and it was perceived by sight or touch. This is all that I can understand by these and the like expressions. For as to what is said of the absolute existence of unthinking things without any relation to their being perceived, that seems perfectly unintelligible. Their *esse* is *percipi,* nor is it possible they should have any existence, out of the minds or thinking things which perceive them.

IV. *The vulgar opinion involves a contradiction.*—It is indeed an opinion *strangely* prevailing amongst men, that houses, mountains, rivers, and in a word all sensible objects have an existence natural or real, distinct from their being perceived by the understanding. But with how great an assurance and acquiescence soever this principle may be entertained in the world ; yet whoever shall find in his heart to call it in question, may, if I

[1] First argument in support of the author's theory.

mistake not, perceive it to involve a manifest contradiction. [For what are the forementioned objects but the things we *perceive* by sense, and what do we perceive *besides our own ideas or sensations ;* and is it not plainly repugnant that any one of these or any combination of them should exist unperceived ?]

V. *Cause of this prevalent error.*—[If we thoroughly examine this tenet, it will, perhaps, be found at bottom to depend on the doctrine of *abstract ideas.* For can there be a nicer strain of abstraction than to distinguish the existence of sensible objects from their being perceived, so as to conceive them existing unperceived ?] Light and colours, heat and cold, extension and figures, in a word the things we see and feel, what are they but so many sensations, notions, ideas, or impressions on the sense ; and is it possible to separate, even in thought, any of these from perception ? For my part I might as easily divide a thing from itself. I may indeed divide in my thoughts or conceive apart from each other those things which, perhaps, I never perceived by sense so divided. ☞ Thus I imagine the trunk of a human body without the limbs, or conceive the smell of a rose without thinking on the rose itself. So far I will not deny I can abstract, if that may properly be called *abstraction*, which extends only to the conceiving separately such objects as it is possible may really exist or be actually perceived asunder. But my conceiving or imagining power does not extend beyond the possibility of real existence or perception. Hence as it is impossible for me to see or feel any thing without an actual sensation of that thing, so is it impossible for me to conceive in my thoughts any sensible thing or object distinct from the sensation or perception of it.[1]

VI. Some truths there are so near and obvious to the mind, that a man need only open his eyes to see them. Such I take this important one to be, to wit, that all the choir of heaven and furniture of the earth, in a word all those bodies which compose the mighty frame of the world, have not any subsistence without a mind, that

[1] "In truth the object and the sensation are the same thing, **and** cannot therefore be abstracted from each other."—Edit. 1710.

their *being* (*esse*) is to be perceived or known; that consequently so long as they are not actually perceived by me, or do not exist in my mind or that of any other *created spirit*, they must either have no existence at all, *or else subsist in the mind of some eternal spirit* : it being perfectly unintelligible and involving all the absurdity of abstraction, to attribute to any single part of them an existence independent of a spirit.[1] To be convinced of which, the reader need only reflect and try to separate in his own thoughts the being of a sensible thing from its being perceived.

VII. *Second argument.*[2]—[From what has been said, it follows, there is *not any other substance than spirit*, or that which perceives.] But for the fuller proof of this point, let it be considered, the sensible qualities are colour, figure, motion, smell, taste, and such like, that is, the ideas perceived by sense. [Now for an idea to exist in an unperceiving thing, is a manifest contradiction ; for *to have an idea is all one as to perceive :* that therefore wherein colour, figure, and the like qualities exist, must perceive them ; hence it is clear there can be no *unthinking* substance or *substratum* of those ideas.]

VIII. *Objection.—Answer.*—[But say you, though the ideas themselves do not exist without the mind, yet there may be things *like* them whereof they are copies or resemblances, which things exist without the mind, in an unthinking substance.] [I *answer*, an idea can be like nothing but an idea ; a colour or figure can be like nothing but another colour or figure. If we look but ever so little into our thoughts, we shall find it impossible for us to conceive a likeness except only between our ideas.]. [Again, I ask whether those supposed originals or external things, of which our ideas are the pictures or representations, be themselves perceivable

---

[1] "To make this appear with all the light and evidence of an axiom, it seems sufficient if I can but awaken the reflection of the reader, that he may take an impartial view of his own meaning, and turn his thoughts upon the subject itself, free and disengaged from all embarrass of words and prepossession in favour of received mistakes."—Edit. 1710.
[2] Vide sect. iii. and xxv.

or no? if they are, *then they are ideas,* and we have gained our point; but if you say they are not, I appeal to any one whether it be sense, to assert a colour is like something which is invisible; hard or soft, like something which is intangible; and so of the rest.]

IX. *The philosophical notion of matter involves a contradiction.*—Some there are who make a *distinction* betwixt *primary* and *secondary* qualities: by the former, they mean extension, figure, motion, rest, solidity or impenetrability, and number: by the latter they denote all other sensible qualities, as colours, sounds, tastes, and so forth. The ideas we have of these they acknowledge not to be the resemblances of any thing existing without the mind or unperceived; but they will have our ideas of the primary qualities to be patterns or images of things which exist without the mind, in an unthinking substance which they call *matter.* [By *matter* therefore we are to understand an inert, senseless substance, in which extension, figure and motion, *do actually subsist.* But it is evident from what we have already shown, that extension, figure, and motion, are *only ideas existing in the mind,* and that an idea can be like nothing but another idea, and that consequently neither they nor their archetypes can exist in an *unperceiving* substance.] Hence it is plain, that the very notion of what is called *matter,* or *corporeal substance,* involves a contradiction in it.[1]

X. *Argumentum ad hominem.*—They who assert that figure, motion, and the rest of the primary or original qualities, do exist without the mind, in unthinking substances, do at the same time acknowledge that colours, sounds, heat, cold, and such like secondary qualities, do not, which they tell us are sensations existing *in the mind alone,* that depend on and are occasioned by the different size, texture, and motion

[1] " Insomuch that I should not think it necessary to spend more time in exposing its absurdity. But because the tenet of the existence of matter seems to have taken so deep a root in the minds of philosophers, and draws after it so many ill consequences, I choose rather to be thought prolix and tedious, than omit any thing that might conduce to the full discovery and extirpation of the prejudice."—Edit. 1710.

of the minute particles of matter. This they take for
an undoubted truth, which they can demonstrate beyond
all exception. [Now if it be certain, that those original
qualities *are inseparably united with the other sensible
qualities*, and not, even in thought, capable of being
abstracted from them, it plainly follows that they exist
only in the mind. But I desire any one to reflect and
try, whether he can, by any abstraction of thought,
conceive the extension and motion of a body, without
all other sensible qualities.] For my own part, I see
evidently that it is not in my power to frame an idea
of a body extended and moved, but I must withal give
it some colour or other sensible quality which is *acknowledged* to exist only in the mind. In short, extension,
figure, and motion, abstracted from all other qualities,
are inconceivable. Where therefore the other sensible
qualities are, there must these be also, to wit, in the
mind and nowhere else.

XI. *A second argumentum ad hominem.*—[Again, *great*
and *small*, *swift* and *slow*, *are allowed to exist no where
without the mind*, being entirely *relative*, and changing
as the frame or position of the organs of sense varies.
The extension therefore which exists without the mind,
is neither great nor small, the motion neither swift nor
slow, that is, they are nothing at all. But, say you, they
are extension in general, and motion in general: thus we
see how much the tenet of extended, moveable substances existing without the mind, depends on that
strange doctrine of *abstract ideas*.] And here I cannot
but remark, how nearly the vague and indeterminate
description of matter or corporeal substance, which the
modern philosophers are run into by their own principles, resembles that antiquated and so much ridiculed
notion of *materia prima*, to be met with in Aristotle and
his followers. [Without extension solidity cannot be
conceived; since therefore it has been shown that extension exists not in an unthinking substance, the same
must also be true of solidity.]

XII. [That *number* is entirely *the creature of the mind*,
even though the other qualities be allowed to exist with-

out, will be evident to whoever considers, that the same thing bears a different denomination of number, as the mind views it with different respects.] Thus, the same extension is one, or three, or thirty-six, according as the mind considers it with reference to a yard, a foot, or an inch. Number is so visibly relative, and dependent on men's understanding, that it is strange to think how any one should give it an absolute existence without the mind. We say, one book, one page, one line; all these are equally units, though some contain several of the others. And in each instance it is plain, the unit relates to some particular combination of ideas arbitrarily put together by the mind.

XIII. *Unity*, I know, some will have to be *a simple or uncompounded idea*, accompanying all other ideas into the mind. That I have any such idea, answering the word *unity*, I do not find; and if I had, methinks I could not miss finding it; on the contrary, it should be the most familiar to my understanding, since it is said to accompany all other ideas, and to be perceived by all the ways of sensation and reflection. To say no more, it is an *abstract idea*.

XIV. *A third argumentum ad hominem.*—I shall further add, that after the same manner as modern philosophers prove certain sensible qualities to have no existence in matter, or without the mind, the same thing may be likewise proved of all other sensible qualities whatsoever. Thus, for instance, it is said that heat and cold are affections only of the mind, and not at all patterns of real beings, existing in the corporeal substances which excite them, for that the same body which appears cold to one hand, seems warm to another. [Now why may we not as well argue that figure and extension are not patterns or resemblances of qualities existing in matter, because to the same eye at different stations, or eyes of a different texture at the same station, they appear various, and cannot therefore be the images of any thing *settled and determinate without the mind?*] Again, it is proved that *sweetness* is not really in the sapid thing, because, the thing remaining unaltered, the sweetness is changed into bitter, as in case of a fever or otherwise vit:ated palate. Is it not as reasonable to say, that *motion* is not without the mind, since if the succession of ideas in the mind become swifter, the motion, it is acknowledged, shall appear slower without any alteration in any external object.

XV. *Not conclusive as to extension.*—In short, let any one consider those arguments which are thought manifestly to prove that colours and tastes exist only in the mind, and he shall find they may with equal force be brought to prove the same thing of extension, figure, and motion. [Though it must be confessed, this method of arguing doth not so much prove that there is no extension or colour in an outward object, as that we do not know by *sense* which is the *true* extension or colour of the object.] But the arguments foregoing plainly show it to be impossible that any colour or extension at all, or other sensible quality whatsoever, should ex'st in an *unthinking* subject without the mind, or in truth, that there should be any such thing as an outward object.

XVI. But let us examine a little the received opinion. It is said *extension* is *a mode* or accident *of matter*, and that matter is the *substratum* that supports it. Now I desire that you would explain what is meant by matter's *supporting* extension : say you, I have no idea of matter, and therefore cannot explain it. I answer, though you have no positive, yet if you have any meaning at all, you must at least have a relative idea of matter ; though you know not what it is, yet you must be supposed to know what relation it bears to accidents, and what is meant by its supporting them. It is evident *support* cannot here be taken in its usual or literal sense, as when we say that pillars support a building : in what sense therefore must it be taken ? [1]

XVII. *Philosophical meaning of " material substance" divisible into two parts.*—[If we inquire into what the most accurate philosophers declare themselves to mean

[1] " For my part, I am not able to discover any sense at all that can be applicable to it."—Edit. 1710.

by *material substance*, we shall find them acknowledge, they have no other meaning annexed to those sounds, but the idea of *being in general*, together *with the relative notion of its supporting accidents*.] The general idea of being appeareth to me the most abstract and incomprehensible of all other; and as for its supporting accidents, this, as we have just now observed, cannot be understood in the common sense of those words; it must therefore be taken in some other sense, but what that is they do not explain. [So that when I consider the *two parts* or branches which make the signification of the words *material substance*, I am convinced there is no distinct meaning annexed to them.] But why should we trouble ourselves any further, in discussing this material *substratum* or support of figure and motion, and other sensible qualities? does it not suppose they have an existence without the mind? and is not this a direct repugnancy, and altogether inconceivable?

XVIII. *The existence of external bodies wants proof.*— [But though it were possible that solid, figured, moveable substances may exist without the mind, corresponding to the ideas we have of bodies, yet *how is it possible for us to know this?* either we must know it by sense, or by reason.] [As for our senses, by them we have the knowledge *only of our sensations*, ideas, or those things that are immediately perceived by sense, call them what you will: but they do not inform us that things exist without the mind, or unperceived, like to those which are perceived.] This the materialists themselves acknowledge. It remains therefore that if we have any knowledge at all of external things, it must be by *reason*, inferring their existence from what is immediately perceived by sense. [But (I do not see) what reason can induce us to believe the existence of bodies without the mind, from what we perceive, since the very patrons of matter themselves do not pretend, there is *any necessary connexion betwixt them and our ideas*. I say, it is granted on all hands (and what happens in dreams, frenzies, and the like, puts it beyond dispute) that *it is possible we might be affected with all the ideas we have now, though no bodies existed without, resembling them.*] Hence it is evident the supposition of external bodies is not necessary for the producing our ideas : since it is granted they are produced sometimes, and might possibly be produced always, in the same order we see them in at present, without their concurrence.

XIX. *The existence of external bodies affords no explication of the manner in which our ideas are produced.*— But though we might possibly have all our sensations without them, yet perhaps it may be thought *easier* to conceive and explain the *manner* of their production, by supposing external bodies in their likeness rather than otherwise ; and so it might be at least probable there are such things as bodies that excite their ideas in our minds. [But neither can this be said ; for though we give the materialists their external bodies, they, by their own confession, are never the nearer knowing how our ideas are produced : since they own themselves unable to comprehend in what manner *body can act upon spirit*, or how it is possible it should imprint any idea in the mind.] Hence it is evident, the production of ideas or sensations in our minds, can be no reason why we should suppose matter or corporeal substances, *since that is acknowledged to remain equally inexplicable with or without this supposition.* [If therefore it were possible for bodies to exist without the mind, yet to hold they do so must needs be a very precarious opinion ; since it is to suppose, without any reason at all, that God has created innumerable beings *that are entirely useless, and serve to no manner of purpose.*

XX. *Dilemma.*—In short, if there were external bodies, it is impossible we should ever come to know it ; and if there were not, we might have the very same reasons to think there were that we have now. [Suppose, what no one can deny possible, an intelligence, without the help of external bodies, to be affected with the same train of sensations or ideas that you are, imprinted in the same order and with like vividness in his mind. I ask, whether that intelligence hath not all the reason to believe the existence of corporeal substances,

represented by his ideas, and exciting them in his mind,
that you can possibly have for believing the same thing?]
Of this there can be no question; which one consideration is enough to make any reasonable person suspect
the strength of whatever arguments he may think himself to have for the existence of bodies without the
mind.

XXI. [Were it necessary to add any *further proof
against the existence of matter*, after what has been said,
I could instance several of those errors and difficulties
(not to mention impieties) which have sprung from that
tenet.] It has occasioned numberless controversies and
disputes in philosophy, and not a few of greater moment
in religion. But I shall not enter into the detail of
them in this place, as well because I think arguments
à posteriori are unnecessary for confirming what has
been, if I mistake not, sufficiently demonstrated *à priori*,
as because I shall hereafter find occasion to say somewhat of them.

XXII. I am afraid I have given cause to think me
needlessly prolix in handling this subject. For to what
purpose is it to dilate on that which may be demonstrated with the utmost evidence in a line or two, to any
one that is capable of the least reflection? it is but
looking into your own thoughts, and so trying whether
you can conceive it possible for a sound, or figure, or
motion, or colour, to exist without the mind, or unperceived. This easy trial may make you see, that what
you contend for is a downright contradiction. Insomuch that I am content to put the whole upon this
issue; if you can but *conceive* it possible for one extended moveable substance, or in general, for any one
idea, or any thing like an idea, to exist otherwise than in
a mind perceiving it, I shall readily give up the cause:
and as for all that *compages* of external bodies which you
contend for, I shall grant you its existence, though (1)
*you cannot either give me any reason why you believe
it exists*,[1] or (2) *assign any use to it when it is supposed to exist*.[2] I say, the bare possibility of your

[1] Vide sect. lviii.   [2] Vide sect. lx.

opinion's being true, shall pass for an argument that it is so.[1]

XXIII. [But say you, surely there is nothing easier than to imagine trees, for instance, in a park, or books existing in a closet, and nobody by to perceive them. I answer, you may so, there is no difficulty in it]: [but what is all this, I beseech you, more than framing in your mind certain ideas which you call *books* and *trees*, and at the same time omitting to frame the idea of any one that may perceive them? *but do not you yourself perceive or think of them all the while?*] this therefore is nothing to the purpose; it only shows you have the power of imagining or forming ideas in your mind; [but it doth not show that you can conceive it possible the objects of your thought may exist without the mind: to make out this, *it is necessary that you conceive them existing unconceived or unthought-of, which is a manifest repugnancy.*] [When we do our utmost to conceive the existence of external bodies, we are all the while only contemplating our own ideas. But the mind, taking no notice of itself, is deluded to think it can and doth conceive bodies existing unthought-of or without the mind; though at the same time they are apprehended by or exist in itself.] A little attention will discover to any one the truth and evidence of what is here said, and make it unnecessary to insist on any other proofs against the existence of material substance.

XXIV. *The absolute existence of unthinking things are words without a meaning.*—It is very obvious, upon the least inquiry into our own thoughts, to know whether it be possible for us to understand what is meant by the *absolute existence of sensible objects in themselves or without the mind.* To me it is evident those words mark out either a direct contradiction, or else nothing at all. And to convince others of this, I know no readier or fairer way, than to entreat they would calmly attend to their own thoughts: and if by this attention the emptiness or repugnancy of those expressions does appear,

[1] *i.e.* although your argument be deficient in the two requisites of an hypothesis.—Ed.

surely nothing more is requisite for their conviction. It is on this therefore that I insist, to wit, that the *absolute* existence of unthinking things are words without a meaning, or which include a contradiction. This is what I repeat and inculcate, and earnestly recommend to the attentive thoughts of the reader.

XXV. *Third argument.*[1]—*Refutation of Locke.*—[All our ideas, sensations, or the things which we perceive, by whatsoever names they may be distinguished, are visibly inactive; there is nothing of power or agency included in them. So that *one idea* or object of thought *cannot produce*, or make *any alteration in another.*] To be satisfied of the truth of this, there is nothing else requisite but a bare observation of our ideas. For since they and every part of them exist only in the mind, it follows that there is nothing in them but what is perceived. But whoever shall attend to his ideas, whether of sense or reflection, will not perceive in them any power or activity; there is therefore no such thing contained in them. A little attention will discover to us that the very being of an idea implies passiveness and inertness in it, insomuch that it is impossible for an idea to do any thing, or, strictly speaking, to be the cause of any thing: neither can it be the resemblance or pattern of any active being, as is evident from Sect. VIII. [Whence it plainly follows that extension, figure, and motion, cannot be the cause of our sensations. To say, therefore, that these are the effects of powers resulting from the configuration, number, motion, and size of corpuscles, must certainly be false.][2]

XXVI. *Cause of ideas.*—We perceive a continual succession of ideas, some are anew excited, others are changed or totally disappear. There is therefore some cause of these ideas whereon they depend, and which produces and changes them. That this cause cannot be any quality or idea or combination of ideas, is clear from the preceding section. It must therefore be a substance; but it has been shown that there is no corporeal or material substance: [it remains therefore that

[1] Vide sect. iii. and vii.   [2] Vide sect. cii.

the *cause of ideas* is an incorporeal active substance or spirit.]

XXVII. *No idea of spirit.*—A spirit is one simple, undivided, active being: as it perceives ideas, it is called the *understanding,* and as it produces or otherwise operates about them, it is called the *will.* Hence there can be no idea formed of a soul or spirit: [for all ideas whatever, being passive and inert (vide Sect. XXV.), they cannot represent unto us, by way of image or *likeness,* that which acts.] A little attention will make it plain to any one, that to have an idea which shall be like that active principle of motion and change of ideas, is absolutely impossible. [Such is the nature of *spirit,* or that which acts, that it cannot be of itself perceived *but only by the effects which it produceth.*] If any man shall doubt of the truth of what is here delivered, let him but reflect and try if he can frame the idea of any power or active being; and whether he hath ideas of two principal powers, marked by the names *will* and *understanding,* distinct from each other as well as from a third idea of substance or being in general, with a relative notion of its supporting or being the subject of the aforesaid powers, which is signified by the name *soul* or *spirit.* This is what some hold; but so far as I can see, the words *will,*[1] *soul, spirit,* do not stand for different ideas, or in truth, for any idea at all, but for something which is very different from ideas, and which being an agent cannot be like unto, or represented by, any idea whatsoever. [Though it must be owned at the same time, that we have some notion of soul, spirit, and the operations of the mind, such as willing, loving, hating, inasmuch as we know or understand the meaning of those words.]

XXVIII. I find I can excite ideas in my mind at pleasure, and vary and shift the scene as oft as I think fit. It is no more than willing, and straightway this or that idea arises in my fancy: and by the same power it is obliterated, and makes way for another. This making and unmaking of ideas doth very properly denominate

---

[1] "Understanding, mind."—Edit. 1710.

the mind active. Thus much is certain, and grounded on experience: but when we talk of unthinking agents, or of exciting ideas exclusive of volition, we only amuse ourselves with words.

XXIX. *Ideas of sensation*[1] *differ from those of reflection or memory.*—[But whatever power I may have over *my own* thoughts, I find the ideas actually perceived by sense have not a like dependence on my will.] When in broad day-light I open my eyes, it is not in my power to choose whether I shall see or no, or to determine what particular objects shall present themselves to my view; and so likewise as to the hearing and other senses, the ideas imprinted on them are not creatures of my will. [There is *therefore some other will or spirit* that *produces them.*]

XXX. *Laws of nature.*—[The ideas of sense are more strong, lively, and *distinct* than those of the imagination; they have likewise a steadiness, order, and coherence, and are not excited at random, as those which are the effects of human wills often are, but in a regular train or series, the admirable connexion whereof sufficiently testifies the wisdom and benevolence of its author.] Now *the set rules or established methods, wherein the mind we depend on excites in us the ideas of sense, are called the laws of nature:* and these we learn by experience, which teaches us that such and such ideas are attended with such and such other ideas, in the ordinary course of things

XXXI. *Knowledge of them necessary for the conduct of worldly affairs.*—[This gives us a sort of foresight, which enables us to regulate our actions for the benefit of life. And without this we should be eternally at a loss: we could not know how to act any thing that might procure us the least pleasure, or remove the least pain of sense.] That food nourishes, sleep refreshes, and fire warms us; that to sow in the seed-time is the way to reap in the harvest, and, in general, that to obtain such or such ends, such or such means are conducive, all this we know, *not by discovering any necessary connexion between*

---

[1] 1st. They do not depend on the will.—2nd. They are distinct.

our ideas, but only by the observation of the settled laws of nature, without which we should be all in uncertainty and confusion, and a grown man no more know how to manage himself in the affairs of life than an infant just born.

XXXII. And yet *this* consistent, *uniform working*, which so evidently displays the goodness and wisdom of that governing Spirit whose will constitutes the laws of nature, is so far from leading our thoughts to him, that it rather *sends them a wandering after second causes*. [For when we perceive certain ideas of sense constantly followed by other ideas, and *we know this is not of our own doing*, we forthwith attribute power and agency to the ideas themselves, and make one the cause of another, than which nothing can be more absurd and unintelligible.] Thus, for example, having observed that when we perceive by sight a certain round luminous figure, we at the same time perceive by touch the idea or sensation called *heat*, we do from thence conclude the sun to be the cause of heat. And in like manner perceiving the motion and collision of bodies to be attended with sound, we are inclined to think the latter an effect of the former.

XXXIII. *Of real things and ideas or chimeras.*—[The ideas imprinted on the senses by the author of nature are called *real things*: and those excited in the imagination, being less regular, vivid, and constant, are more properly termed *ideas*, or *images of things*, which they copy and represent.] But then our sensations, be they never so vivid and distinct, are nevertheless *ideas*, that is, they exist in the mind, or are perceived by it, as truly as the ideas of its own framing. The ideas of sense are allowed to have more reality in them, that is, to be more (1) *strong*, (2) *orderly*, and (3) *coherent* than the creatures of the mind : but this is no argument that they exist without the mind. They are also (4) *less dependent on the spirit*,[1] or thinking substance which perceives them, in that they are excited by the will of another and more powerful spirit : yet still they are *ideas*, and certainly no

[1] Vide sect. xxix.—Note.

idea, whether faint or strong, can exist otherwise than in a mind perceiving it.

XXXIV. *First general objection. — Answer.*—Before we proceed any further, it is necessary to spend some time in answering objections which may probably be made against the principles hitherto laid down. In doing of which, if I seem too prolix to those of quick apprehensions, I hope it may be pardoned, since all men do not equally apprehend things of this nature ; and I am willing to be understood by every one. [*First* then it will be objected that by the foregoing principles, *all that is real and substantial in nature is banished out of the world :* and instead thereof a chimerical scheme of ideas takes place.] All things that exist, exist only in the mind, that is, they are purely notional. What therefore becomes of the sun, moon, and stars ? What must we think of houses, rivers, mountains, trees, stones ; nay, even of our own bodies? Are all these but so many chimeras and illusions on the fancy ? To all which, and whatever else of the same sort may be objected, [I *answer*, that by the principles premised, we are not deprived of any one thing in nature. Whatever we see, feel, hear, or any wise conceive or understand, remains as secure as ever, and is as real as ever. There is a *rerum natura*, and the distinction between realities and chimeras retains its full force.] This is evident from Sect. xxix., xxx., and xxxiii., where we have shown what is meant by *real things* in opposition to *chimeras*, or ideas of our own framing ; but then they both equally exist in the mind, and in that sense are like *ideas*.

XXXV. *The existence of matter, as understood by philosophers, denied.*[1]—I do not argue against the existence of any one thing that we can apprehend, either by sense or reflection. That the things I see with mine eyes and touch with my hands do exist, really exist, I make not the least question. The only thing whose existence we deny, *is that which philosophers call matter* or corporeal substance. And in doing of this, there is no damage

[1] Vide sect. lxxxiv.

done to the rest of mankind, who, I dare say, will never miss it. The atheist indeed will want the colour of an empty name to support his impiety; and the philosophers may possibly find, they have lost a great handle for trifling and disputation.

XXXVI. *Reality explained.*—If any man thinks this detracts from the existence or reality of things, he is very far from understanding what hath been premised in the plainest terms I could think of. Take here an abstract of what has been said. [There are spiritual substances, minds, or human souls, which will or excite ideas in themselves at pleasure : but these are faint, weak, and unsteady in respect of others they perceive by sense, which being impressed upon them according to certain rules or laws of nature, speak themselves the effects of a mind more powerful and wise than human spirits. These latter are said to have more *reality* in them than the former : by which is meant that they are affecting, orderly, and distinct, and that they are not fictions of the mind perceiving them.] And in this sense, the sun that I see by day is the real sun, and that which I imagine by night is the idea of the former. In the sense here given of *reality*, it is evident that every vegetable, star, mineral, and in general each part of the mundane system, is as much a *real being* by our principles as by any other. Whether others mean any thing by the term *reality* different from what I do, I entreat them to look into their own thoughts and see.

XXXVII. *The philosophic, not the vulgar substance, taken away.*—[It will be urged that thus much at least is true, to wit, that we take away all corporeal substances. To this my answer is, that if the word *substance* be taken in the vulgar sense, for a combination of sensible qualities, such as extension, solidity, weight, and the like : this we cannot be accused of taking away. But if it be taken in a philosophic sense, for the *support* of accidents or *qualities without the mind ;* then indeed I acknowledge that we take it away, if one may be said to take away that which never had any existence, not even in the imagination.]

XXXVIII. But, say you, it sounds very harsh to say we eat and drink ideas, and are clothed with ideas. I acknowledge it does so, the word *idea* not being used in common discourse to signify the several combinations of sensible qualities, which are called *things :* and it is certain that any expression which varies from the familiar use of language, will seem harsh and ridiculous. But this doth not concern the truth of the proposition, which in other words is no more than to say, we are fed and clothed with those things which we perceive immediately by our senses. The hardness or softness, the colour, taste, warmth, figure, and such like qualities, which combined together constitute the several sorts of victuals and apparel, have been shown to exist only in the mind that perceives them; and this is all that is meant by calling them *ideas ;* which word, if it was as ordinarily used as *thing*, would sound no harsher nor more ridiculous than it. I am not for disputing about the propriety, but the truth of the expression. If therefore you agree with me that we eat, and drink, and are clad with the immediate objects of sense, which cannot exist unperceived or without the mind; I shall readily grant it is more proper or conformable to custom, that they should be called things rather than ideas.

XXXIX. *The term idea preferable to thing.*—If it be demanded why I make use of the word *idea*, and do not rather in compliance with custom call them *things*. [I answer, I do it for two reasons : first, because the term *thing*, in contradistinction to *idea*, is generally supposed to denote somewhat existing without the mind : secondly, because *thing* hath a more comprehensive signification than *idea*, including *spirits*, or thinking things, as well as *ideas*.] Since therefore the objects of sense exist only in the mind, and are withal thoughtless and inactive, I chose to mark them by the word *idea*, which implies those properties.

XL. *The evidence of the senses not discredited.*—But. say what we can, some one perhaps may be apt to reply, he will still believe his senses, and never suffer any arguments, how plausible soever, to prevail over the certainty of them. Be it so, assert the evidence of sense as high as you please, we are willing to do the same. That what I see, hear, and feel *doth exist, that is* to say, *is perceived by me,* I no more doubt than I do of my own being. But I do not see how the testimony of sense can be alleged as a proof for the existence of any thing which is not perceived by sense. We are not for having any man turn *sceptic,* and disbelieve his senses; on the contrary, we give them all the stress and assurance imaginable; nor are there any principles more opposite to scepticism than those we have laid down,[1] as shall be hereafter clearly shown.

XLI. *Second objection.—Answer.—*Secondly, it will be *objected* that there is a great difference betwixt real fire, for instance, and the idea of fire, betwixt dreaming or imagining one's self burnt, and actually being so: this and the like may be urged in opposition to our tenets. [To all which the *answer* is evident from what hath been already said, and I shall only add in this place, that if real fire be very different from the idea of fire, so also is the real pain that it occasions, very different from the idea of the same pain: and yet nobody will pretend that real pain either is, or can possibly be, in an unperceiving thing or without the mind, any more than its idea.]

XLII. *Third objection.—Answer.—*Thirdly, it will be objected that we see things actually without or at a distance from us, and which consequently do not exist in the mind, it being absurd that those things which are seen at the distance of several miles, should be as near to us as our own thoughts. [In answer to this, I desire it may be considered, that in a *dream* we do oft perceive things as existing at a great distance off, and yet for all that, those things are acknowledged to have their existence only in the mind.]

XLIII. But for the fuller clearing of this point, it may be worth while to consider, how it is that we perceive distance and things placed at a distance by sight. For that we should in truth see *external* space, and bodies

---

[1] They extirpate the very root of scepticism, "the fallacy of the senses."—Ed.

actually existing in it, some nearer, others further off, seems to carry with it some opposition to what hath been said, of their existing nowhere without the mind. The consideration of this difficulty it was that gave birth to my Essay towards a new Theory of Vision, which was published not long since. [Wherein it is shown (1) that *distance* or outness is *neither immediately* of itself *perceived* by sight, nor yet apprehended or judged of by lines and angles, or any thing that hath a necessary connexion with it: but (2) that it is *only suggested* to our thoughts, by certain visible ideas and sensations attending vision, which in their own nature have no manner of similitude or relation, either with distance, or things placed at a distance. But by a connexion taught us *by experience*, they come to signify and suggest them to us, after the same manner that *words* of any language suggest the ideas they are made to stand for. ☞ Insomuch that a man *born* blind, and afterwards made to see, would not, at first sight, think the things he saw to be without his mind, or at any distance from him. See Sect. XLI. of the forementioned treatise.

XLIV. The ideas of sight and touch make two species, entirely distinct and heterogeneous. *The former are marks and prognostics of the latter.* That the proper objects of sight neither exist without the mind, nor are the images of external things, was shown even in that treatise. Though throughout the same, the contrary be supposed true of tangible objects: not that to suppose that vulgar error was necessary for establishing the notions therein laid down, but because it was beside my purpose to examine and refute it in a discourse concerning *vision*. [So that in strict truth the ideas of sight, when we apprehend by them distance and things placed at a distance, do not suggest or mark out to us things *actually* existing at a distance, but only admonish us what ideas of touch will be imprinted in our minds at such and such distances of time, and in consequence of such or such actions.] It is, I say, evident from what has been said in the foregoing parts of this treatise, and in Sect. CXLVII., and elsewhere of the essay concerning vision, that visible ideas are the language whereby the governing Spirit, on whom we depend, informs us what tangible ideas he is about to imprint upon us, in case we excite this or that motion in our own bodies. But for a fuller information in this point, I refer to the essay itself.

XLV. *Fourth objection, from perpetual annihilation and creation.—Answer.—*[Fourthly, it will be objected, that from the foregoing principles it follows, things are every moment annihilated and created anew.] The objects of sense exist only when they are perceived : the trees therefore are in the garden, or the chairs in the parlour, no longer than while there is somebody by to perceive them. Upon *shutting my eyes*, all the furniture in the room is reduced to nothing, and barely upon opening them it is again created. [In *answer* to all which, I refer the reader to what has been said in Sec. III., IV., &c., and desire he will consider whether he means any thing by the actual existence of an idea, distinct from its being perceived.] For my part, after the nicest inquiry I could make, I am not able to discover that any thing else is meant by those words. And I once more entreat the reader to sound his own thoughts, and not suffer himself to be imposed on by words. If he can conceive it possible either for his ideas or their archetypes to exist without being perceived, then I give up the cause : but if he cannot, he will acknowledge it is unreasonable for him to stand up in defence of he knows not what, and pretend to charge on me as an absurdity the not assenting to those propositions which at bottom have no meaning in them.

XLVI. *Argumentum ad hominem.—*[It will not be amiss to observe, how far the received principles of philosophy are themselves chargeable with those pretended absurdities.] [(1) It is thought strangely absurd that upon closing my eyelids all the visible objects round me should be reduced to nothing ; and yet is not this what philosophers commonly acknowledge when they agree on all hands, that light and colours, which alone are the proper and immediate objects of sight, are mere sensations, that exist no

longer than they are perceived?] [(2) Again, it may
to some perhaps seem very incredible, that things
should be every moment creating; yet this very notion
is commonly taught in the schools. For the *schoolmen*,
though they acknowledge the existence of matter, and
that the whole mundane fabric is framed out of it, are
nevertheless of opinion that it cannot subsist without
the divine conservation, which by them is expounded
to be a continual creation.

XLVII. [(3) Further, a little thought will discover
to us, that though we allow the existence of matter or
corporeal substances, yet it will unavoidably follow
from the principles which are now generally admitted,
that the *particular* bodies, of what kind soever, do none
of them exist whilst they are not perceived.] For (1) it
is evident from Sect. xi. and the following sections,
that the matter philosophers contend for is an incomprehensible somewhat, *which hath none of those particular
qualities whereby the bodies falling under our senses are
distinguished one from another.* (2) But to make this
more plain, it must be remarked, that the infinite divisibility of matter is now universally allowed, at least by
the most approved and considerable philosophers, who,
on the received principles, demonstrate it beyond all
exception. Hence it follows, that there is an infinite
number of parts in each particle of matter, which are
not perceived by sense. The reason, therefore, that
any particular body seems to be of a finite magnitude,
or exhibits only a finite number of parts to sense, is,
not because it contains no more, since in itself it contains an infinite number of parts, *but because the sense
is not acute enough to discern them.* In proportion,
therefore, as the sense is rendered more acute, it perceives a greater number of parts in the object; that
is, the object appears greater, and its figure varies,
those parts in its extremities which were before unperceivable, appearing now to bound it in very different
lines and angles from those perceived by an obtuser
sense. And, at length, after various changes of size
and shape, when the sense becomes infinitely acute,

the body shall seem infinite. During all which, there is no alteration in the body, but only in the sense. *Each body, therefore, considered in itself, is infinitely extended, and consequently void of all shape or figure.* From which it follows, that though we should grant the existence of matter to be ever so certain, yet it is withal as certain, the materialists themselves are by their own principles forced to acknowledge, that neither the particular bodies perceived by sense, nor any thing like them, exist without the mind. [Matter, I say, and each particle thereof, is according to them infinite and shapeless, *and it is the mind that frames all that variety of bodies which compose the visible world, any one whereof does not exist longer than it is perceived.*]

XLVIII. If we consider it, the objection proposed in Sect. XLV. will not be found reasonably charged on the principles we have premised, so as in truth to make any objection at all against our notions. [For though we hold, indeed, the objects of sense to be nothing else but ideas which cannot exist unperceived, yet we may not hence conclude they have no existence, except only while they are perceived by *us*, since *there may be some other spirit that perceives them, though we do not.*] Whereever bodies are said to have no existence without the mind, I would not be understood to mean this or that particular mind, but *all minds whatsoever.* It does not therefore follow from the foregoing principles, that bodies are annihilated and created every moment, or exist not at all during the intervals between our perception in them.

XLIX. *Fifth objection.—Answer.*—[Fifthly, it may perhaps be *objected*, that if extension and figure exist only in the mind, it follows that the mind is extended and figured ; since extension is a mode or attribute, which (to speak with the schools) is predicated of the subject in which it exists.] I *answer*, (1) Those qualities are in the mind *only as they are perceived by it*, that is, not by way of *mode* or *attribute*, but only by way of *idea ;* and it no more follows, that the soul or mind is extended because extension exists in it alone, than it does that it is red or blue, because those colours are *on all hands* acknowledged to exist in it, and nowhere else.] [(2) As to what philosophers say of subject and mode, that seems very groundless and unintelligible.] ☞ For instance, in this proposition, a die is hard, extended, and square; they will have it that the word *die* denotes a subject or substance, distinct from the hardness, extension, and figure, which are predicated of it, and in which they exist. This I cannot comprehend: [to me a die seems to be nothing distinct from those things which are termed its modes or accidents. And to say a die is hard, extended, and square, is not to attribute those qualities to a subject distinct from and supporting them, but only an explication of the meaning of the word *die*.]

L. *Sixth objection, from natural philosophy.—Answer.* —[Sixthly, you will say there have been a great many things explained by matter and motion: take away these, and you destroy the whole corpuscular philosophy, and undermine those mechanical principles which have been applied with so much success to account for the *phenomena*.] In short, whatever advances have been made, either by ancient or modern philosophers, in the study of nature, do all proceed on the supposition, that corporeal substance or matter doth really exist. To this I *answer*, that there is not any one *phenomenon* explained on that supposition, which may not as well be explained without it, as might easily be made appear by an *induction of particulars*. [To explain the *phenomena*, is all one as to show, why upon such and such occasions we are affected with such and such ideas. But (1) how matter should operate on a spirit, or produce any idea in it, is what no philsopher will pretend to explain. It is therefore evident, there can be no use of matter in natural philosophy.] [Besides, (2) they who attempt to account for things, do it not by *corporeal substance,* but by figure, motion, and other qualities, which are in truth no more than mere ideas, and therefore cannot be the cause of any thing, as hath been already shown.] See Sect. xxv.

LI. *Seventh objection.—Answer.*—[Seventhly, it will upon this be demanded whether it does not seem *absurd to take away natural causes, and ascribe every thing to the immediate operation of spirits ?*] We must no longer say upon these principles that fire heats, or water cools, but that a spirit heats, and so forth. Would not a man be deservedly laughed at, who should talk after this manner? I *answer*, he would so ; in such things we ought to *think with the learned, and speak with the vulgar.* They who to demonstration are convinced of the truth of the Copernican system, do nevertheless say the sun rises, the sun sets, or comes to the meridian : and if they affected a contrary style in common talk, it would without doubt appear very ridiculous. A little reflection on what is here said will make it manifest, that the common use of language would receive no manner of alteration or disturbance from the admission of our tenets.

LII. [*In the ordinary affairs of life, any phrases may be retained,* so long as they excite in us proper sentiments, or dispositions to act in such a manner as is necessary for our *well-being,* how false soever they may be, if taken in a strict and *speculative sense.* Nay, this is unavoidable, since propriety being regulated by *custom,* language is suited to the *received* opinions, which are not always the truest.] Hence it is impossible, even in the most rigid philosophic reasonings, so far to alter the bent and genius of the tongue we speak, as never to give a handle for cavillers to pretend difficulties and inconsistencies. But a fair and ingenuous reader will collect the sense from the scope and tenor and connexion of a discourse, making allowances for those inaccurate modes of speech which use has made inevitable.

LIII. [As to the *opinion that there are no corporeal causes,* this has been heretofore maintained by some of the schoolmen, as it is of late by others among the modern philosophers, who though they allow matter to exist, yet will have God alone to be the immediate efficient cause of all things.] These men saw, that amongst all the objects of sense, there was none which had any power or activity included in it, and that by consequence this was likewise true of whatever bodies they supposed to exist without the mind, like unto the immediate objects of sense. [But then, that they should suppose an innumerable multitude of created beings, which they acknowledge are not capable of producing any one effect in nature, and which therefore are made to no manner of purpose, since God might have done every thing as well without them ; this I say, though we should allow it possible, must yet be a very unaccountable and extravagant supposition.]

LIV. *Eighth objection.—Twofold answer.*—[In the eighth place, the universal concurrent assent of mankind may be thought by some an invincible argument in behalf of matter, or the existence of external things.] Must we suppose the whole world to be mistaken ? and if so, what cause can be assigned of so widespread and predominant an error ? I answer, *first*, That upon a narrow inquiry, it will not perhaps be found, so many as is imagined do really believe the existence of matter or things without the mind. Strictly speaking, to believe that which involves a contradiction, or has no meaning in it, is impossible : and whether the foregoing expressions are not of that sort, I refer it to the impartial examination of the reader. [In one sense indeed, men may be said to believe that matter exists, that is, they *act* as if the immediate cause of their sensations, which affects them every moment and is so nearly present to them, were some senseless, unthinking being.] But that they should clearly apprehend any meaning marked by those words, and form thereof a settled *speculative* opinion, is what I am not able to conceive. This is not the only instance wherein men impose upon themselves, by imagining they believe those propositions they have often heard, though at bottom they have no meaning in them.

LV. But *secondly*, though we should grant a notion to be ever so universally and stedfastly adhered to, yet this is but a weak argument of its truth, to whoever considers what a vast number of prejudices and false opinions are every where embraced with the utmost tenaciousness, by the unreflecting (which are the far greater) part of mankind. ☞ There was a time when the antipodes and motion of the earth were looked upon as monstrous absurdities, even by men of learning : and if it be considered what a small proportion they bear to the rest of mankind, we shall find that at this day, those notions have gained but a very inconsiderable footing in the world.

LVI. *Ninth objection. — Answer. —* [But it is demanded, that we assign *a cause of this prejudice,* and account for its obtaining in the world. To this I *answer,* That men knowing they perceived several ideas, *whereof they themselves were not the authors,* as not being excited from within, nor depending on the operation of their wills, this made them maintain, those ideas or objects of perception had an *existence independent of, and without the mind,* without ever dreaming that a contradiction was involved in those words.] [But philosophers having plainly seen that the immediate objections of perception do not exist without the mind, *they in some degree* corrected the mistake of the vulgar, but at the same time run into another which seems no less absurd, to wit, that there are certain objects really existing without the mind, or having a subsistence distinct from being perceived, *of which our ideas are only images* or resemblances, imprinted by those objects on the mind.] And this notion of the philosophers owes its origin to the same cause with the former, namely, their being conscious that they were not the authors of their own sensations, which they evidently knew were imprinted from without, and which therefore must have some cause distinct from the minds on which they are imprinted.

LVII. But *why they should suppose the ideas of sense to be excited in us by things in their likeness,* and not rather have recourse to *spirit* which alone can act, may be accounted for, [*first,* because they were not aware of the repugnancy there is, (1) as well in supposing things like unto our ideas existing without, as (2) attributing to them *power or activity.*] [*Secondly,* because the supreme spirit, which excites those ideas in our minds, is not marked out and limited to our view *by any particular finite collection of sensible ideas*, as human agents are by their size, complexion, limbs, and motions.] [And *thirdly*, because his operations are regular and uniform.] Whenever the course of nature is interrupted by a miracle, men are ready to own the presence of a superior agent. But when we see things go on in the ordinary course, they do not excite in us any reflection; their order and concatenation, though it be an argument of the greatest wisdom, power, and goodness in their creator, is yet so constant and familiar to us, that we do not think them the immediate effects of a *free spirit*: especially since inconstancy and mutability in acting, though it be an imperfection, is looked on as a mark of *freedom*.

LVIII. *Tenth objection.—Answer.—*Tenthly, it will be objected, that the notions we advance are inconsistent with several sound truths in philosophy and mathematics. ☞ [For example, *the motion of the earth* is now universally admitted by astronomers, as a truth grounded on the clearest and most convincing reasons; but on the foregoing principles, there can be no such thing. For motion being only an idea, it follows that if it be not perceived, it exists not; but the motion of the earth is not perceived by sense.] I *answer*, that tenet, if rightly understood, will be found to agree with the principles we have premised; [for the question, whether the earth moves or no, amounts in reality to no more than this, to wit, whether we have reason to conclude from what hath been observed by astronomers, that if we were placed in such and such circumstances, and such or such a position and distance, both from the earth and sun, we should perceive the former to move among the choir of the planets, and appearing in all respects like one of them: and this, by the established rules of nature, which we have no reason to mistrust, is reasonably collected from the phenomena.]

LIX. [We may, from the experience we have had of the train and succession of ideas in our minds, often

make, I will not say uncertain conjectures, but sure and
well-grounded predictions, concerning the ideas we shall
be affected with, pursuant to a great train of actions,
and be enabled to pass a right judgment of what would
have appeared to us, in case we were in circumstances
very different from those we are in at present.] [Herein
consists the knowledge of nature, which may preserve
its use and certainty very consistently with what hath
been said.] It will be easy to apply this to whatever
objections of the like sort may be drawn from the
magnitude of the stars, or any other discoveries in
astronomy or nature.

LX. *Eleventh objection.*—[In the eleventh place, it
will be demanded *to what purpose serves that curious
organization of plants*, and *the admirable mechanism in
the parts of animals?*] Might not vegetables grow, and
shoot forth leaves and blossoms, and animals perform
all their motions, as well without as with all that variety
of internal parts so elegantly contrived and put together,
*which being ideas have nothing powerful or operative in
them, nor have any necessary connexion with the effects
ascribed to them?* If it be a spirit that immediately produces every effect by a *fiat*, or act of his will, we must
think all that is fine and artificial in the works, whether
of man or nature, to be made in vain. ☞ By this
doctrine, though an *artist* hath made the spring and
wheels, and every movement of a watch, and adjusted
them in such a manner as he knew would produce the
motions he designed; yet he must think all this done
to no purpose, and that it is an intelligence which
directs the index, and points to the hour of the day.
If so, why may not the intelligence do it, without his
being at the pains of making the movements, and
putting them together? Why does not an empty case
serve as well as another? And how comes it to pass,
that whenever there is any fault in the going of a watch,
there is some corresponding disorder to be found in the
movements, which being mended by a skilful hand, all
is right again?

The like may be said of all the clock-work of nature,

great part whereof is so wonderfully fine and subtile, as scarce to be discerned by the best microscope. In short it will be asked, how upon our principles any tolerable account can be given, or any final cause assigned of an innumerable multitude of bodies and machines framed with the most exquisite art, which in the common philosophy have very apposite uses assigned them, and serve to explain abundance of phenomena.

LXI. *Answer.*—To all which I answer, *first*, that though there were some difficulties relating to the administration of providence, and the uses by it assigned to the several parts of nature, which I could not solve by the foregoing principles, yet this objection could be of small weight against the truth and certainty of those things which may be proved *à priori*, with the utmost evidence. *Secondly*, but neither are the received principles free from the like difficulties; for it may still be demanded, to what end God should take those round-about methods of effecting things by instruments and machines, which no one can deny might have been effected by the *mere command of his will*, without all that *apparatus*: nay, (*thirdly*,) if we narrowly consider it, we shall find the objection may be retorted with greater force on those who hold the existence of those machines without the mind; for it has been made evident, that solidity, bulk, figure, motion, and the like, *have no activity* or *efficacy* in them, so as to be capable of producing any one effect in nature. See Sect. xxv. [Whoever therefore supposes them to exist (allowing the supposition possible) when they are not perceived, does it manifestly to no purpose; since the only use that is assigned to them, as they exist unperceived, is that they produce those perceivable effects, which in truth cannot be ascribed to any thing but spirit.]

LXII. (*Fourthly.*)—[But to come nearer the difficulty, it must be observed, that though the fabrication of all those parts and organs be not absolutely necessary to the *producing any effect*, yet it is necessary to the producing of things *in a constant, regular way, according to the laws of nature.* There are certain general laws that run through the whole chain of natural effects : these are learned by the observation and study of nature, and are by men applied (1) as well to the framing artificial things for the use and ornament of life, as (2) to the explaining the various *phenomena :*] which explication consists ónly in showing the conformity any particular phenomenon hath to the general laws of nature, or which is the same thing, in discovering the *uniformity* there is in the production of natural effects ; as will be evident to whoever shall attend to the several instances, wherein philosophers pretend to account for appearances. That there is a great and conspicuous use in these regular constant methods of working observed by the supreme agent, hath been shown in Sect. xxxi. And it is no less visible, that a particular size, figure, motion, and disposition of parts are necessary, though not absolutely to the producing any effect, yet to the producing it according to the standing mechanical laws of nature. ☞ Thus, for instance, it cannot be denied that God, or the intelligence which sustains and rules the ordinary course of things, might, if he were minded to produce a miracle, cause all the motions on the dial-plate of a watch, though nobody had ever made the movements, and put them in it : but yet if he will act agreeably to the rules of mechanism, by him for wise ends established and maintained in the creation, it is necessary that those actions of the watchmaker, whereby he makes the movements and rightly adjusts them, precede the production of the aforesaid motions ; as also that any disorder in them be attended with the perception of some corresponding disorder in the movements, which being once corrected, all is right again.

LXIII. It may indeed on some occasions be *necessary, that the author of nature display his overruling power* in producing some appearance out of his ordinary series of things. Such exceptions from the general rules of nature are proper to *surprise and awe men* into an acknowledgment of the divine being : [but then they are to be used but seldom, (1) otherwise there

is a plain reason why they should fail of that effect.]
[(2) Besides, God seems to choose the *convincing our
reason* of his attributes by the works of nature, which
discover so much harmony and contrivance in their
make, and are such plain indications of wisdom and
beneficence in their author, rather than to *astonish* us
into a belief of his being by anomalous and surprising
events.]

LXIV. *To set this matter in a yet clearer light*, I shall
observe that what has been objected in Sect. LX. amounts
in reality to no more than this : ideas are not any how
and at random produced, there being a certain order
and connexion between them, like to that of cause and
effect : there are also several combinations of them,
made in a very regular and artificial manner, which
seem like so many instruments in the hand of nature,
that being hid, as it were, behind the scenes, have a
secret operation in producing those appearances which
are seen on the theatre of the world, being themselves
discernible only to the curious eye of the philosopher.
But since one idea cannot be the cause of another, to
what purpose is that connexion ? and since those instruments, being barely *inefficacious perceptions* in the mind,
are not subservient to the production of natural effects :
it is demanded why they are made, or, in other words,
what reason can be assigned why God should make us,
upon a close inspection into his works, behold so great
variety of ideas, so artfully laid together, and so much
according to rule ; it not being credible, that he would
be at the expense (if one may so speak) of all that art
and regularity to no purpose ?

LXV. [To all which my *answer* is, *first*, that the connexion of ideas does not imply the relation of *cause* and
effect, but only of a mark or *sign* with the thing *signified*.]
☞ The *fire* which I see is not the cause of the pain I
suffer upon my approaching it, but the mark that fore-
warns me of it. In like manner, the noise that I hear
is not the effect of this or that motion or collision of the
ambient bodies, but the sign thereof. [*Secondly*, the
reason why ideas are formed into machines, that is,

artificial and regular combinations, is the same with that for combining letters into words. That a few original ideas may be made to signify a *great number of effects and actions*, it is necessary they be variously combined together : and to the end their use be *permanent and universal*, these combinations must be made by *rule*, and with *wise contrivance*.] By this means abundance of information is conveyed unto us concerning what we are to expect from such and such actions, and what methods are proper to be taken, for the exciting such and such ideas : which in effect is all that I conceive to be distinctly meant, when it is said that by discerning the figure, texture, and mechanism of the inward parts of bodies, whether natural or artificial, we may attain to know the several uses and properties depending thereon, or the nature of the thing.

LXVI. *Proper employment of the natural philosopher.* —Hence it is evident, that those *things* which, *under the notion of a cause co-operating* or concurring *to the production of effects, are altogether inexplicable*, and run us into great absurdities, may be very naturally explained, and have a proper and obvious use assigned them, when they are considered only as marks or signs for our information. [And it is the *searching after, and endeavouring to understand those signs* (this language, if I may so call it) *instituted by the author of nature*, that ought to be the employment of the natural philosopher, and not the pretending to explain things by corporeal causes ; which doctrine seems to have too much estranged the minds of men from that active principle, that supreme and wise spirit, "in whom we live, move, and have our being."]

LXVII.—*Twelfth objection.—Answer.*—In the twelfth place, it may perhaps be objected, that though it be clear from what has been said, that there can be no such thing as an inert, senseless, extended, solid, figured, moveable substance, existing without the mind, such as philosophers describe matter : [yet if any man shall leave out of his idea of *matter*, the positive ideas of extension, figure, solidity, and motion, and say that he means only by that word an inert senseless substance, that exists without the mind, or unperceived, which is the *occasion of our ideas*, or at the presence whereof God is pleased to excite ideas in us :] it doth not appear, but that matter taken in this sense may possibly exist. [In *answer* to which I say *first*, that it seems no less absurd to suppose a substance without accidents, than it is to suppose accidents without a substance. But *secondly*, though we should grant this unknown substance may possibly exist, yet *where can it be supposed to be ?* that it exists not in the mind is agreed, and that it exists not in place is no less certain ; *since all* (place or) *extension exists only in the mind*, as hath been already proved. It remains therefore that it exists no where at all.]

LXVIII. *Matter supports nothing, an argument against its existence.*—Let us examine a little the description that is here given us of *matter*. It neither acts, nor perceives, nor is perceived : for this is all that is meant by saying it is an *inert, senseless, unknown* substance ; which is a definition entirely made up of negatives, excepting only the relative notion of its standing under or supporting : but then it must be observed, that it *supports* nothing at all ; and how nearly this comes to the description of a *nonentity*, I desire may be considered. But, say you, it is the *unknown occasion, at the presence of which* ideas are excited in us by the will of God. [Now I would fain know how any thing can be *present* to us, which is neither perceivable by sense nor reflection, nor capable of producing any idea in our minds, nor is at all extended, nor hath any form, nor exists in any place.] The words *to be present*, when thus applied, must needs be taken in some abstract and strange meaning, and which I am not able to comprehend.

LXIX. [Again,[1] let us examine what is meant by *occasion ;* so far as I can gather from the common use of language, that word signifies, either the agent which *produces any effect*, or else something that is *observed to accompany*, or go before it, in the ordinary course of things.] But when it is applied to matter as above

---

[1] Vide sect. lxvii. for the first argument to show that matter is not the *occasion* of our ideas.—Ed.

described, it can be taken in neither of those senses. [For matter is said to be passive and inert, and so cannot be an *agent* or efficient cause. It is also *unperceivable*, as being devoid of all sensible qualities, and so cannot be the occasion of our perceptions in the latter sense:] ☞ as when the *burning my finger* is said to be the occasion of the pain that attends it. What therefore can be meant by calling matter an *occasion?* this term is either used in no sense at all, or else in some sense very distant from its received signification.

LXX. [You will perhaps say that *matter*, though it be not perceived by us, *is* nevertheless *perceived by God*, to whom it is the occasion of exciting ideas in our minds.] For, say you, since we observe our sensations to be imprinted in an *orderly and constant manner*, it is but reasonable to suppose there are certain constant and regular occasions of their being produced. That is to say, that there are certain permanent and distinct parcels of matter, corresponding to our ideas, which, though they do not excite them in our minds, or any ways immediately affect us, as being altogether passive and unperceivable to us, they are nevertheless to God, by whom they are perceived, as it were so many occasions to remind him when and what ideas to imprint on our minds: *that so things may go on in a constant, uniform manner.*

LXXI. [In *answer* to this I observe, that as the notion of matter is here stated, the question is no longer concerning the existence of a thing distinct from *spirit* and *idea*, from perceiving and being perceived: but whether there are not certain ideas, of I know not what sort, in the mind of God, which are so many marks or notes that direct him how to produce sensations in our minds, in a constant and regular method]: ☞ much after the same manner as a musician is directed by the notes of music to produce that harmonious train and composition of sound, which is called a *tune;* though they who hear the music do not perceive the notes, and may be entirely ignorant of them. But this notion of

matter [1] seems too extravagant to deserve a confutation.
[Besides, it is in effect no objection against what we
have advanced, to wit, that there is no senseless, *unperceived substance*.]

LXXII. *The order of our perceptions shows the goodness of God, but affords no proof of the existence of matter.*
—If we follow the light of reason, we shall, from the
constant, uniform method of our sensations, collect the
goodness and wisdom of the *spirit* who excites them in
our minds. But this is all that I can see reasonably
concluded from thence. To me, I say, it is evident
that the being of a *spirit infinitely wise, good, and powerful* is abundantly sufficient to explain all the appearances of nature. But as for *inert, senseless matter*,
nothing that I perceive has any the least connexion
with it, or leads to the thoughts of it. And I would
fain see any one explain any the meanest *phenomenon* in
nature by it, or show any manner of reason, though in
the lowest rank of probability, that he can have for its
existence; or even make any tolerable sense or meaning
of that supposition. For as to its being an occasion,
we have, I think, evidently shown that with regard to us
it is no occasion: it remains therefore that it must be,
if at all, the occasion to God of exciting ideas in us;
and what this amounts to, we have just now seen.

LXXIII. [It is worth while to reflect a little on the
motives which induced men *to suppose the existence of
material substance*]; that so having observed the gradual
ceasing and expiration of those motives or reasons,
we may proportionably withdraw the assent that was
grounded on them. *First*, therefore, it was thought
that colour, figure, motion, and the rest of the sensible
qualities or accidents, did really exist without the mind;
[and for this reason, it *seemed needful to suppose some
unthinking substratum or substance wherein they did exist,
since they could not be conceived to exist by themselves*.]
Afterwards, (*secondly*) in process of time, men being
convinced that colours, sounds, and the rest of the

[1] (Which after all is *the only intelligible one* that I can pick, from
what is said of unknown occasions.)—Edit. 1710.

sensible secondary qualities had no existence without
the mind, they stripped this *substratum* or material substance of those qualities, leaving only the *primary ones*,
figure, motion, and such like, which they still conceived
to exist without the mind, and consequently to stand in
need of a material support. But it having been shown,
that none, even of these, can possibly exist otherwise
than in a spirit or mind which perceives them, it follows that we have no longer any reason to suppose the
being of *matter*. Nay that it is utterly impossible there
should be any such thing, so long as that word is taken
to denote an *unthinking substratum* of qualities or accidents, wherein they exist without the mind.

LXXIV. But though it be allowed by the *materialists*
themselves, that matter was thought of only for the sake
of supporting accidents ; and the reason entirely ceasing,
one might expect the mind should naturally, and without
any reluctance at all, quit the belief of what was solely
grounded thereon. Yet the prejudice is riveted so deeply
in our thoughts, that we can scarce tell how to part with
it, and are therefore inclined, since the *thing* itself is
indefensible, at least to retain the *name ;* which we
apply to I know not what abstracted and indefinite
notions of *being* or *occasion*, though without any show of
reason, at least so far as I can see. For what is there
on our part, or what do we perceive amongst all the
ideas, sensations, notions, which are imprinted on our
minds, either by sense or reflection, from whence may
be inferred the existence of an inert, thoughtless, unperceived occasion ? and on the other hand, on the part of
an *all-sufficient spirit*, what can there be that should
make us believe, or even suspect, he is *directed* by an
inert occasion to excite ideas in our minds?

LXXV. *Absurdity of contending for the existence of
matter as the occasion of ideas.*—It is a very extraordinary instance of the force of prejudice, and much to be
lamented, that the mind of man retains so great a fond-
ness, against all the evidence of reason, for a stupid,
thoughtless *somewhat*, by the interposition whereof it
would, as it were, screen itself from the providence of

God, and remove him further off from the affairs of the world. But though we do the utmost we can, to secure the belief of *matter*, though when reason forsakes us, we endeavour to support our opinion on the bare possibility of the thing, and though we indulge ourselves in the full scope of an imagination not regulated by reason, to make out that poor *possibility*, yet the upshot of all is, that there are certain *unknown ideas* in the mind of God ; for this, if any thing, is all that I conceive to be meant by *occasion* with regard to God. And this, at the bottom, is no longer contending for the *thing*, but for the *name*.

LXXVI. Whether therefore there are such ideas in the mind of God, and whether they may be called by the name *matter*, I shall not dispute. But if you stick to the notion of an *unthinking* substance, or support of extension, motion, and other sensible qualities, then to me is it most evidently impossible there should be any such thing. Since is it a plain repugnancy, that those qualities should exist in or be supported by an unperceiving substance.

LXXVII. *That a substratum not perceived, may exist, unimportant.*—[But say you, though it be granted that there is no thoughtless support of extension, and the other qualities or accidents *which we perceive ;* yet there may, perhaps, be some inert unperceiving substance, or *substratum* of *some other qualities*, as incomprehensible to us as colours are to a man born blind, *because we have not a sense adapted to them*.] But if we had a new sense, we should possibly no more doubt of their existence, than a blind man made to see does of the existence of light and colours. [I answer, *first*, if what you mean by the word *matter* be only the *unknown support of unknown qualities*, it is no matter whether there is such a thing or not, since it no way concerns us : and I do not see the advantage there is in disputing about we know not *what*, and we know not *why*.]

LXXVIII. [But *secondly*, if we had *a new sense*,[1] it *could only furnish us with new ideas or sensations :* and

1 Vide sect. cxxxvi.

then we should have the same reason against their existing in an unperceiving substance, that has been already
offered with relation to figure, motion, colour, and the
like.] Qualities, as hath been shown, are nothing else
but *sensations* or *ideas*, which exist only in a *mind* perceiving them ; and this is true not only of the ideas we
are acquainted with at present, but likewise of all possible
ideas whatsoever.

LXXIX. But you will *insist*, what if (1) I have no
reason to believe the existence of matter, what if (2)
I can assign any use to it, or (3) explain any thing by it,
or even (4) conceive what is meant by that word ? yet
still it is no contradiction to say that matter exists, and
that this matter is *in general* a *substance*, or *occasion of
ideas ;* though, indeed, to go about to unfold the meaning, or adhere to any particular explication of those
words, may be attended with great difficulties. I *answer*,
when words are used without a meaning, you may put
them together as you please, without danger of running
into a contradiction. You may say, for example, that
twice two is equal to *seven*, so long as you declare you
do not take the words of that proposition in their usual
acceptation, but for marks of you know not what. And
by the same reason you may say, there is an inert
thoughtless substance without accidents, which is the
occasion of our ideas. And we shall understand just as
much by one proposition, as the other.

LXXX. [In the last place, you will *say*, what if we
give up the cause of material substance, and assert, that
matter is an unknown *somewhat*, neither substance nor
accident, spirit nor idea, inert, thoughtless, indivisible,
immoveable, unextended, existing in no place ?] for, say
you, whatever may be urged against *substance* or *occasion*,
or any other positive or relative notion of matter, hath
no place at all, so long as this *negative definition of
matter* is adhered to. I *answer*, you may, if so it shall
seem good, use the word *matter* in the same sense that
other men use *nothing*, and so make those terms con-
vertible in your style. For after all, this is what appears
to me to be the result of that definition, the parts whereof

when I consider with attention, either collectively, or separate from each other, I do not find that there is any kind of effect or impression made on my mind, different from what is excited by the term *nothing*.

LXXXI. [You will *reply* perhaps, that in the foresaid definition is included, what doth *sufficiently* distinguish it from nothing, the positive, abstract idea of *quiddity*, *entity*, or *existence*.] I own indeed, that those who pretend to the faculty of framing abstract general ideas, do talk as if they had such an idea, which is, say they, the most abstract and general notion of all, that is to me the most incomprehensible of all others. That there are a great variety of spirits of different orders and capacities, whose faculties, both in number and extent, are far exceeding those the author of my being has bestowed on me, I see no reason to deny. And for me to pretend to determine by my own few, stinted, narrow inlets of perception, what ideas the inexhaustible power of the supreme spirit may imprint upon them, were certainly the utmost folly and presumption. Since there may be, for ought that I know, innumerable sorts of ideas or sensations, as different from one another, and from all that I have perceived, as colours are from sounds. But how ready soever I may be to acknowledge the scantiness of my comprehension, with regard to the endless variety of spirits and ideas, that might possibly exist, yet for any one to pretend to a notion of entity or existence, *abstracted* from *spirit* and *idea*, from perceiving and being perceived, is, I suspect, a downright repugnancy and trifling with words. It remains that we consider the objections which may possibly be made on the part of religion.

LXXXII. *Objections derived from the scriptures answered*.[1]—Some [2] there are who think, that though the arguments for the real existence of bodies, which are drawn from reason, be allowed not to amount to demonstration, yet (first) the *holy scriptures* are so clear in the point, as will sufficiently convince every good Christian,

[1] And concluded in sect. xcv.
[2] Malebranche. Vide sect. lxxxiv.

that bodies do really exist, and are something more than mere ideas; there being in holy writ innumerable facts related, which evidently suppose the reality of timber, and stone, mountains, and rivers, and cities, and human bodies. [To which I *answer*, that no sort of writings whatever, sacred or profane, which use those and the like words in the *vulgar acceptation*, or so as to have a meaning in them, are in danger of having their truth called in question by our doctrine. That all those things do really exist, that there are bodies, even corporeal substances, when taken *in the vulgar sense*, has been shown to be agreeable to our principles]: and the difference betwixt *things* and *ideas*, *realities* and *chimeras*, has been distinctly explained.[1] [And I do not think, that either what philosophers call *matter*, or the existence of objects without the mind, is any where mentioned in scripture.]

LXXXIII. *No objection as to language tenable.* — [Again, whether there be or be not external things, it is agreed on all hands, that the proper use of words is the marking our conceptions, or things *only as they are known and perceived by us;* whence it plainly follows, that in the tenets we have laid down, there is nothing inconsistent with the right use and significancy of *language,* and that discourse of what kind soever, so far as it is intelligible, remains undisturbed.] But all this seems so manifest, from what hath been set forth in the premises, that it is needless to insist any further on it.

LXXXIV. But (secondly)[2] it will be urged, that *miracles do,* at least, *lose much of their* stress and *import by our principles.* ☞ What must we think of Moses' rod, was it not *really* turned into a serpent, or was there only a change of *ideas* in the minds of the spectators? And can it be supposed, that our Saviour did no more at the marriage-feast in Cana, than impose on the sight, and smell, and taste of the guests, so as to create in them the appearance or idea only of wine? The same may be said of all other miracles: which, in consequence

1 Sect. xxix., xxx., xxxiii., xxxvi., &c.
2 Sect. lxxxii.

of the foregoing principles, must be looked upon only as so many cheats, or illusions of fancy. To this I reply, that the rod was changed into a real serpent, and the water into real wine. That this doth not, in the least, contradict what I have elsewhere said, will be evident from Sect. xxxiv., xxxv. But this business of *real* and *imaginary* hath been already so plainly and fully explained, and so often referred to, and the difficulties about it are so easily answered from what hath gone before, that it were an affront to the reader's understanding, to resume the explication of it in this place. ☞ I shall only observe, that if at table all who were present should see, and smell, and taste, and drink wine, and find the effects of it, with me there could be no doubt of its reality. [So that at bottom, the scruple concerning real miracles hath no place at all on ours, but only on the received principles, and, consequently, maketh rather *for*, than *against*, what hath been said.]

LXXXV. *Consequences of the preceding tenets.*—Having done with the objections, which I endeavoured to propose in the clearest light, and given them all the force and weight I could, we proceed in the next place to take a view of our tenets *in their consequences.* [Some of these appear at first sight, as that several difficult and obscure questions, on which abundance of speculation hath been thrown away, are entirely banished from philosophy. Whether (1) corporeal substance can think? whether (2) matter be infinitely divisible? and (3) how it operates on spirit? These, and the like inquiries, have given infinite amusement to philosophers in all ages.] But depending on the existence of *matter*, they have no longer any place on our principles. Many other advantages there are, as well with regard to *religion* as the *sciences*, which it is easy for any one to deduce from what hath been premised. But this will appear more plainly in the sequel.[1]

LXXXVI. *The removal of matter gives certainty to*

[1] (1) Many philosophic speculations banished: (2) Scepticism extirpated: (3) Atheists and fatalists deprived of their chief support: (4) Idolatry exposed: (5) Socinianism refuted.

knowledge.—[From the principles we have laid down, it follows, human knowledge may naturally be reduced to two heads, that of *ideas* and that of *spirits.*] Of each of these I shall treat in order. And first, as to ideas or unthinking things, our knowledge of these hath been very much obscured and confounded, and we have been led into very dangerous errors, by supposing a two-fold existence of the objects of sense, the one *intelligible*, or in the mind, the other *real* and without the mind : whereby unthinking things are thought to have a natural subsistence of their own, distinct from being perceived by spirits. [This, which, if I mistake not, hath been shown to be a most groundless and absurd notion, is *the very root of scepticism ;* for so long as men thought that real things subsisted without the mind, and that their knowledge was only so far forth *real* as it was conformable to *real things*, it follows, they could not be certain that they had any real knowledge at all. For how can it be known, that the things which are perceived are conformable to those which are not perceived, or exist without the mind?]

LXXXVII. Colour, figure, motion, extension, and the like, considered only as so many *sensations* in the mind, are perfectly known, there being nothing in them which is not perceived. But if they are looked on as notes or images, referred to *things* or *archetypes* existing without the mind, then are we involved all in *scepticism*. We see only the appearances, and not the real qualities of things. [What may be the extension, figure, or motion of any thing really and absolutely, or in itself, it is impossible for us to know, but only the *proportion* or the *relation* they bear to our senses.] Things remaining the same, our ideas vary, and which of them, or even whether any of them at all represent the true quality really existing in the thing, it is out of our reach to determine. So that, for ought we know, all we see, hear, and feel, may be only phantom and vain chimera, and not at all agree with the real things, existing in *rerum natura*. All this scepticism follows, from our supposing a difference between *things* and *ideas*, and that the former have a subsistence without the mind, or unperceived. It were easy to dilate on this subject, and show how the arguments urged by sceptics in all ages, depend on the supposition of external objects.[1]

LXXXVIII. *If there be external matter, neither the nature nor existence of things can be known.*—So long as we attribute a real existence to unthinking things, distinct from their being perceived, it is not only impossible for us to know with evidence (1) the nature of any real unthinking being, but even (2) that it exists. Hence it is, that we see philosophers distrust their senses, and doubt of the existence of heaven and earth, of every thing they see or feel, even of their own bodies. And after all their labour and struggle of thought, they are forced to own, we cannot attain to any self-evident or demonstrative knowledge of the existence of sensible things. But all this doubtfulness, which so bewilders and confounds the mind, and makes *philosophy* ridiculous in the eyes of the world, vanishes, if we annex a meaning to our words, and do not amuse ourselves with the terms *absolute*, *external*, *exist*, and such like, signifying we know not what. I can as well doubt of my own being, as of the being of those things which I actually perceive by sense : [it being a manifest contradiction, that any sensible object should be immediately perceived by sight or touch, and, at the same time, have no existence in nature, since the very existence of an un-thinking being consists in *being perceived*.]

LXXXIX. *Of thing or being.*—Nothing seems of more importance, towards erecting a firm system of sound and real knowledge, which may be proof against the assaults of scepticism, than to lay the beginning in a distinct explication of what is meant by *thing*, *reality*, *existence* : for in vain shall we dispute concerning the real existence of things, or pretend to any knowledge thereof, so long as we have not fixed the meaning of those words. [*Thing or being*[2] is the most general name of all; it comprehends under it two kinds entirely distinct and hetero-

---

[1] " But this is too obvious to need being insisted on."—Edit. 1710.

[2] Vide sect. xxxix.

geneous, and which have nothing common but the name, to wit, *spirits* and *ideas*. The former are *active, indivisible* (incorruptible) *substances :* the latter are *inert, fleeting*, (perishable passions,) or *dependent beings*, which subsist not by themselves, but are supported by, or exist in minds or spiritual substances.[1] We comprehend our own existence by inward feeling or reflection, and that of other spirits by reason. We may be said to have some knowledge or notion of our own minds, of spirits and active beings, whereof, in a strict sense, we have not ideas. In like manner we know and have a notion of relations between things or ideas, which relations are distinct from the ideas or things related, inasmuch as the latter may be perceived by us without our perceiving the former. [To me it seems that ideas, spirits, and relations, are all, in their respective kinds, the object of human knowledge and subject of discourse : and that the term *idea* would be improperly extended to signify every thing we know or have any notion of.]

XC. *External things either imprinted by or perceived by some other mind.*—[Ideas imprinted on the senses are real things, or do really exist ; this we do not deny, but we deny (1) they can subsist without the minds which perceive them, or (2) that they are resemblances of any archetypes existing without the mind : (1) since the very being of a sensation or idea consists in being perceived, and (2) an idea can be like nothing but an idea.] [Again, the *things perceived by sense may be termed external*, with regard to their origin, in that they are not generated from within, by the mind itself, but (1) *imprinted by a spirit distinct from that which perceives them.* Sensible objects may likewise be said to be without the mind, in another sense, namely, (2) *when they exist in some other mind.* Thus when I shut my eyes, the things I saw may still exist, but it must be in another mind.]

XCI. *Sensible qualities real.*—It were a mistake to think, that what is here said derogates in the least from the reality of things. [It is acknowledged, on the re-

---

[1] The remainder of the section does not appear in the edition of 1710.

ceived principles, that extension, motion, and, in a word, all sensible qualities, have need of a support, as not being able to subsist by themselves. But the objects perceived by sense are allowed to be nothing but combinations of those qualities, and, consequently, cannot subsist by themselves. *Thus far it is agreed on all hands.*] So that in denying the things perceived by sense, an existence independent of a substance, or support wherein they may exist, we detract nothing from the received opinion of their *reality*, and are guilty of no innovation in that respect. All the difference is, that according to us the unthinking beings perceived by sense have no existence distinct from being perceived, and cannot therefore exist in any other substance, than those *unextended, indivisible substances,* or *spirits, which act, and think, and perceive them:* whereas philosophers vulgarly hold, that the sensible qualities exist in an *inert, extended, unperceiving substance,* which they call *matter,* to which they attribute a natural subsistence, exterior to all thinking beings, or distinct from being perceived by any mind whatsoever, even the eternal mind of the Creator, wherein they suppose only ideas of the corporeal substances created by him : if indeed they allow them to be at all *created.*

XCII. *Objections of atheists overturned.*—For as we have shown the doctrine of matter, or corporeal substance, to have been the main pillar and support of scepticism, so likewise upon the same foundation have been raised all the impious schemes of atheism and irreligion. [Nay, so great a difficulty hath it been thought, *to conceive matter produced out of nothing,* that the most celebrated among the ancient philosophers, even of these who maintained the being of a God, have thought matter to be uncreated and coeternal with him.] How great a friend material substance hath been to atheists in all ages, were needless to relate. All their monstrous systems have so visible and necessary a dependence on it, that when this corner-stone is once removed, the whole fabric cannot choose but fall to the ground ; insomuch that it is no longer worth while to bestow a particular consideration on the absurdities of every wretched sect of atheists.

XCIII. *And of fatalists also.*—[That impious and profane persons should readily fall in with those systems which favour their inclinations, by deriding immaterial substance, and supposing the soul to be divisible and subject to corruption as the body; which exclude all freedom, intelligence, and design from the formation of things, and instead thereof make a self-existent, stupid, unthinking substance, the root and origin of all beings.] That they should hearken to those who deny a Providence, or inspection of a superior mind over the affairs of the world, attributing the whole series of events either to *blind chance* or *fatal necessity*, arising *from the impulse of one body on another.* All this is very natural. And on the other hand, when men of better principles observe the enemies of religion lay so great a stress on *unthinking matter*, and all of them use so much industry and artifice to reduce every thing to it; methinks they should rejoice to see them deprived of their grand support, and driven from that only fortress, without which your Epicureans, Hobbists, and the like, have not even the shadow of a pretence, but become the most cheap and easy triumph in the world.

XCIV. *Of Idolaters.*—The existence of matter, or bodies unperceived, has not only been the main support of atheists and fatalists, but [on the same principle doth *idolatry* likewise in all its various forms depend.] Did men but consider that the sun, moon, and stars, and every other object of the senses, are only so many sensations in their minds, which have no other existence but barely being perceived, doubtless they would never fall down and worship their own *ideas;* but rather address their homage to that eternal invisible Mind which produces and sustains all things.

XCV. *And Socinians.*—The same absurd principle, by mingling itself with the articles of our faith, hath occasioned no small difficulties to Christians. [☞ For example, about the resurrection, how many scruples and objections have been raised by Socinians and others?

But do not the most plausible of them depend on the supposition, that a body is denominated the same, with regard not to the form or *that which is perceived by sense*, but the material substance which remains the same under several forms?] Take away this *material substance*, about the identity whereof all the dispute is, and mean by *body* what every plain ordinary person means by that word, to wit, that which is immediately seen and felt, which is only a combination of sensible qualities, or ideas: and then their most unanswerable objections come to nothing.[1]

XCVI. *Summary of the consequences of expelling matter.*—Matter being once expelled out of nature, drags with it so many sceptical and impious notions, such an incredible number of disputes and puzzling questions, which have been thorns in the sides of divines, as well as philosophers, and made so much fruitless work for mankind; that if the arguments we have produced against it are not found equal to demonstration (as to me they evidently seem), yet I am sure all friends to knowledge, peace, and religion, have reason to wish they were.

XCVII. Beside the external existence of the objects of perception, another great source of errors and difficulties, with regard to ideal knowledge, is the doctrine of *abstract ideas*, such as it hath been set forth in the introduction. The plainest things in the world, those we are most intimately acquainted with, and perfectly know, when they are considered in an abstract way, appear strangely difficult and incomprehensible. Time, place, and motion, taken in particular or concrete, are what every body knows; but having passed through the hands of a metaphysician, they become too abstract and fine to be apprehended by men of ordinary sense. Bid your servant meet you at such a *time*, in such a *place*, and he shall never stay to deliberate on the meaning of those words: in conceiving that particular time and place, or the motion by which he is to get thither, he

[1] The answers to objections on the ground of religion, which are concluded in this section, were commenced in sect. lxxxii.

finds not the least difficulty. But if *time* be taken, exclusive of all those particular actions and ideas that diversify the day, merely for the *continuation of existence*, or duration in abstract, then it will perhaps gravel even a philosopher to comprehend it.

XCVIII. *Dilemma.*—(For my own part,) whenever I attempt to frame a simple idea of *time*, abstracted from the succession of ideas in my mind, which flows uniformly, and is participated by all beings, I am lost and embrangled in inextricable difficulties. I have no notion of it at all, only I hear others say, it is infinitely divisible, and speak of it in such a manner as leads me to entertain odd thoughts of my existence; [since that doctrine lays one under an absolute necessity of thinking, either (1) that he passes away innumerable ages without a thought, or else (2) that he is annihilated every moment of his life:] both which seem equally absurd. [Time therefore being nothing, *abstracted from the succession of ideas in our minds*, it follows that the duration of any finite spirit must be estimated *by the number of ideas or actions* succeeding each other in that spirit or mind. Hence it is a plain consequence that the soul always thinks:[1] and in truth, whoever shall go about to divide in his thoughts, or abstract the *existence* of a spirit from its *cogitation*, will, I believe, find it no easy task.

XCIX. So likewise, when we attempt to abstract *extension* and *motion* from all other qualities, and consider them by themselves, we presently lose sight of them, and run into great extravagancies.[2] [All which depend on a twofold abstraction: first, it is supposed that extension, for example, may be abstracted from all other sensible qualities; and secondly, that the entity of extension may be abstracted from its being perceived.] But whoever shall reflect, and take care to understand what he says, will, if I mistake not, acknowledge that all sensible qualities are alike *sensations*, and alike *real;*

[1] Vide Locke's Essay on the Human Understanding, Book II., ch. i. sect. 10.

[2] "Hence spring those odd paradoxes *that the fire is not hot*, nor *the wall white*, &c., or that heat and colour are in the objects, nothing but figure and motion."—Edit. 1710.

that where the extension is, there is the colour too, to wit, in his mind, and that their archetypes can exist only in some other *mind*: and that the objects of sense are nothing but those sensations combined, blended, or (if one may so speak) concreted together: none of all which can be supposed to exist unperceived.

C. What it is for a man to be happy, or an object of good, of *happiness*, prescinded from all particular pleasure, or of *goodness*, from every thing that is good, this is what few can pretend to. [So likewise, a man may be just and virtuous, without having precise ideas of *justice* and *virtue*. The opinion that those and the like words stand for general notions *abstracted from all particular persons and actions*, seems to have rendered morality difficult, and the study thereof of less use to mankind.] And in effect,[1] the doctrine of *abstraction* has not a little contributed towards spoiling the most useful parts of knowledge.

CI. *Of natural philosophy and mathematics.*—The two great provinces of speculative science, conversant about ideas received from sense and their relations, are *natural philosophy* and *mathematics*; with regard to each of these I shall make some observations. And first, I shall say somewhat of natural philosophy. On this subject it is that the sceptics triumph: all that stock of arguments they produce to depreciate our faculties, and make mankind appear ignorant and low, are drawn principally from this head, to wit, that we are under an invincible blindness as to the *true* and *real* nature of things. This they exaggerate, and love to enlarge on. We are miserably bantered, say they, by our senses, and amused only with the outside and show of things. The real essence, the internal qualities, and constitution of every the meanest object, is hid from our view; something there is in every drop of water, every grain of sand, which it is beyond the power of human understanding to fathom

---

[1] "One may make a great progress in *school ethics*, without ever being the wiser or better man for it, or knowing how to behave himself, in the affairs of life, more to the advantage of himself, or his neighbours, than he did before. This hint may suffice to let any one see that."—Edit. 1710.

or comprehend. But it is evident from what has been shown, that all this complaint is groundless, and that we are influenced by false principles to that degree as to mistrust our senses, and think we know nothing of those things which we perfectly comprehend.

CII. [One great inducement to our pronouncing ourselves ignorant of the nature of things, is the current opinion *that every thing includes within itself the cause of its properties :* or that there is in each object an inward essence, which is the source whence its discernible qualities flow, and whereon they depend. Some [1] have pretended to account for appearances by *occult qualities*, but of late they are mostly resolved into *mechanical causes,* [2] to wit, the figure, *motion, weight,* and such like qualities of insensible particles : whereas in truth there is no other agent or efficient cause than *spirit*, it being evident that motion, as well as all other *ideas*, is perfectly inert. See Sect. xxv. Hence, to endeavour to explain the production of colours or sounds, by figure, motion, magnitude and the like, must needs be labour in vain. [3] And accordingly, we see the attempts of that kind are not at all satisfactory. Which may be said, in general, of those instances, wherein one *idea* or *quality* is assigned for the cause of another. [I need not say, how many hypotheses and speculations are left out, and how much the study of nature is abridged by this doctrine.]

CIII. *Attraction signifies the effect, not the manner or cause.*—The great mechanical principle now in vogue is *attraction*. That a stone falls to the earth, or the sea swells towards the moon, may to some appear sufficiently explained thereby. But how are we enlightened by being told this is done by attraction? Is it that that word signifies the manner of the tendency, and that it is by the mutual drawing of bodies, instead of their

---

[1] The Peripatetics.
[2] By the Cartesians. Vide Reid on the intellectual Powers, **Essay** II., ch. xviii, sect. 6, 7. Edit. 1843.
[3] Because they are inert.

being impelled or protruded towards each other? but nothing is determined of the manner or action, and it may as truly (for ought we know) be termed *impulse*, or *protrusion*, as *attraction*. Again, the parts of steel we see cohere firmly together, and this also is accounted for by attraction; but in this, as in the other instances, I do not perceive that any thing is signified besides the *effect* itself: for as to the *manner* of the action whereby it is produced, or the *cause* which produces it, these are not so much as aimed at.

CIV. Indeed, if we take a view of the several phenomena, and compare them together, we may observe some likeness and conformity between them. ☞ For example, in the falling of a stone to the ground, in the rising of the sea towards the moon, in cohesion and crystallization, there is something alike, namely a union or mutual approach of bodies. So that any one of these or the like phenomena, may not seem strange or surprising to a man who hath nicely observed and compared the effects of nature. For that only is thought so which is uncommon, or a thing by itself, and out of the ordinary course of our observation. That bodies should tend towards the centre of the earth, is not thought strange, because it is what we perceive every moment of our lives. But that they should have a like gravitation towards the centre of the moon, may seem odd and unaccountable to most men, because it is discerned only in the tides. But a philosopher, whose thoughts take in a larger compass of nature, having observed a certain similitude of appearances, as well in the heavens as the earth, that argue innumerable bodies to have a mutual tendency towards each other, which he denotes by the general name *attraction*, whatever can be reduced to that, he thinks justly accounted for. Thus he explains the tides by the attraction of the terraqueous globe towards the moon, which to him doth not appear odd or anomalous, but only a particular example of a general rule or law of nature.

CV. If therefore we consider the *difference* there is *betwixt natural philosophers and other men*, with regard to their knowledge of the phenomena, we shall find it consists, [not in an exacter knowledge of the *efficient cause* that produces them, for that can be no other than the *will of a spirit*, but only in *a greater largeness of comprehension, whereby analogies, harmonies, and agreements are discovered in the works of nature, and the particular effects explained,*] that is, reduced to general rules (see Sect. LXII.), which rules, grounded on the analogy and uniformness observed in the production of natural effects, are most agreeable, and sought after by the mind ; [for that they extend our prospect beyond what is present, and near to us, and enable us to make *very probable conjectures,* touching things that may have happened at very great distances of time and place, as well as to predict things to come ;] which sort of endeavour towards omniscience is much affected by the mind.

CVI. *Caution as to the use of analogies.*—[But we should proceed warily in such things :[1] for we are apt to lay too great a stress on analogies, and to the prejudice of truth, humour that eagerness of the mind, whereby it is carried to extend its knowledge into general theorems.] ☞ For example, gravitation, or mutual attraction, because it appears in many instances, some are straightway for pronouncing *universal ;* and that to *attract, and be attracted by every other body, is an essential quality inherent in all bodies whatsoever.* Whereas it appears the *fixed stars* have no such tendency towards each other : and so far is that gravitation from being *essential* to bodies, that in some instances a quite contrary principle seems to show itself ; as in the perpendicular *growth of plants,* and the *elasticity of the air.* There is nothing *necessary or essential in the case,* but it depends entirely on the will of the *governing spirit,* who causes certain bodies to cleave together, or tend towards each other, according to various laws, whilst he keeps

---

[1] Vide Reid on the Intellectual Powers, Essay I., ch. iv. sect 4 et seq. 8vo. edit. 1843.
" For besides that this could prove a very pleasing entertainment to the mind, it might be of great advantage, in that it not only discovers to us the (1) *attributes of the Creator,* but may also direct us in several instances to the (2) *proper uses and applications of things.*"

others at a fixed distance; and to some he gives a quite contrary tendency to fly asunder, just as he sees convenient.

CVII. After what has been premised, I think we may lay down *the following conclusions. First,* it is plain philosophers amuse themselves in vain, when they inquire for any natural efficient cause distinct from a *mind* or *spirit. Secondly,* considering the whole creation is the workmanship of a *wise and good agent,* it should seem to become philosophers to employ their thoughts (contrary to what some hold) about the *final causes of things :* [1] [(3) and I must confess, I see no reason why pointing out *the various ends* to which natural things are adapted, and for which they were originally with unspeakable wisdom contrived, should not be thought one good way of accounting for them,] and altogether worthy a philosopher. *Thirdly,* from what hath been premised no reason can be drawn, why the *history of nature should* not still *be studied,* and observations and experiments made, which, that they are of use to mankind, and enable us to draw any general conclusions, is not the result of any *immutable habitudes,* or relations between things themselves, but only of God's goodness and kindness to men in the administration of the world. See Sect. xxx., xxxi. *Fourthly,* by a diligent observation of the phenomena within our view, we may *discover the general laws of nature, and from them deduce the other phenomena,* I do not say *demonstrate ;* for all deductions of that kind depend on a supposition that the Author of nature always operates uniformly, and in a constant observance of those rules we take for principles : *which we cannot evidently know.*

CVIII. *Three analogies.*[2]—Those men who frame general rules from the phenomena, and afterwards derive the phenomena from those rules, seem to consider signs rather than causes. A man may well understand natural

---

[1] This advantage threefold : (1) it would help in discovering the attributes of the Creator ; (2) in directing us to the proper uses of things ; (3) in pointing out the ends to which natural things are adapted.

[2] (1) Speaking. (2) Writing. (3) Reading.

signs without knowing their *analogy* or being able to (1) *say* by what rule a thing is so or so.[1] [And as it is very possible (2) to *write* improperly *through too strict an observance of general grammar rules :* so in arguing from general rules of nature, it is not impossible we may extend the analogy too far, and by that means run into mistakes.]

CIX. [As in (3) *reading* other books, a wise man will choose to fix his thoughts on the *sense* and apply it to use, rather than lay them out in *grammatical remarks* on the language ; so in perusing the volume of nature, it seems beneath the dignity of the mind to affect an exactness in reducing *each particular phenomenon to general rules*, or showing how it follows from them.] We should propose to ourselves nobler views, such as (1) to recreate and exalt the mind, with a prospect of the beauty, *order*, extent, and variety of natural things : hence, by proper inferences, (2) to enlarge our notions of the grandeur, wisdom, and beneficence of the Creator : and lastly, (3) to make the several parts of the creation, so far as in us lies, subservient to the ends they were designed for, God's glory, and the sustentation and comfort of ourselves and fellow-creatures.

CX. The best key for the aforesaid analogy, or natural science, will be easily acknowledged to be a certain celebrated treatise of *mechanics :*[2] in the entrance of which justly admired treatise, time, space, and motion, are distinguished into *absolute* and *relative*, *true* and *apparent*,

---

[1] In the edition of 1710, sect. cviii. commences as follows : "It appears from sect. lxvi. (66) that the steady, consistent methods of nature may not unfitly be styled the language of its Author, by which he discovers his attributes to our view, and directs us how to act for the convenience and felicity of life. And to me, those men who frame general rules from the *phenomena*, and afterwards derive the *phenomena* from those rules, seem to be grammarians, and their art the grammar of nature. [Two ways there are of learning a language, either by *rule* or by *practice*.] A man may be well read in the language of nature, without understanding the grammar of it, or being able to say by what rule a thing is so or so."

[2] This section is much altered and abridged from the edition of 1710, in which the commencement is thus given : " The best grammar of the kind we are speaking of, will be easily acknowledged to be a treatise of Mechanics, demonstrated and applied to nature, by a philosopher of a

mathematical and *vulgar :* [which distinction, as it is at large explained by the author, doth suppose those quantities to have an existence without the mind : and that they are ordinarily conceived with relation to sensible things, to which nevertheless, in their own nature, they bear no relation at all.]

CXI. As for *time*, as it is there taken in an absolute or abstracted sense, for the duration or perseverance of the existence of things, I have nothing more to add concerning it, after what hath been already said on that subject, Sect. xcvii., xcviii. For the rest, this celebrated author holds there is an *absolute space*, which, being unperceivable to sense, remains in itself similar and immoveable : and relative space to be the measure thereof, which being moveable, and defined by its situation in respect of sensible bodies, is vulgarly taken for immoveable space. *Place* he defines to be that part of space which is occupied by any body. And according as the space is absolute or relative, so also is the place. *Absolute motion* is said to be the translation of a body from absolute place to absolute place, as relative motion is from one relative place to another. And because the parts of absolute space do not fall under our senses, instead of them we are obliged to use their sensible measures : and so define both place and motion with respect to bodies, which we regar⁴ as immoveable. But it is said, in philosophical matters we must *abstract* from our senses, since it may be, that none of those bodies which seem to be quiescent, are truly so : and the same thing which is moved relatively, may be really at rest. As likewise one and the same body may be in relative rest and motion, or even moved with contrary relative motions at the same time, according as its place is variously defined. All which ambiguity is to be found

neighbouring nation, whom all the world admire.[1] I shall not take upon me to make remarks on that extraordinary person ; only some things he has advanced, so directly opposite to the doctrine we have hitherto laid down, that we should be wanting in the regard due to the authority of so great a man, did we not take some notice of them."

---

[1] *Newton.*

in the apparent motions, but not at all in the true or absolute, which should therefore be alone regarded in philosophy. And the true, we are told, are distinguished from apparent or relative motions by the following properties. First, in true or absolute motion, all *parts* which preserve the same position with respect to the whole, partake of the motions of the whole. Secondly, the *place* being moved, that which is placed therein is also moved: so that a body moving in a place which is in motion, doth participate the motion of its place. Thirdly, *true motion* is never generated or changed, otherwise than by force impressed on the *body itself*. Fourthly, true motion is always changed by *force impressed* on the *body moved*. Fifthly, in circular motion *barely relative,* there is no centrifugal force, which nevertheless in that which is true or absolute, is proportional to the quantity of motion.

CXII. *Motion, whether real or apparent, relative.*— But notwithstanding what hath been said, it doth not appear to me, that there can be any motion other than *relative :* so that to conceive motion, there must be at least conceived two bodies, whereof the distance or position in regard to each other is varied. Hence if there was one only body in being, it could not possibly be moved. This seems evident, in that the idea I have of motion doth necessarily include relation.[1]

CXIII. *Apparent motion denied.*—But though in every motion it be necessary to conceive more bodies than one, yet it may be that one only is moved, namely that on which the force causing the change of distance is impressed, or in other words, that to which the action is applied. For however some may define relative motion, so as to term that body *moved*, which changes its distance from some other body, whether the force or action causing that change were applied to it, or no : yet as relative motion is that which is perceived by sense, and regarded in the ordinary affairs of life, it should seem that every

---

[1] " This to me seems very evident, in that the idea I have of motion does necessarily involve *relation* in it. Whether others can conceive it otherwise, a little attention may satisfy them."—Edit. 1710, 8vo.

man of common sense knows what it is, as well as the best philosopher: now I ask any one, whether in this sense of motion as he walks along the streets, the stones he passes over may be said to *move*, because they change distance with his feet? [To me it seems, that though motion includes a relation of one thing to another, yet *it is not necessary that each term of the relation be denominated from it.*] As a man may think of somewhat which doth not think, so a body may be moved to or from another body, which is not therefore itself in motion.[1]

CXIV. As the *place* happens to be variously defined, the motion which is related to it varies. ☞ A man in a ship may be said to be quiescent, with relation to the sides of the vessel, and yet move with relation to the land. Or he may move eastward in respect of the one, and westward in respect of the other. In the common affairs of life, men never go beyond the earth to define the place of any body: and what is quiescent in respect of that, is accounted *absolutely* to be so. But philosophers, who have a greater extent of thought, and juster notions of the system of things, discover even the earth itself to be moved. [In order therefore to fix their notions, they seem to conceive the corporeal world as finite, and the utmost unmoved walls or shell thereof to be the place whereby they estimate true motions.] If we sound our own conceptions, I believe we may find all the absolute motion we can frame an idea of, to be at bottom no other than relative motion thus defined. For as hath been already observed, absolute motion exclusive of all external relation is incomprehensible: and to this kind of relative motion, all the above-mentioned properties, causes, and effects ascribed to absolute motion, will, if I mistake not, be found to agree. As to what is said of the centrifugal force, that it doth not at all belong to circular relative motion: I do not see how this follows from the experiment which is brought to prove it. See *Philosophiæ Naturalis Principia Mathe-*

1 " I mean *relative* motion, for other I am not able to conceive."— Edit. 1710.

matica, in Schol. Def. VIII. For the water in the vessel, at that time wherein it is said to have the greatest relative circular motion, hath, I think, no motion at all; as is plain from the foregoing section.

CXV. [For to denominate a body *moved*, it is requisite, *first*, that it change its distance or situation with regard to some other body: and *secondly*, that the force or action occasioning that change be applied to it.] If either of these be wanting, I do not think that agreeable to the sense of mankind, or the propriety of language, a body can be said to be in motion. I grant indeed, that it is possible for us to think a body, which we see change its distance from some other, to be moved, though it have no force applied to it, (in which sense there may be apparent motion,) but then it is, because the force causing the change of distance is *imagined* by us to be applied or impressed on that body thought to move. Which indeed shows we are capable of mistaking a thing to be in motion which is not, and that is all;[1] but does not prove that, in the common acceptation of *motion*, a body is moved merely because it changes distance from another; since as soon as we are un-deceived, and find that the moving force was not com-municated to it, we no longer hold it to be moved. [So on the other hand, when one only body, the parts whereof preserve a given position between themselves, is imagined to exist; some there are who think that it can be moved all manner of ways, though without any change of distance or situation to any other bodies; which we should not deny, if they meant only that it might have an impressed force, which, *upon the bare creation of other bodies, would produce a motion of some certain quantity* and determination.] But that an actual motion (distinct from the impressed force, or power productive of change of place, in case there were bodies present whereby to define it) can exist in such a single body, I must confess I am not able to comprehend.

CXVI. *Any idea of pure space relative.*—From what hath been said, it follows that *the philosophic considera-*

---

[1] The remainder of the section is taken from the edition of 1710.

tion of motion doth not imply the being of an absolute space, distinct from that which is perceived by sense, and related to bodies : which that it cannot exist without the mind, is clear upon the same principles, that demonstrate the like of all other objects of sense. And perhaps, if we inquire narrowly, we shall find we cannot even frame an idea of *pure space exclusive of all body*. This, I must confess, seems impossible, as being a most abstract idea. When I excite a motion in some part of my body, if it be free or without resistance, I say there is *space :* but if I find a resistance, then I say there is *body :* and in proportion as the resistance to motion is lesser or greater, I say the *space* is more or less *pure*. So that when I speak of pure or empty space, it is not to be supposed, that the word *space* stands for an idea distinct from, or conceivable without body and motion. Though indeed *we are apt to think every noun substantive stands for a distinct idea*, that may be separated from all others : which hath occasioned infinite mistakes. [When therefore supposing, all the world to be annihilated besides my own body, I say there still remains *pure space :* thereby nothing else is meant, but only that I conceive it possible for the limbs of my body to be moved on all sides without the least resistance : but if that too were annihilated, then there could be no motion, and consequently no space.] Some perhaps may think the sense of seeing doth furnish them with the idea of pure space; but it is plain from what we have elsewhere shown, that the ideas of space and distance are not obtained by that sense. See the Essay concerning Vision.

CXVII. What is here laid down seems to put an end to all those disputes and difficulties which have sprung up amongst the learned concerning the nature of *pure space*. [But the chief advantage arising from it is, that we are freed from that dangerous *dilemma*, to which several who have employed their thoughts on this subject imagine themselves reduced, to wit, of thinking either that real space is God, or else that there is something beside God which is eternal, uncreated, infinite, indivisible, immutable.] Both which may justly be thought pernicious and absurd notions. It is certain that not a few divines, as well as philosophers of great note, have, from the difficulty they found in conceiving either limits or annihilation of space, concluded it must be *divine*. And some of late have set themselves particularly to show, that the incommunicable attributes of God agree to it. Which doctrine, how unworthy soever it may seem of the divine nature, yet I do not see how we can get clear of it, so long as we adhere to the received opinions.

CXVIII. *The errors arising from the doctrines of abstraction and external material existences, influence mathematical reasonings.* — Hitherto of *natural philosophy:* we come now to make some inquiry concerning that other great branch of speculative knowledge, to wit, *mathematics.* These, how celebrated soever they may be for their clearness and certainty of demonstration, which is hardly any where else to be found, cannot nevertheless be supposed altogether free from mistakes, if in their principles there lurks some secret error, which is common to the professors of those sciences with the rest of mankind. Mathematicians, though they deduce their theorems from a great height of evidence, yet their first principles are limited by the consideration of quantity ; and they do not ascend into any inquiry concerning those transcendental maxims, which influence all the particular sciences, each part whereof, mathematics not excepted, doth consequently participate of the errors involved in them. That the principles laid down by mathematicians are true, and their way of deduction from those principles clear and incontestable, we do not deny. But we hold, there may be certain erroneous maxims of greater extent than the object of mathematics, and for that reason not expressly mentioned, though tacitly supposed throughout the whole progress of that science ; and that the ill effects of those secret, unexamined errors are diffused through all the branches thereof. [To be plain, we suspect the mathematicians are, as well as other men, concerned in the errors (1) arising from the doctrine of abstract general ideas, and (2) the existence of objects without the mind.]

CXIX. *Arithmetic* hath been thought to have for its object *abstract* ideas of *number*. Of which to understand the properties and mutual habitudes is supposed no mean part of speculative knowledge. The opinion of the pure and intellectual nature of numbers in abstract, hath made them in esteem with those philosophers, who seem to have affected an uncommon fineness and elevation of thought. It hath set a price on the most trifling numerical speculations, which in practice are of no use, but serve only for amusement : and hath therefore so far infected the minds of some, that they have dreamt of mighty *mysteries* involved in numbers, and attempted the explication of natural things by them. But if we inquire into our own thoughts, and consider what hath been premised, we may perhaps entertain a low opinion of those high flights and abstractions, and look on all inquiries about numbers, only as so many *difficiles nugæ*, so far as they are not subservient to practice, and promote the benefit of life.

CXX. [*Unity in abstract* we have before considered in Sect. XIII., from which and what has been said in the Introduction, it plainly follows *there is not any such idea*. But number being defined a *collection of units*, we may conclude that, if there be no such thing as unity or unit in abstract, there are no ideas of number *in abstract* denoted by the numeral names and figures.] The theories therefore in arithmetic, if they are abstracted from the names and figures, as likewise from all use and practice, as well as from the particular things numbered, can be supposed to have nothing at all for their object. Hence we may see, how entirely the science of numbers is subordinate to practice, and how jejune and trifling it becomes, when considered as a matter of mere speculation.

CXXI. However since there may be some, who, deluded by the specious show of discovering abstracted verities, waste their time in arithmetical theorems and problems, which have not any use : it will not be amiss, if we more fully consider, and expose the vanity of that pretence ; and this will plainly appear, by taking a view of arithmetic in its infancy, and observing what it was that originally put men on the study of that science, and to what scope they directed it. It is natural to think that at first men, for ease of memory and help of computation, made use of counters, or in writing of single strokes, points, or the like, each whereof was made to signify a unit, that is, some one thing of whatever kind they had occasion to reckon. Afterwards they found out the more compendious ways, of making one character stand in place of several strokes, or points. And lastly, the notation of the Arabians or Indians came into use, wherein, by the repetition of a few characters or figures, and varying the signification of each figure according to the place it obtains, all numbers may be most aptly expressed : which seems to have been done in imitation of language, so that an exact analogy is observed betwixt the notation by figures and names, the nine simple figures answering the nine first numeral names and places in the former, corresponding to denominations in the latter. And agreeably to those conditions of the simple and local value of figures, were contrived methods of finding from the given figures or marks of the parts, what figures, and how placed, are proper to denote the whole, or *vice versâ*. And having found the sought figures, the same rule or analogy being observed throughout, it is easy to read them into words ; and so the number becomes perfectly known. For then the number of any particular things is said to be known, when we know the names or figures (with their due arrangement) that according to the standing analogy belong to them. For these signs being known, we can, by the operations of arithmetic, know the signs of any part of the particular sums signified by them ; and thus computing in signs (because of the connexion established betwixt them and the distinct multitudes of things, whereof one is taken for a unit), we may be able rightly to sum up, divide, and proportion the things themselves that we intend to number.

CXXII. [In *arithmetic* therefore we regard not the *things* but the *signs*, which nevertheless are not regarded for their own sake, but because they *direct us how to act* with relation to things, and dispose rightly of them.] [Now agreeably to what we have before observed of words in general (Sect. XIX. Introd.), it happens here likewise, that abstract ideas are thought to be signified by numeral names or characters, while they do not suggest *ideas of particular things* to our minds.] I shall not at present enter into a more particular dissertation on this subject; but only observe that it is evident from what hath been said, those things which pass for abstract truths and theorems concerning numbers are, in reality, conversant about no object distinct from particular numerable things, except only names and characters; which originally came to be considered on no other account but their being *signs*, or capable to represent aptly whatever particular things men had need to compute. Whence it follows, that to study them for their own sake would be just as wise, and to as good purpose, as if a man, neglecting the true use or original intention and subserviency of language, should spend his time in impertinent criticisms upon words, or reasonings and controversies purely verbal.

CXXIII. From numbers we proceed to speak of *extension*, which considered as relative, is the object of *geometry*. The *infinite* divisibility of *finite* extension, though it is not expressly laid down, either as an axiom or theorem in the elements of that science, yet is throughout the same every where supposed, and thought to have so inseparable and essential a connexion with the principles and demonstrations in geometry, that mathematicians never admit it into doubt, or make the least question of it. And as this notion is the source from whence do spring all those amusing geometrical paradoxes, which have such a direct repugnancy to the plain common sense of mankind, and are admitted with so much reluctance into a mind not yet debauched by learning; so is it the principal occasion of all that nice and extreme subtilty, which renders the study of *mathematics* so difficult and tedious. [Hence, if we can make it appear that no finite extension contains innumerable parts, or is infinitely divisible, it follows that we shall at once clear the science of geometry from a great number of difficulties and contradictions, which have ever been esteemed a reproach to human reason, and withal make the attainment thereof a business of much less time and pains than it hitherto hath been.]

CXXIV. [Every particular *finite extension*, which may possibly be the object of our thought, is an *idea* existing only in the mind, and consequently *each part thereof* must be perceived. If therefore I cannot perceive innumerable parts in any finite extension that I consider, it is certain that they are not contained in it]: but it is evident, that I cannot distinguish innumerable parts in any particular line, surface, or solid, which I either perceive by sense, or figure to myself in my mind: wherefore I conclude they are not contained in it. Nothing can be plainer to me, than that the extensions I have in view are no other than my own ideas, and it is no less plain, that I cannot resolve any one of my ideas into an infinite number of other ideas, that is, that they are not infinitely divisible. If by *finite extension* be meant something distinct from a finite idea, I declare I do not know what that is, and so cannot affirm or deny any thing of it. But if the terms *extension, parts*, and the like, are taken in any sense conceivable, that is, for ideas; then to say a finite quantity or extension consists of parts infinite in number, is so manifest a contradiction, that every one at first sight acknowledges it to be so. And it is impossible it should ever gain the assent of any reasonable creature, who is not brought to it by gentle and slow degrees, as a converted gentile to the belief of *transubstantiation*. Ancient and rooted prejudices do often pass into principles: and those propositions which once obtain the force and credit of a *principle*, are not only themselves, but likewise whatever is deducible from them, thought privileged from all examination. And there is no absurdity so gross, which by this means the mind of man may not be prepared to swallow.

CXXV. [(1) He whose understanding is prepossessed with the *doctrine of abstract general ideas*, may be persuaded, that (whatever be thought of the ideas of sense) extension in *abstract* is infinitely divisible. (2) And one who thinks the objects of sense exist *without the mind*, will perhaps in virtue thereof be brought to admit, that a line but an inch long may contain innumerable parts really existing, though too small to be discerned.] These errors are grafted as well in the minds of *geometricians*, as of other men, and have a like influence on their reasonings; and it were no difficult thing, to show how the arguments from geometry, made use of to support the infinite divisibility of extension, are bottomed on them. [At present we shall only observe in general, whence it is that the mathematicians are all so fond and tenacious of this doctrine.

CXXVI. It hath been observed in another place, that the theorems and demonstrations in geometry are conversant about *universal* ideas. Sect. xv. Introd.] Where it is explained in what sense this *ought* to be understood, to wit, that the particular lines and figures included in the diagram, are supposed to stand for innumerable others of different sizes : or in other words, the geometer considers them abstracting from their magnitude : which doth not imply that he forms an abstract idea, but only that he cares not what the particular magnitude is, whether great or small, but looks on that as a thing indifferent to the demonstration : [hence it follows, that a line in the scheme, but an inch long, must be spoken of as though it contained ten thousand parts, since it is regarded not in itself, but as it is universal; and it is universal only in its signification, whereby it represents innumerable lines greater than itself, in which may be distinguished ten thousand parts or more, though there may not be above an inch in it. After this manner *the properties of the lines signified are* (*by a very usual figure*) *transferred to the sign,* and thence through mistake thought to appertain to it considered in its own nature.]

CXXVII. Because there is no number of parts so great, but it is possible there may be a line containing more, the inch-line is said to contain parts more than any assignable number; which is true, not of the inch taken absolutely, but only for the things signified by it. But men not retaining that distinction in their thoughts, slide into a belief that the small particular line described on paper contains in itself parts innumerable. There is no such thing as the ten-thousandth part of an *inch;* but there is of a *mile* or *diameter of the earth*, which may be signified by that inch. When therefore I delineate a triangle on paper, and take one side not above an inch, for example, in length, to be the *radius;* this I consider as divided into ten thousand or a hundred thousand parts, or more. For though the ten-thousandth part of that line, considered in itself, is nothing at all, and consequently may be neglected without any error or inconveniency; yet these described lines being only marks standing for greater quantities, whereof it may be the ten-thousanth part is very considerable, it follows, that to prevent notable errors in practice, the *radius* must be taken of ten thousand parts, or more.

CXXVIII. *Lines which are infinitely divisible.*—From what hath been said the reason is plain why, to the end any theorem may become universal in its use, it is necessary we speak of the lines described on paper, as though they contained parts which really they do not. In doing of which, if we examine the matter throughly, we shall perhaps discover that we cannot conceive an inch itself as consisting of, or being divisible into a thousand parts, [but only some other line which is far greater than an inch, and represented by it.] And that when we say a line is *infinitely divisible*, we must mean a line which is *infinitely great.* What we have here observed seems to be the chief cause, why to suppose the infinite divisibility of finite extension hath been thought necessary in geometry.

CXXIX. The several *absurdities* and contradictions which flowed *from this false principle* might, one would think, have been esteemed so many demonstrations against it. [But by I know not what *logic*, it is held that proofs *à posteriori* are not to be admitted against propositions relating to infinity. As though it were not impossible even for an infinite mind to reconcile contradictions. Or as if any thing absurd and repugnant could have a necessary connexion with truth, or flow from it.] But whoever considers the weakness of this pretence, will think it was contrived on purpose to humour the laziness of the mind, which had rather acquiesce in an indolent scepticism, than be at the pains to go through with a severe examination of those principles it hath ever embraced for true.

CXXX. Of late the *speculations about infinites* have run so high, and grown to such strange notions, as have occasioned no small scruples and disputes among the geometers of the present age. Some there are of great note, who, not content with holding that finite lines may be divided into an infinite number of parts, do yet further maintain, that each of those infinitesimals is itself subdivisible into an infinity of other parts, or infinitesimals of a second order, and so on *ad infinitum*. These, I say, assert there are infinitesimals of infinitesimals of infinitesimals, without ever coming to an end. So that according to them an inch doth not barely contain an infinite number of parts, but an infinity of an infinity of an infinity *ad infinitum* of parts. Others there be who hold all orders of infinitesimals below the first to be nothing at all, thinking it with good reason absurd, to imagine there is any positive quantity or part of extension, which though multiplied infinitely, can ever equal the smallest given extension. And yet on the other hand it seems no less absurd, to think the square, cube, or other power of a positive real root, should itself be nothing at all; which they who hold infinitesimals of the first order, denying all of the subsequent orders, are obliged to maintain.

CXXXI. *Objection of mathematicians. — Answer.—* Have we not therefore reason to conclude, that they are *both* in the wrong, and that there is in effect no such thing as parts infinitely small, or an infinite number of parts contained in any finite quantity? But you will say, that if this doctrine obtains, it will follow (1) that the very *foundations of geometry are destroyed:* and those great men who have raised that science to so astonishing a height, have been all the while building a castle in the air. [To this it may be *replied,* that whatever is useful in geometry and promotes the benefit of human life, doth still remain firm and unshaken on our principles.] That science, considered as *practical,* will rather receive advantage than any prejudice from what hath been said. But to set this in a due light, may be the subject of a distinct inquiry. For the rest, though it should follow that some of the more intricate and subtle parts of *speculative mathematics* may be pared off without any prejudice to truth; yet I do not see what damage will be thence derived to mankind. On the contrary, it were highly to be wished, that men of great abilities and obstinate application would draw off their thoughts from those amusements, and employ them in the study of such things as lie nearer the concerns of life, or have a more direct influence on the manners.

CXXXII. *Second objection of mathematicians.—Answer.*—If it be said that several theorems undoubtedly true, are discovered by methods in which *infinitesimals* are made use of, which could never have been, if their existence included a contradiction in it. [I *answer,* that upon a thorough examination it will not be found, that in any instance it is necessary to make use of or conceive infinitesimal parts of finite lines, or even quantities less than the *minimum sensibile:* nay, it will be evident this is never done, it being impossible.][1]

CXXXIII. *If the doctrine were only an hypothesis it should be respected for its consequences.*—By what we have

---

[1] The following passage is added in the edition of 1710:—" And whatever mathematicians may think of *fluxions* or the *differential calculus* and the like, a little reflection will show them, that in working by those methods, they do not conceive or imagine lines or surfaces less than what are perceivable to sense. They may, indeed, call those little and almost insensible quantities *infinitesimals* or *infinitesimals of infinitesimals,* if they please: but at bottom this is all, they being in truth finite, nor does the solution of problems require the supposing any other. But this will be more clearly made out hereafter."

premised, it is plain that very numerous and *important errors have taken their rise from those false principles*, which were impugned in the foregoing parts of this treatise. And the opposites of those erroneous tenets at the same time appear to be most fruitful principles, from whence do flow innumerable consequences highly advantageous to true philosophy as well as to religion. Particularly, *matter or the absolute existence of corporeal objects*, hath been shown to be that wherein the most avowed and pernicious enemies of all knowledge, whether human or divine, have ever placed their chief strength and confidence. And surely, if by distinguishing the real existence of unthinking things from their being perceived, and allowing them a substance of their own out of the minds of spirits, (1) *no one thing is explained in nature*; but on the contrary a great many inexplicable difficulties arise: if (2) *the supposition of matter is barely precarious*, as not being grounded on so much as one single reason: if (3) *its consequences cannot endure* the *light of examination* and free inquiry, but screen themselves under the dark and general pretence of *infinites being incomprehensible*: if withal (4) the removal of this *matter* be not attended with the least evil consequence, if it be not even missed in the world, but every thing as well, nay much easier conceived without it: if lastly, (5) both *sceptics* and *atheists* are for ever silenced upon supposing only spirits and ideas, and this scheme of things is perfectly agreeable both to *reason* and *religion*: methinks we may expect it should be admitted and firmly embraced, though it were proposed only as an *hypothesis*, and the existence of matter had been allowed possible, which yet I think we have evidently demonstrated that it is not.

CXXXIV. True it is, that in consequence of the foregoing principles, several disputes and speculations, which are esteemed no mean parts of learning, are rejected as useless. But how great a prejudice soever against our notions, this may give to those who have already been deeply engaged, and made large advances in studies of that nature: yet by others, we hope it will not be thought any just ground of dislike to the principles and tenets herein laid down, that they abridge the labour of study, and make human sciences more clear, compendious, and attainable, than they were before.

CXXXV. HAVING despatched what we intended to say concerning the knowledge of *ideas*, the method we proposed leads us, in the next place, to treat of *spirits :* [1] with regard to which, perhaps human knowledge is not so deficient as is vulgarly imagined. [The great reason that is assigned for our being thought ignorant of the nature of spirits, is, our not having an idea of it.] But surely it ought not to be looked on as a defect in a human understanding, that it does not perceive the idea of *spirit*, if it is *manifestly impossible there should be any such idea*. And this, if I mistake not, has been demonstrated in Sect. XXVII.; to which I shall here add [that a spirit has been shown to be the only substance or support, wherein the unthinking beings or ideas can exist : but that this *substance* which supports or perceives ideas should itself be an *idea*, or like an *idea*, is evidently absurd.]

CXXXVI. *Objection.—Answer.*—[It will perhaps be said, that we want a sense [2] (as some have imagined) proper to know substances withal, which if we had, we might know our own soul, as we do a triangle.   To this I *answer*, that in case we had a new sense bestowed upon us, we could only receive thereby *some new sensations or ideas of sense*.   But I believe nobody will say, that what he means by the terms *soul* and *substance*, is only some particular sort of idea or sensation.]   We may therefore infer, that all things duly considered, it is not more reasonable to think our faculties defective, in that they do not furnish us with an idea of spirit or *active thinking* substance, than it would be if we should blame them for not being able to comprehend a *round square*.

CXXXVII. From the opinion (1) that *spirits are to be known after the manner of an idea* [3] or sensation, have risen many absurd and heterodox tenets, and much

[1] Vide sect. xxvii.   [2] Vide sect. lxxviii.
[3] Vide sect. cxxxix.

scepticism about the nature of the soul. [It is even probable, that this opinion may have produced a doubt in some, whether they had any soul at all distinct from their body, since upon inquiry they could not find *they had an idea of it.*] That an *idea*, which is inactive, and the existence whereof consists in being perceived, should be the image or likeness of an agent subsisting by itself, seems no need to other refutation, than barely attending to what is meant by those words. [But perhaps you will say, that though an *idea* cannot resemble a *spirit*, in its thinking, acting, or subsisting by itself, yet it may in some other respects: and it is not necessary that an idea or image be in all respects like the original.]

CXXXVIII. [*I answer*, if it does not in those mentioned, it is impossible it should represent it in any other thing. Do but leave out the power of willing, thinking, and perceiving ideas, and there remains nothing else wherein the idea can be like a spirit.] For by the word *spirit* we mean only that which thinks, wills, and perceives; this, and this alone, constitutes the signification of that term. If, therefore, it is impossible that any degree of those powers should be represented in an idea, it is evident there can be no idea of a spirit.

CXXXIX. [But it will be objected, (2)[1] that if there is no *idea* signified by the terms *soul, spirit,* and *substance*, they are wholly insignificant, or have no meaning in them. I answer, those words do mean or signify a real thing, which is neither an idea nor like an idea, but that which perceives ideas, and wills, and reasons about them.] What I am myself, that which I denote by the term I, is the same with what is meant by *soul* or *spiritual substance.* If it be said that this is only quarrelling at a word, and that since the immediate significations of other names are, by common consent, called *ideas*, no reason can be assigned, why that which is signified by the name *spirit* or *soul*, may not partake in the same appellation. [I answer, all the unthinking objects of the mind agree, in that they are *entirely passive*, and their existence consists only in being perceived: whereas a soul or

[1] Vide sect. cxxxvii.

spirit is an active being, whose existence consists not in being perceived, but *in perceiving ideas* and thinking. It is therefore necessary, *in order to prevent equivocation*, and confounding natures perfectly disagreeing and unlike, that we distinguish between *spirit* and *idea*. See Sect. XXVII.]

CXL. *Our idea of spirit.*—[In a large sense indeed, we may be said to have an idea, or rather a notion of *spirit*, that is, (1) we understand the meaning of the word, otherwise we could not affirm or deny any thing of it. Moreover, (2) as we conceive the ideas that are in the minds of other spirits by means of our own, which we suppose to be *resemblances* of them : so we know other spirits by means of our own soul, which in that sense is the image or idea of them, it having a like respect to other spirits, that blueness or heat by me perceived hath to those ideas perceived by another.] [1]

CXLI. *The natural immortality of the soul is a necessary consequence of the foregoing doctrine.* [2]—[It must not be supposed, that they who assert the natural immortality of the soul are of opinion that it is *absolutely incapable of annihilation*, even by the infinite power of the Creator who first gave it being : but only that it is not liable to be broken or dissolved by the *ordinary laws of nature or motion.*] They, indeed, who hold the soul of man to be only a thin vital flame, or system of animal spirits, make it perishing and corruptible as the body, since there is nothing more easily dissipated than such a being, which it is naturally impossible should survive the ruin of the tabernacle wherein it is enclosed. And this notion hath been greedily embraced and cherished by the worst part of mankind, as the most effectual antidote against all impressions of virtue and religion. But it hath been made evident, that bodies, of what frame or texture soever, are barely passive ideas in the mind, which is more distant and heterogeneous from

---

[1] Vide Reid on the Intellectual Powers.   Essay ii. ch. x. sect. 13. —Edit. 1843.

[2] " But before we attempt to prove that, it is fit that we explain the meaning of that tenet."—Original edition.

them, than light is from darkness. [We have shown that the soul is indivisible, incorporeal, unextended, and it is consequently *incorruptible*. Nothing can be plainer, than that the motions, changes, decays, and dissolutions, which we hourly see befall natural bodies (and which is what we mean by the *course of nature*), cannot possibly affect an *active, simple, uncompounded* substance : such a being therefore is indissoluble by the force of nature, that is to say, *the soul of man is* naturally *immortal*.]

CXLII. After what hath been said, it is I suppose plain, that *our souls* are *not to be known in the same manner as senseless*, inactive *objects*, or by way of *idea*. *Spirits* and *ideas* are things so wholly different, that when we say *they exist, they are known*, or the like, these words must not be thought to signify any thing common to both natures. There is nothing alike or common in them : and to expect that by any multiplication or enlargement of our faculties, we may be enabled to know a spirit as we do a triangle, seems as absurd as if we should hope to *see a sound*. This is inculcated because I imagine it may be of moment towards clearing several important questions, and preventing some very dangerous errors concerning the nature of the soul. We may not, I think, strictly be said to have an idea of an active being, or of an action, although we may be said to have a notion of them. I have some knowledge or notion of my mind, and its acts about ideas, inasmuch as I know or understand what is meant by those words. What I know, that I have some notion of. I will not say that the terms *idea* and *notion* may not be used convertibly, if the world will have it so. But yet it conduceth to clearness and propriety, that we distinguish things very different by different names. It is also to be remarked, that, all relations including an act of the mind, we cannot so properly be said to have an idea, but rather a notion of the relations or habitudes between things. But if, in the modern way, the word *idea* is extended to spirits, and relations, and acts ; this is, after all, an affair of verbal concern.

CXLIII. It will not be amiss to add, that the doctrine

of *abstract ideas* hath had no small share in *rendering those sciences intricate* and obscure, *which are* particularly *conversant about spiritual things*. [Men have imagined they could frame abstract notions of the *powers and acts of the mind*, and consider them prescinded, as well from the mind or spirit itself, as from their respective objects and effects.] Hence a great number of dark and ambiguous terms, presumed to stand for abstract notions, have been introduced into metaphysics and morality, and from these have grown infinite distractions and disputes amongst the learned.

CXLIV.[1] [But nothing seems more to have contributed towards engaging men in controversies and mistakes, with regard to the nature and operations of the mind, *than the being used to speak of those things in terms borrowed from sensible ideas*.] ☞ For example, the will is termed the *motion* of the soul : this infuses a belief, that the mind of man is as a ball in motion, impelled and determined by the objects of sense, as necessarily as that is by the stroke of a racket. Hence arise endless scruples and errors of dangerous consequence in morality. All which, I doubt not, may be cleared, and truth appear plain, uniform, and consistent, could but philosophers be prevailed on to retire into themselves, and attentively consider their own meaning.

CXLV. *Knowledge of spirits not immediate.*—[From what hath been said, it is plain that *we* cannot *know the existence of other spirits* otherwise than *by their operations*, or *the ideas by them excited in us*. I perceive several motions, changes, and combinations of ideas, that inform me there are certain particular agents *like myself*, which accompany them, and concur in their production.] [Hence the knowledge I have of other spirits is *not immediate*, as is the knowledge of my ideas; but depending on the intervention of ideas, by me referred to

---

[1] We are said to have an idea of spirit because (1) an opinion of spirit may be had in the manner of an idea.—Sect. cxl. (2) It has been thought practicable to have an abstract idea of the powers and acts of the mind.—Sect. cxliii. (3) These powers are spoken of in terms borrowed from sensible objects.—Sect. cxliv.

agents or spirits distinct from myself, as effects or con-comitant signs.]

CXLVI. But though there be some things which convince us human agents are concerned in producing them; yet it is evident to every one, that those things which are called the works of nature, that is, the far greater part of the ideas or sensations perceived by us, are not produced by, or dependent on, the wills of men. There is therefore some other spirit that causes them, since it is repugnant that they should subsist by themselves. See Sect. XXIX. But if we attentively consider the constant regularity, order, and concatenation of natural things, the surprising magnificence, beauty, and perfection of the larger, and the exquisite contrivance of the smaller parts of the creation, together with the exact harmony and correspondence of the whole, but, above all, the never enough admired laws of pain and pleasure, and the instincts or natural inclinations, appetites, and passions of animals; I say if we consider all these things, and at the same time attend to the meaning and import of the attributes, one, eternal, infinitely wise, good, and perfect, we shall clearly perceive that they belong to the aforesaid spirit, *who works all in all, and by whom all things consist.*

CXLVII. *The existence of God more evident than that of man.*—Hence it is evident, that God is known as certainly and immediately as any other mind or spirit whatsoever, distinct from ourselves. [We may even assert, that the existence of God is far more evidently perceived than the existence of men; because the effects of nature are infinitely *more numerous and considerable* than those ascribed to human agents.] There is not any one mark that denotes a man, or effect produced by him, which doth not more strongly evince the being of that Spirit who is the *Author of nature*. [For it is evident that in affecting other persons, the will of man hath no other object than barely the *motion of the limbs of his body;* but that such a motion should be attended by, or excite *any idea in the mind of another*, depends wholly on the will of the Creator.] He alone it is who, "upholding all things by the word of his power," maintains that intercourse between spirits, whereby they are able to perceive the existence of each other. And yet this pure and clear light, which enlightens every one, is itself invisible (to the greatest part of mankind).[1]

CXLVIII. It seems to be a *general pretence of the unthinking* herd, that *they cannot see God*. Could we but see him, say they, as we see a man, we should believe that he is, and believing obey his commands. But, alas, we need only open our eyes to see the sovereign Lord of all things with a more full and clear view, than we do any one of our fellow-creatures. Not that I imagine we see God (as some will have it) by a direct and immediate view, or see corporeal things, not by themselves, but by seeing that which represents them in the essence of God, which doctrine is, I must confess, to me incomprehensible. But I shall explain my meaning. A human spirit or person is not perceived by sense, as not being an idea; when therefore we see the colour, size, figure, and motions of a man, we perceive only certain sensations or ideas excited in our own minds: and these being exhibited to our view in sundry distinct collections, serve to mark out unto us the existence of finite and created spirits like ourselves. [Hence it is plain, we do not see a man, if by *man* is meant that which lives, moves, perceives, and thinks as we do: but only such a certain collection of ideas, as directs us to think there is a distinct principle of thought and motion like to ourselves, accompanying and represented by it.] And after the same manner we see God; all the difference is, that whereas some one finite and narrow assemblage of ideas denotes a particular human mind, whithersoever we direct our view, we do at all times and in all places perceive manifest tokens of the divinity: every thing we see, hear, feel, or anywise perceive by sense, being a sign or effect of the power of God; as is our perception of those very motions which are produced by men.

CXLIX. It is therefore plain, that *nothing can be more*

[1] Orig. Edit.

evident to any one that is capable of the least reflection, *than the existence of God*, or a Spirit who is intimately present to our minds, producing in them all that variety of ideas or sensations, which continually affect us, on whom we have an absolute and entire dependence, in short, *in whom we live, and move, and have our being.* That the discovery of this great truth, which lies so near and obvious to the mind, should be attained to by the reason of so very few, is a sad instance of the stupidity and inattention of men, who, though they are surrounded with such clear manifestations of the Deity, are yet so little affected by them, that they seem as it were blinded with excess of light.

CL. *Objection on behalf of nature.—Answer.*—[But you will say, hath nature no share in the production of natural things, and must they be all ascribed to the immediate and sole operation of God? I answer, if by *nature* is meant only the visible *series* of effects, or sensations imprinted on our minds according to certain fixed and general laws: then it is plain, that nature taken in this sense cannot produce any thing at all. But if by *nature* is meant some being distinct from God, as well as from the laws of nature, and things perceived by sense, I must confess that word is to me an empty sound, without any intelligible meaning annexed to it.] Nature in this acceptation is a vain *chimera*, introduced by those heathens, who had not just notions of the omnipresence and infinite perfection of God. But it is more unaccountable, that it should be received among Christians professing belief in the holy scriptures, which constantly ascribe those effects to the *immediate hand of God*, that heathen philosophers are wont to impute to *nature.* " The Lord, he causeth the vapours to ascend ; he maketh lightnings with rain ; he bringeth forth the wind out of his treasures," Jer. x. 13. " He turneth the shadow of death into the morning, and maketh the day dark with night," Amos v. 8. " He visiteth the earth, and maketh it soft with showers : he blesseth the springing thereof, and crowneth the year with his goodness, so that the pastures are clothed with flocks, and the valleys are covered over with corn." See Psalm lxv. But notwithstanding that this is the constant language of scripture ; yet we have I know not what aversion from believing, that God concerns himself so nearly in our affairs. Fain would we suppose him at a great distance off, and substitute some blind unthinking deputy in his stead, though (if we may believe St. Paul) he be " not far from every one of us."

CLI. *Objection to the hand of God being the immediate cause, threefold.—Answer.*—[It will I doubt not be objected, (1) that the slow and gradual methods observed in the production of natural things, do not seem to have for their cause the *immediate* hand of an *almighty agent*. (2) Besides, monsters, untimely births, fruits blasted in the blossom, rains falling in desert places, (3) miseries incident to human life, are so many arguments that the whole frame of nature is not immediately actuated and superintended by a spirit of infinite wisdom and goodness.] But the answer to this objection is in a good measure plain from Sect. LXII., it being visible, that the aforesaid methods of nature are absolutely necessary, in order to working by the most simple and general rules, and after *a steady and consistent manner ;* which argues both the *wisdom* and *goodness* of God.[1] [Such is the artificial contrivance of this mighty machine of nature, that whilst its motions and various phenomena strike on our senses, the hand which actuates the whole is itself unperceivable to men of flesh and blood. " Verily," saith the prophet, " thou art a God that hidest thyself," Isaiah xlv. 15. But though God conceal himself from the eyes of the sensual and lazy, who will not be at the least expense of thought ; yet to an unbiassed and attentive mind, nothing can be more plainly legible, than the intimate presence of an all-wise Spirit, who fashions, regulates, and sustains the whole system of being.

---

[1] " (*First*) For it doth hence follow, that the finger of God is not so conspicuous to the resolved and careless sinner, which gives him an opportunity to harden in his impiety, and grow ripe for vengeance. Vide sect. lvii."—Edit. 1710.

(*Secondly*,) [1] it is clear from what we have elsewhere observed, that the operating according to general and stated laws, is so necessary *for our guidance in the affairs of life*,] and letting us into the secret of nature, that without it, all reach and compass of thought, all human sagacity and design could serve to no manner of purpose : it were even impossible there should be any such faculties or powers in the mind. See Sect. XXXI. Which one consideration abundantly outbalances whatever particular inconveniences may thence arise.

CLII. [We should *further consider*, (1) that the very blemishes and defects of nature are not without their use, in that they make an agreeable sort of variety, and augment the beauty of the rest of the creation, as shades in a picture serve to set off the brighter and more enlightened parts.] (2) [We would likewise do well to examine, whether our taxing the waste of seeds and embryos, and accidental destruction of plants and animals, before they come to full maturity, as an *imprudence* in the author of nature, be not the effect of *prejudice* contracted by our familiarity with impotent and saving mortals.] In *man* indeed a thrifty management of those things, which *he cannot procure without much pains* and industry, may be esteemed *wisdom*. But we must not imagine, that the inexplicably fine machine of an animal or vegetable costs the great Creator any more pains or trouble in its production than a pebble doth : nothing being more evident, than that an omnipotent spirit can indifferently produce every thing by a mere *fiat* or act of his will. [Hence it is plain, that the splendid profusion of natural things should not be interpreted weakness or prodigality in the agent who produces them, but rather he looked on as an argument of the riches of his power.]

CLIII. As for the *mixture of pain*, or uneasiness which is *in the world*, pursuant to the general laws of nature, and the actions of finite imperfect spirits : this, in the state we are in at present, is indispensably necessary to our well-being. But our prospects are *too narrow* :

[1] The first argument is contained in the preceding note.

we take, for instance, the idea of *some one particular pain* into our thoughts, and account it *evil;* whereas if we enlarge our view, so as to comprehend the various ends, connexions, and dependencies of things, on what occasions and in what proportions we are affected with pain and pleasure, the nature of human freedom, and the design with which we are put into the world; [we shall be forced to acknowledge that those particular things, which considered in themselves appear to be *evil*, have the nature of *good*, when considered as *linked with the whole system of beings.*]

CLIV. *Atheism and Manicheism would have few supporters if mankind were in general attentive.*—From what hath been said it will be manifest to any considering person, that it is merely for want of attention and comprehensiveness of mind, that there are any favourers of *atheism* or the *Manichean heresy* to be found. Little and unreflecting souls may indeed burlesque the works of Providence, the beauty and order whereof they have not capacity, or will not be at the pains, to comprehend. But those who are masters of any justness and extent of thought, and are withal used to reflect, can never sufficiently admire the divine traces of wisdom and goodness that shine throughout the economy of nature. But what truth is there which shineth so strongly on the mind, that by an aversion of thought, a wilful shutting of the eyes, we may not escape seeing it? Is it therefore to be wondered at, if the generality of men, who are ever intent on business or pleasure, and little used to fix or open the eye of their mind, should not have all that conviction and evidence of the being of God, which might be expected in reasonable creatures?

CLV. We should rather *wonder, that men can be found so stupid as to neglect*, than that neglecting they should be unconvinced of such an evident and momentous truth. And yet it is to be feared that too many of parts and leisure, who live in Christian countries, are merely through a supine and dreadful negligence sunk into a sort of *atheism*. Since it is downright impossible, that a soul pierced and enlightened with a thorough sense of the omnipresence, holiness, and justice of that Almighty Spirit, should persist in a remorseless violation of his laws. We ought therefore earnestly to meditate and dwell on those important points; that so we may attain conviction without all scruple, that "the eyes of the Lord are in every place beholding the evil and the good;" that he is with us and keepeth us in all places whither we go, and giveth us bread to eat, and raiment to put on; that he is present and conscious to our innermost thoughts; and that we have a most absolute and immediate dependence on him. A clear view of which great truths cannot choose but fill our heart with an awful circumspection and holy fear, which is the strongest incentive to *virtue,* and the best guard against *vice.*

CLVI. For after all, what deserves the first place in our studies, is the consideration of God, and our *duty;* which to promote, as it was the main drift and design of my labours, so shall I esteem them altogether useless and ineffectual if by what I have said I cannot inspire my readers with a pious sense of the presence of God: and having shown the falseness or vanity of those barren speculations, which make the chief employment of learned men, the better dispose them to reverence and embrace the salutary truths of the gospel, which to know and to practise is the highest perfection of human nature.

THREE DIALOGUES
BETWEEN HYLAS AND PHILONOUS,
IN OPPOSITION TO SCEPTICS
AND ATHEISTS

THREE DIALOGUES

THE FIRST DIALOGUE

Philonous. GOOD morrow, Hylas: I did not expect to find you abroad so early.

Hylas. It is indeed something unusual: but my thoughts were so taken up with a subject I was discoursing of last night, that finding I could not sleep, I resolved to rise and take a turn in the garden.

Phil. It happened well, to let you see what innocent and agreeable pleasures you lose every morning. Can there be a pleasanter time of the day, or a more delightful season of the year? That purple sky, those wild but sweet notes of birds, the fragrant bloom upon the trees and flowers, the gentle influence of the rising sun, these and a thousand nameless beauties of nature inspire the soul with secret transports; its faculties too being at this time fresh and lively, are fit for these meditations, which the solitude of a garden and tranquillity of the morning naturally dispose us to. But I am afraid I interrupt your thoughts; for you seemed very intent on something.

Hyl. It is true, I was, and shall be obliged to you if you will permit me to go on in the same vein; not that I would by any means deprive myself of your company, for my thoughts always flow more easily in conversation with a friend, than when I am alone: but my request is, that you would suffer me to impart my reflections to you.

Phil. With all my heart, it is what I should have requested myself, if you had not prevented me.

Hyl. I was considering the odd fate of those men who

have in all ages, through an affectation of being distinguished from the vulgar, or some unaccountable
turn of thought, pretended either to believe nothing at
all, or to believe the most extravagant things in the
world. This however might be borne, if their paradoxes
and scepticism did not draw after them some consequences of general disadvantage to mankind. But the
mischief lieth here; that when men of less leisure see
them who are supposed to have spent their whole time
in the pursuits of knowledge, professing an entire ignorance of all things, or advancing such notions as are
repugnant to plain and commonly received principles,
they will be tempted to entertain suspicions concerning
the most important truths, which they had hitherto held
sacred and unquestionable.

Phil. I entirely agree with you, as to the ill tendency of
the affected doubts of some philosophers, and fantastical
conceits of others. I am even so far gone of late in
this way of thinking, that I have quitted several of the
sublime notions I had got in their schools for vulgar
opinions. And I give it you on my word, since this
revolt from metaphysical notions to the plain dictates
of nature and common sense, I find my understanding
strangely enlightened, so that I can now easily comprehend a great many things which before were all
mystery and riddle.

Hyl. I am glad to find there was nothing in the
accounts I heard of you.

Phil. Pray, what were those?

Hyl. You were represented in last night's conversation, as one who maintained the most extravagant opinion
that ever entered into the mind of man, to wit, that there
is no such thing as *material substance* in the world.

Phil. That there is no such thing as what philosophers
call *material substance*, I am seriously persuaded: but
if I were made to see any thing absurd or sceptical in
this, I should then have the same reason to renounce
this, that I imagine I have now to reject the contrary
opinion.

Hyl. What! can any thing be more fantastical, more

repugnant to common sense, or a more manifest piece of scepticism, than to believe there is no such thing as *matter*?

Phil. Softly, good Hylas. What if it should prove, that you who hold there is, are by virtue of that opinion a greater sceptic, and maintain more paradoxes and repugnancies to common sense, than I who believe no such thing?

Hyl. You may as soon persuade me, the part is greater than the whole, as that, in order to avoid absurdity and scepticism, I should ever be obliged to give up my opinion in this point.

Phil. Well then, are you content to admit that opinion for true, which upon examination shall appear most agreeable to common sense, and remote from scepticism?

Hyl. With all my heart. Since you are for raising disputes about the plainest things in nature, I am content for once to hear what you have to say.

Phil. Pray, Hylas, what do you mean by a *sceptic*?

Hyl. I mean what all men mean, one that doubts of every thing.

Phil. He then who entertains no doubt concerning some particular point, with regard to that point cannot be thought a *sceptic.*

Hyl. I agree with you.

Phil. Whether doth doubting consist in embracing the affirmative or negative side of a question?

Hyl. In neither; for whoever understands English, cannot but know that *doubting* signifies a suspense between both.

Phil. He then that denieth any point, can no more be said to doubt of it than he who affirmeth it with the same degree of assurance.

Hyl. True.

Phil. And consequently, for such his denial is no more to be esteemed a *sceptic* than the other.

Hyl. I acknowledge it.

Phil. How cometh it to pass then, Hylas, that you pronounce me a *sceptic*, because I deny what you affirm, to wit, the existence of matter? Since, for ought you can tell, I am as peremptory in my denial, as you in your affirmation.

Hyl. Hold, Philonous, I have been a little out in my definition ; but every false step a man makes in discourse is not to be insisted on. I said, indeed, that a *sceptic* was one who doubted of every thing ; but I should have added, or who denies the reality and truth of things.

Phil. What things? Do you mean the principles and theorems of sciences? but these you know are universal intellectual notions, and consequently independent of matter ; the denial therefore of this doth not imply the denying them.

Hyl. I grant it. But are there no other things? What think you of distrusting the senses, of denying the real existence of sensible things, or pretending to know nothing of them? Is not this sufficient to denominate a man a *sceptic?*

Phil. Shall we therefore examine which of us it is that denies the reality of sensible things, or professes the greatest ignorance of them ; since, if I take you rightly, he is to be esteemed the greatest *sceptic?*

Hyl. That is what I desire.

Phil. What mean you by sensible things?

Hyl. Those things which are perceived by the senses. Can you imagine that I mean any thing else?

Phil. Pardon me, Hylas, if I am desirous clearly to apprehend your notions, since this may much shorten our inquiry. Suffer me then to ask you this further question. Are those things only perceived by the senses which are perceived immediately? or may those things properly be said to be *sensible*, which are perceived mediately, or not without the intervention of others?

Hyl. I do not sufficiently understand you.

Phil. In reading a book, what I immediately perceive are the letters, but mediately, or by means of these, are suggested to my mind the notions of God, virtue, truth, &c. Now that the letters are truly sensible things, or perceived by sense, there is no doubt : but I would know whether you take the things suggested by them to be so too.

Hyl. No, certainly, it were absurd to think *God* or *virtue* sensible things, though they may be signified and suggested to the mind by sensible marks, with which they have an arbitrary connexion.

Phil. It seems then, that by *sensible things* you mean those only which can be perceived immediately by sense.

Hyl. Right.

Phil. Doth it not follow from this, that though I see one part of the sky red, and another blue, and that my reason doth thence evidently conclude there must be some cause of that diversity of colours, yet that cause cannot be said to be a sensible thing, or perceived by the sense of seeing?

Hyl. It doth.

Phil. In like manner, though I hear variety of sounds, yet I cannot be said to hear the causes of those sounds.

Hyl. You cannot.

Phil. And when by my touch I perceive a thing to be hot and heavy, I cannot say with any truth or propriety, that I feel the cause of its heat or weight.

Hyl. To prevent any more questions of this kind, I tell you once for all, that by *sensible things* I mean those only which are perceived by sense, and that in truth the senses perceive nothing which they do not perceive immediately: for they make no inferences. The deducing therefore of causes or occasions from effects and appearances, which alone are perceived by sense, entirely relates to reason.

Phil. This point then is agreed between us, that *sensible things are those only which are immediately perceived by sense.* You will further inform me, whether we immediately perceive by sight any thing beside light, and colours, and figures: or by hearing any thing but sounds: by the palate, any thing besides tastes: by the smell, besides odours: or by the touch, more than tangible qualities.

Hyl. We do not.

Phil. It seems therefore, that if you take away all sensible qualities, there remains nothing sensible.

Hyl. I grant it.

Phil. Sensible things therefore are nothing else but so many sensible qualities, or combinations of sensible qualities.

Hyl. Nothing else.

Phil. Heat then is a sensible thing.

Hyl. Certainly.

Phil. Doth the reality of sensible things consist in being perceived? or, is it something distinct from their being perceived, and that bears no relation to the mind?

Hyl. To *exist* is one thing, and to be *perceived* is another.

Phil. I speak with regard to sensible things only; and of these I ask, whether by their real existence you mean a subsistence exterior to the mind, and distinct from their being perceived?

Hyl. I mean a real absolute being, distinct from, and without any relation to their being perceived.

Phil. Heat, therefore, if it be allowed a real being, must exist without the mind.

Hyl. It must.

Phil. Tell me, Hylas, is this real existence equally compatible to all degrees of heat, which we perceive: or is there any reason why we should attribute it to some, and deny it others? and if there be, pray let me know that reason.

Hyl. Whatever degree of heat we perceive by sense, we may be sure the same exists in the object that occasions it.

Phil. What, the greatest as well as the least?

Hyl. I tell you, the reason is plainly the same in respect of both: they are both perceived by sense; nay, the greater degree of heat is more sensibly perceived; and consequently, if there is any difference, we are more certain of its real existence than we can be of the reality of a lesser degree.

Phil. But is not the most vehement and intense degree of heat a very great pain?

Hyl. No one can deny it.

Phil. And is any unperceiving thing capable of pain or pleasure?

Hyl. No certainly.

Phil. Is your material substance a senseless being, or a being endowed with sense and perception?

Hyl. It is senseless without doubt.

Phil. It cannot therefore be the subject of pain.

Hyl. By no means.

Phil. Nor consequently of the greatest heat perceived by sense, since you acknowledge this to be no small pain.

Hyl. I grant it.

Phil. What shall we say then of your external object; is it a material substance, or no?

Hyl. It is a material substance with the sensible qualities inhering in it.

Phil. How then can a great heat exist in it, since you own it cannot in a material substance? I desire you would clear this point.

Hyl. Hold, Philonous; I fear I was out in yielding intense heat to be a pain. It should seem rather, that pain is something distinct from heat, and the consequence or effect of it.

Phil. Upon putting your hand near the fire, do you perceive one simple uniform sensation, or two distinct sensations?

Hyl. But one simple sensation.

Phil. Is not the heat immediately perceived?

Hy₁. It is.

Phil. And the pain?

Hyl. True.

Phil. Seeing therefore they are both immediately perceived at the same time, and the fire affects you only with one simple, or uncompounded idea, it follows that this same simple idea is both the intense heat immediately perceived, and the pain; and consequently, that the intense heat immediately perceived, is nothing distinct from a particular sort of pain.

Hyl. It seems so.

Phil. Again, try in your thoughts, Hylas, if you can conceive a vehement sensation to be without pain, or pleasure.

H 4⁸3

Hyl. I cannot.

Phil. Or can you frame to yourself an idea of sensible pain or pleasure in general, abstracted from every particular idea of heat, cold, tastes, smells, &c.?

Hyl. I do not find that I can.

Phil. Doth it not therefore follow, that sensible pain is nothing distinct from those sensations or ideas, in an intense degree?

Hyl. It is undeniable; and to speak the truth, I begin to suspect a very great heat cannot exist but in a mind perceiving it.

Phil. What! are you then in that *sceptical* state of suspense, between affirming and denying?

Hyl. I think I may be positive in the point. A very violent and painful heat cannot exist without the mind.

Phil. It hath not therefore, according to you, any real being.

Hyl. I own it.

Phil. Is it therefore certain, that there is no body in nature really hot?

Hyl. I have not denied there is any real heat in bodies. I only say, there is no such thing as an intense real heat.

Phil. But did you not say before, that all degrees of heat were equally real: or if there was any difference, that the greater were more undoubtedly real than the lesser?

Hyl. True: but it was, because I did not then consider the ground there is for distinguishing between them, which I now plainly see. And it is this: because intense heat is nothing else but a particular kind of painful sensation; and pain cannot exist but in a perceiving being; it follows that no intense heat can really exist in an unperceiving corporeal substance. But this is no reason why we should deny heat in an inferior degree to exist in such a substance.

Phil. But how shall we be able to discern those degrees of heat which exist only in the mind, from those which exist without it?

Hyl. That is no difficult matter. You know, the

least pain cannot exist unperceived; whatever therefore
degree of heat is a pain, exists only in the mind. But
as for all other degrees of heat, nothing obliges us to
think the same of them.

Phil. I think you granted before, that no unperceiving being was capable of pleasure, any more than
of pain.

Hyl. I did.

Phil. And is not warmth, or a more gentle degree of
heat than what causes uneasiness, a pleasure?

Hyl. What then?

Phil. Consequently it cannot exist without the mind
in any unperceiving substance, or body.

Hyl. So it seems.

Phil. Since therefore, as well those degrees of heat
that are not painful, as those that are, can exist only
in a thinking substance; may we not conclude that
external bodies are absolutely incapable of any degree
of heat whatsoever?

Hyl. On second thoughts, I do not think it so evident
that warmth is a pleasure, as that a great degree of heat
is a pain.

Phil. I do not pretend that warmth is as great a
pleasure as heat is a pain. But if you grant it to be
even a small pleasure, it serves to make good my
conclusion.

Hyl. I could rather call it an *indolence*. It seems to
be nothing more than a privation of both pain and
pleasure. And that such a quality or state as this
may agree to an unthinking substance, I hope you
will not deny.

Phil. If you are resolved to maintain that warmth, or
a gentle degree of heat, is no pleasure, I know not how
to convince you otherwise, than by appealing to your
own sense. But what think you of cold?

Hyl. The same that I do of heat. An intense degree
of cold is a pain; for to feel a very great cold, is to
perceive a great uneasiness: it cannot therefore exist
without the mind; but a lesser degree of cold may, as
well as a lesser degree of heat.

Phil. Those bodies therefore, upon whose application to our own we perceive a moderate degree of heat, must be concluded to have a moderate degree of heat or warmth in them; and those, upon whose application we feel a like degree of cold, must be thought to have cold in them.

Hyl. They must.

Phil. Can any doctrine be true that necessarily leads a man into an absurdity?

Hyl. Without doubt it cannot.

Phil. Is it not an absurdity to think that the same thing should be at the same time both cold and warm?

Hyl. It is.

Phil. Suppose now one of your hands hot, and the other cold, and that they are both at once put into the same vessel of water, in an intermediate state; will not the water seem cold to one hand, and warm to the other?

Hyl. It will.

Phil. Ought we not therefore by your principles to conclude, it is really both cold and warm at the same time, that is, according to your own concession, to believe an absurdity?

Hyl. I confess it seems so.

Phil. Consequently, the principles themselves are false, since you have granted that no true principle leads to an absurdity.

Hyl. But after all, can any thing be more absurd than to say, *there is no heat in the fire?*

Phil. To make the point still clearer; tell me, whether in two cases exactly alike, we ought not to make the same judgment?

Hyl. We ought.

Phil. When a pin pricks your finger, doth it not rend and divide the fibres of your flesh?

Hyl. It doth.

Phil. And when a coal burns your finger, doth it any more?

Hyl. It doth not.

Phil. Since therefore you neither judge the sensation

itself occasioned by the pin, nor any thing like it to be in the pin; you should not, conformably to what you have now granted, judge the sensation occasioned by the fire, or any thing like it, to be in the fire.

Hyl. Well, since it must be so, I am content to yield this point, and acknowledge, that heat and cold are only sensations existing in our minds : but there still remain qualities enough to secure the reality of external things.

Phil. But what will you say, Hylas, if it shall appear that the case is the same with regard to all other sensible qualities, and that they can no more be supposed to exist without the mind, than heat and cold?

Hyl. Then indeed you will have done something to the purpose; but that is what I despair of seeing proved.

Phil. Let us examine them in order. What think you of tastes, do they exist without the mind, or no?

Hyl. Can any man in his senses doubt whether sugar is sweet, or wormwood bitter?

Phil. Inform me, Hylas. Is a sweet taste a particular kind of pleasure or pleasant sensation, or is it not?

Hyl. It is.

Phil. And is not bitterness some kind of uneasiness or pain?

Hyl. I grant it.

Phil. If therefore sugar and wormwood are unthinking corporeal substances existing without the mind, how can sweetness and bitterness, that is, pleasure and pain, agree to them?

Hyl. Hold, Philonous; I now see what it was deluded me all this time. You asked whether heat and cold, sweetness and bitterness, were not particular sorts of pleasure and pain; to which I answered simply, that they were. Whereas I should have thus distinguished : those qualities, as perceived by us, are pleasures or pains, but not as existing in the external objects. We must not therefore conclude absolutely, that there is no heat in the fire, or sweetness in the sugar, but only that heat or sweetness, as perceived by us, are not in the fire or sugar. What say you to this?

Phil. I say it is nothing to the purpose. Our discourse

proceeded altogether concerning sensible things, which you defined to be the things we *immediately perceive by our senses*. Whatever other qualities therefore you speak of, as distinct from these, I know nothing of them, neither do they at all belong to the point in dispute. You may indeed pretend to have discovered certain qualities which you do not perceive, and assert those insensible qualities exist in fire and sugar. But what use can be made of this to your present purpose, I am at a loss to conceive. Tell me then once more, do you acknowledge that heat and cold, sweetness and bitterness (meaning those qualities which are perceived by the senses), do not exist without the mind?

Hyl. I see it is to no purpose to hold out, so I give up the cause as to those mentioned qualities. Though I profess it sounds oddly, to say that sugar is not sweet.

Phil. But for your further satisfaction, take this along with you: that which at other times seems sweet, shall to a distempered palate appear bitter. And nothing can be plainer, than that divers persons perceive different tastes in the same food, since that which one man delights in, another abhors. And how could this be, if the taste was something really inherent in the food?

Hyl. I acknowledge I know not how.

Phil. In the next place, odours are to be considered. And with regard to these, I would fain know, whether what hath been said of tastes doth not exactly agree to them? Are they not so many pleasing or displeasing sensations?

Hyl. They are.

Phil. Can you then conceive it possible that they should exist in an unperceiving thing?

Hyl. I cannot.

Phil. Or can you imagine, that filth and ordure affect those brute animals that feed on them out of choice with the same smells which we perceive in them?

Hyl. By no means.

Phil. May we not therefore conclude of smells, as of the other forementioned qualities, that they cannot exist in any but a perceiving substance or mind?

Hyl. I think so.

Phil. Then as to sounds, what must we think of them: are they accidents really inherent in external bodies, or not?

Hyl. That they inhere not in the sonorous bodies, is plain from hence; because a bell struck in the exhausted receiver of an air-pump, sends forth no sound. The air therefore must be thought the subject of sound.

Phil. What reason is there for that, Hylas?

Hyl. Because when any motion is raised in the air, we perceive a sound greater or lesser, in proportion to the air's motion; but without some motion in the air, we never hear any sound at all.

Phil. And granting that we never hear a sound but when some motion is produced in the air, yet I do not see how you can infer from thence, that the sound itself is in the air.

Hyl. It is this very motion in the external air, that produces in the mind the sensation of *sound*. For striking on the drum of the ear, it causeth a vibration, which by the auditory nerves being communicated to the brain, the soul is thereupon affected with the sensation called *sound*.

Phil. What! is sound then a sensation?

Hyl. I tell you, as perceived by us, it is a particular sensation in the mind.

Phil. And can any sensation exist without the mind?

Hyl. No, certainly.

Phil. How then can sound, being a sensation, exist in the air, if by the *air* you mean a senseless substance existing without the mind.

Hyl. You must distinguish, Philonous, between sound, as it is perceived by us, and as it is in itself; or, (which is the same thing) between the sound we immediately perceive, and that which exists without us. The former indeed is a particular kind of sensation, but the latter is merely a vibrative or undulatory motion in the air.

Phil. I thought I had already obviated that distinction by the answer I gave when you were applying it in a like case before. But to say no more of that;

are you sure then that sound is really nothing but motion?

Hyl. I am.

Phil. Whatever therefore agrees to real sound, may with truth be attributed to motion.

Hyl. It may.

Phil. It is then good sense to speak of *motion*, as of a thing that is *loud*, *sweet*, *acute*, or *grave*.

Hyl. I see you are resolved not to understand me. Is it not evident, those accidents or modes belong only to sensible sound, or *sound* in the common acceptation of the word, but not to *sound* in the real and philosophic sense, which, as I just now told you, is nothing but a certain motion of the air?

Phil. It seems then there are two sorts of sound, the one vulgar, or that which is heard, the other philosophical and real.

Hyl. Even so.

Phil. And the latter consists in motion.

Hyl. I told you so before.

Phil. Tell me, Hylas, to which of the senses, think you, the idea of motion belongs: to the hearing?

Hyl. No, certainly, but to the sight and touch.

Phil. It should follow then, that according to you, real sounds may possibly be *seen* or *felt*, but never *heard*.

Hyl. Look you, Philonous, you may if you please make a jest of my opinion, but that will not alter the truth of things. I own, indeed, the inferences you draw me into sound something oddly: but common language, you know, is framed by, and for the use of the vulgar: we must not therefore wonder, if expressions adapted to exact philosophic notions, seem uncouth and out of the way.

Phil. Is it come to that? I assure you, I imagine myself to have gained no small point, since you make so light of departing from common phrases and opinions; it being a main part of our inquiry, to examine whose notions are widest of the common road, and most repugnant to the general sense of the world. But can you think it no more than a philosophical paradox, to

say that *real sounds are never heard*, and that the idea of
them is obtained by some other sense. And is there nothing in this contrary to nature and the truth of things?

Hyl. To deal ingenuously, I do not like it. And after
the concessions already made, I had as well grant that
sounds too have no real being without the mind.

Phil. And I hope you will make no difficulty to
acknowledge the same of colours.

Hyl. Pardon me; the case of colours is very different.
Can any thing be plainer, than that we see them on the
objects?

Phil. The objects you speak of are, I suppose, corporeal substances existing without the mind.

Hyl. They are.

Phil. And have true and real colours inhering in
them?

Hyl. Each visible object hath that colour which we
see in it.

Phil. How! is there any thing visible but what we
perceive by sight.

Hyl. There is not.

Phil. And do we perceive any thing by sense, which
we do not perceive immediately?

Hyl. How often must I be obliged to repeat the same
thing? I tell you, we do not.

Phil. Have patience, good Hylas; and tell me once
more whether there is any thing immediately perceived
by the senses, except sensible qualities. I know you
asserted there was not: but I would now be informed,
whether you still persist in the same opinion.

Hyl. I do.

Phil. Pray, is your corporeal substance either a
sensible quality or made up of sensible qualities?

Hyl. What a question that is! who ever thought it
was?

Phil. My reason for asking was, because in saying,
each visible object hath that colour which we see in it, you
make visible objects to be corporeal substances; which
implies either that corporeal substances are sensible
qualities, or else that there is something beside sensible

qualities perceived by sight: but as this point was formerly agreed between us, and is still maintained by you, it is a clear consequence, that your corporeal substance is nothing distinct from sensible qualities.

Hyl. You may draw as many absurd consequences as you please, and endeavour to perplex the plainest things; but you shall never persuade me out of my senses. I clearly understand my own meaning.

Phil. I wish you would make me understand it too. But since you are unwilling to have your notion of corporeal substance examined, I shall urge that point no further. Only be pleased to let me know, whether the same colours which we see, exist in external bodies, or some other.

Hyl. The very same.

Phil. What! are then the beautiful red and purple we see on yonder clouds, really in them? Or do you imagine they have in themselves any other form than that of a dark mist or vapour?

Hyl. I must own, Philonous, those colours are not really in the clouds as they seem to be at this distance. They are only apparent colours.

Phil. Apparent call you them? how shall we distinguish these apparent colours from real?

Hyl. Very easily. Those are to be thought apparent, which, appearing only at a distance, vanish upon a nearer approach.

Phil. And those I suppose are to be thought real, which are discovered by the most near and exact survey.

Hyl. Right.

Phil. Is the nearest and exactest survey made by the help of a microscope, or by the naked eye?

Hyl. By a microscope, doubtless.

Phil. But a microscope often discovers colours in an object different from those perceived by the unassisted sight. And in case we had microscopes magnifying to any assigned degree; it is certain, that no object whatsoever viewed through them, would appear in the same colour which it exhibits to the naked eye.

Hyl. And what will you conclude from all this?

You cannot argue that there are really and naturally no colours on objects; because by artificial managements they may be altered, or made to vanish.

Phil. I think it may evidently be concluded from your own concessions, that all the colours we see with our naked eyes, are only apparent as those on the clouds, since they vanish upon a more close and accurate inspection, which is afforded us by a microscope. Then as to what you say by way of prevention; I ask you, whether the real and natural state of an object is better discovered by a very sharp and piercing sight, or by one which is less sharp.

Hyl. By the former without doubt.

Phil. Is it not plain from *dioptrics*, that microscopes make the sight more penetrating, and represent objects as they would appear to the eye, in case it were naturally endowed with a most exquisite sharpness?

Hyl. It is.

Phil. Consequently the microscopical representation is to be thought that which best sets forth the real nature of the thing, or what it is in itself. The colours therefore by it perceived, are more genuine and real, than those perceived otherwise.

Hyl. I confess there is something in what you say.

Phil. Besides, it is not only possible but manifest, that there actually are animals, whose eyes are by nature framed to perceive those things, which by reason of their minuteness escape our sight. What think you of those inconceivably small animals perceived by glasses? must we suppose they are all stark blind? Or, in case they see, can it be imagined their sight hath not the same use in preserving their bodies from injuries, which appears in that of all other animals? And if it hath, is it not evident, they must see particles less than their own bodies, which will present them with a far different view in each object, from that which strikes our senses? Even our own eyes do not always represent objects to us after the same manner. In the *jaundice*, every one knows that all things seem yellow. Is it not therefore highly probable, those animals in whose eyes we discern a very different texture from that of ours, and whose bodies abound with different humours, do not see the same colours in every object that we do? From all of which, should it not seem to follow that all colours are equally apparent, and that none of those which we perceive are really inherent in any outward object?

Hyl. It should.

Phil. The point will be past all doubt, if you consider, that in case colours were real properties or affections inherent in external bodies, they could admit of no alteration, without some change wrought in the very bodies themselves; but is it not evident from what hath been said, that upon the use of microscopes, upon a change happening in the humours of the eye, or a variation of distance, without any manner of real alteration in the thing itself, the colours of any object are either changed, or totally disappear? Nay, all other circumstances remaining the same, change but the situation of some objects, and they shall present different colours to the eye. The same thing happens upon viewing an object in various degrees of light. And what is more known, than that the same bodies appear differently coloured by candle-light from what they do in the open day? Add to these the experiment of a prism, which, separating the heterogeneous rays of light, alters the colour of any object; and will cause the whitest to appear of a deep blue or red to the naked eye. And now tell me, whether you are still of opinion, that every body hath its true, real colour inhering in it; and if you think it hath, I would fain know further from you, what certain distance and position of the object, what peculiar texture and formation of the eye, what degree or kind of light is necessary for ascertaining that true colour, and distinguishing it from apparent ones.

Hyl. I own myself entirely satisfied, that they are all equally apparent; and that there is no such thing as colour really inhering in external bodies, but that it is altogether in the light. And what confirms me in this opinion, is, that in proportion to the light, colours are still more or less vivid; and if there be no light, then are there no colours perceived. Besides, allowing there are colours on external objects, yet how is it possible for us to perceive them? For no external body affects the mind, unless it act first on our organs of sense. But the only action of bodies is motion; and motion cannot be communicated otherwise than by impulse. A distant object therefore cannot act on the eye, nor consequently make itself or its properties perceivable to the soul. Whence it plainly follows, that it is immediately some contiguous substance, which operating on the eye occasions a perception of colours: and such is light.

Phil. How! is light then a substance?

Hyl. I tell you, Philonous, external light is nothing but a thin fluid substance, whose minute particles being agitated with a brisk motion, and in various manners reflected from the different surfaces of outward objects to the eyes, communicate different motions to the optic nerves; which being propagated to the brain, cause therein various impressions: and these are attended with the sensations of red, blue, yellow, &c.

Phil. It seems, then, the light doth no more than shake the optic nerves.

Hyl. Nothing else.

Phil. And consequent to each particular motion of the nerves the mind is affected with a sensation, which is some particular colour.

Hyl. Right.

Phil. And these sensations have no existence without the mind.

Hyl. They have not.

Phil. How then do you affirm that colours are in the light, since by *light* you understand a corporeal substance external to the mind?

Hyl. Light and colours, as immediately perceived by us, I grant cannot exist without the mind. But in themselves they are only the motions and configurations of certain insensible particles of matter.

Phil. Colours then, in the vulgar sense, or taken for

the immediate objects of sight, cannot agree to any but a perceiving substance.

Hyl. That is what I say.

Phil. Well then, since you give up the point as to those sensible qualities, which are alone thought colours by all mankind beside, you may hold what you please with regard to those invisible ones of the philosophers. It is not my business to dispute about them; only I would advise you to bethink yourself, whether, considering the inquiry we are upon, it be prudent for you to affirm *the red and blue which we see are not real colours, but certain unknown motions and figures which no man ever did or can see, are truly so.* Are not these shocking notions, and are not they subject to as many ridiculous inferences, as those you were obliged to renounce before in the case of sounds?

Hyl. I frankly own, Philonous, that it is in vain to stand out any longer. Colours, sounds, tastes, in a word, all those termed *secondary qualities,* have certainly no existence without the mind. But by this acknowledgment I must not be supposed to derogate any thing from the reality of matter or external objects, seeing it is no more than several philosophers maintain, who nevertheless are the furthest imaginable from denying matter. For the clearer understanding of this, you must know sensible qualities are by philosophers divided into *primary* and *secondary.* The former are extension, figure, solidity, gravity, motion, and rest. And these they hold exist really in bodies. The latter are those above enumerated; or briefly, all sensible qualities beside the primary, which they assert are only so many sensations or ideas existing no where but in the mind. But all this, I doubt not, you are already apprised of. For my part, I have been a long time sensible there was such an opinion current among philosophers, but was never thoroughly convinced of its truth till now.

Phil. You are still then of opinion, that extension and figures are inherent in external unthinking substances.

Hyl. I am.

Phil. But what if the same arguments which are

brought against secondary qualities, will hold proof against these also?

Hyl. Why then I shall be obliged to think, they too exist only in the mind.

Phil. Is it your opinion, the very figure and extension which you perceive by sense, exist in the outward object or material substance?

Hyl. It is.

Phil. Have all other animals as good grounds to think the same of the figure and extension which they see and feel?

Hyl. Without doubt, if they have any thought at all.

Phil. Answer me, Hylas. Think you the senses were bestowed upon all animals for their preservation and well-being in life? or were they given to men alone for this end?

Hyl. I make no question but they have the same use in all other animals.

Phil. If so, is it not necessary they should be enabled by them to perceive their own limbs, and those bodies which are capable of harming them?

Hyl. Certainly.

Phil. A mite therefore must be supposed to see his own foot, and things equal or even less than it, as bodies of some considerable dimension; though at the same time they appear to you scarce discernible, or at best as so many visible points.

Hyl. I cannot deny it.

Phil. And to creatures less than the mite they will seem yet larger.

Hyl. They will.

Phil. Insomuch that what you can hardly discern, will to another extremely minute animal appear as some huge mountain.

Hyl. All this I grant.

Phil. Can one and the same thing be at the same time in itself of different dimensions?

Hyl. That were absurd to imagine.

Phil. But from what you have laid down it follows, that both the extension by you perceived, and that per-

ceived by the mite itself, as likewise all those perceived
by lesser animals, are each of them the true extension of
the mite's foot, that is to say, by your own principles you
are led into an absurdity.

Hyl. There seems to be some difficulty in the point.

Phil. Again, have you not acknowledged that no real
inherent property of any object can be changed, without
some change in the thing itself ?

Hyl. I have.

Phil. But as we approach to or recede from an object,
the visible extension varies, being at one distance ten or
a hundred times greater than at another.   Doth it not
therefore follow from hence likewise, that it is not really
inherent in the object ?

Hyl. I own I am at a loss what to think.

Phil. Your judgment will soon be determined, if you
will venture to think as freely concerning this quality, as
you have done concerning the rest.   Was it not admitted
as a good argument, that neither heat nor cold was in
the water, because it seemed warm to one hand, and
cold to the other ?

Hyl. It was.

Phil. Is it not the very same reasoning to conclude,
there is no extension or figure in an object, because to
one eye it shall seem little, smooth, and round, when at
the same time it appears to the other, great, uneven, and
angular ?

Hyl. The very same.   But doth this latter fact ever
happen ?

Phil. You may at any time make the experiment, by
looking with one eye bare, and with the other through a
microscope.

Hyl. I know not how to maintain it, and yet I am
loath to give up *extension*, I see so many odd consequences following upon such a concession.

Phil. Odd, say you ?   After the concessions already
made, I hope you will stick at nothing for its oddness.
But on the other hand should it not seem very odd, if
the general reasoning which includes all other sensible
qualities did not also include extension ?   If it be

allowed that no idea nor any thing like an idea can exist in an unperceiving substance, then surely it follows, that no figure or mode of extension, which we can either perceive or imagine, or have any idea of, can be really inherent in matter ; not to mention the peculiar difficulty there must be, in conceiving a material substance, prior to and distinct from extension, to be the *substratum* of extension. Be the sensible quality what it will, figure, or sound, or colour ; it seems alike impossible it should subsist in that which doth not perceive it.

Hyl. I give up the point for the present, reserving still a right to retract my opinion, in case I shall hereafter discover any false step in my progress to it.

Phil. That is a right you cannot be denied. Figures and extension being despatched, we proceed next to *motion.* Can a real motion in any external body be at the same time both very swift and very slow?

Hyl. It cannot.

Phil. Is not the motion of a body swift in a reciprocal proportion to the time it takes up in describing any given space? Thus a body that describes a mile in an hour, moves three times faster than it would in case it described only a mile in three hours.

Hyl. I agree with you.

Phil. And is not time measured by the succession of ideas in our minds?

Hyl. It is.

Phil. And is it not possible ideas should succeed one another twice as fast in your mind, as they do in mine, or in that of some spirit of another kind.

Hyl. I own it.

Phil. Consequently the same body may to another seem to perform its motion over any space in half the time that it doth to you. And the same reasoning will hold as to any other proportion : that is to say, according to your principles (since the motions perceived are both really in the object) it is possible one and the same body shall be really moved the same way at once, both very swift and very slow. How is this consistent either with common sense, or with what you just now granted?

Hyl. I have nothing to say to it.

Phil. Then as for *solidity:* either you do not mean any sensible quality by that word, and so it is beside our inquiry : or if you do, it must be either hardness or resistance. But both the one and the other are plainly relative to our senses : it being evident, that what seems hard to one animal, may appear soft to another, who hath greater force and firmness of limbs. Nor is it less plain, that the resistance I feel is not in the body.

Hyl. I own the very sensation of resistance, which is all you immediately perceive, is not in the *body*, but the cause of that sensation is.

Phil. But the causes of our sensations are not things immediately perceived, and therefore not sensible. This point I thought had been already determined.

Hyl. I own it was ; but you will pardon me if I seem a little embarrassed : I know not how to quit my old notions.

Phil. To help you out, do but consider, that if extension be once acknowledged to have no existence without the mind, the same must necessarily be granted of motion, solidity, and gravity, since they all evidently suppose extension. It is therefore superfluous to inquire particularly concerning each of them. In denying extension, you have denied them all to have any real existence.

Hyl. I wonder, Philonous, if what you say be true, why those philosophers who deny the secondary qualities any real existence, should yet attribute it to the primary. If there is no difference between them, how can this be accounted for ?

Phil. It is not my business to account for every opinion of the philosophers. But among other reasons which may be assigned for this, it seems probable, that pleasure and pain being rather annexed to the former than the latter, may be one. Heat and cold, tastes and smells, have something more vividly pleasing or disagreeable than the ideas of extension, figure, and motion, affect us with. And it being too visibly absurd to hold, that pain or pleasure can be in an unperceiving substance, men are more easily weaned from believing the external existence of the secondary, than the primary qualities. You will be satisfied there is something in this, if you recollect the difference you made between an intense and more moderate degree of heat, allowing the one a real existence, while you denied it to the other. But after all, there is no rational ground for that distinction; for surely an indifferent sensation is as truly *a sensation*, as one more pleasing or painful; and consequently should not any more than they be supposed to exist in an unthinking subject.

Hyl. It is just come into my head, Philonous, that I have somewhere heard of a distinction between absolute and sensible extension. Now though it be acknowledged that *great* and *small*, consisting merely in the relation which other extended beings have to the parts of our own bodies, do not really inhere in the substances themselves; yet nothing obliges us to hold the same with regard to *absolute extension*, which is something abstracted from *great* and *small*, from this or that particular magnitude or figure. So likewise as to motion, *swift* and *slow* are altogether relative to the succession of ideas in our own minds. But it doth not follow, because those modifications of motion exist not without the mind, that therefore absolute motion abstracted from them doth not.

Phil. Pray what is it that distinguishes one motion, or one part of extension from another? Is it not something sensible, as some degree of swiftness or slowness, some certain magnitude or figure peculiar to each?

Hyl. I think so.

Phil. These qualities therefore, stripped of all sensible properties, are without all specific and numerical differences, as the schools call them.

Hyl. They are.

Phil. That is to say, they are extension in general, and motion in general.

Hyl. Let it be so.

Phil. But it is a universally received maxim, that *every thing which exists is particular*. How then can motion in general, or extension in general, exist in any corporeal substance?

Hyl. I will take time to solve your difficulty.

Phil. But I think the point may be speedily decided. Without doubt you can tell, whether you are able to frame this or that idea. Now I am content to put our dispute on this issue. If you can frame in your thoughts a distinct abstract idea of motion or extension, divested of all those sensible modes, as swift and slow, great and small, round and square, and the like, which are acknowledged to exist only in the mind, I will then yield the point you contend for. But if you cannot, it will be unreasonable on your side to insist any longer upon what you have no notion of.

Hyl. To confess ingenuously, I cannot.

Phil. Can you even separate the ideas of extension and motion, from the ideas of all those qualities which they who make the distinction term *secondary*?

Hyl. What! is it not an easy matter, to consider extension and motion by themselves, abstracted from all other sensible qualities? Pray how do the mathematicians treat of them?

Phil. I acknowledge, Hylas, it is not difficult to form general propositions and reasonings about those qualities, without mentioning any other; and in this sense to consider or treat of them abstractedly. But how doth it follow that because I can pronounce the word *motion* by itself, I can form the idea of it in my mind exclusive of body? Or because theorems may be made of extension and figures, without any mention of *great* or *small*, or any other sensible mode or quality; that therefore it is possible such an abstract idea of extension, without any particular size or figure, or sensible quality, should be distinctly formed, and apprehended by the mind? Mathematicians treat of quantity, without regarding what other sensible qualities it is attended with, as being altogether indifferent to their demonstrations. But when laying aside the words, they contemplate the bare ideas, I believe you will find, they are not the pure abstracted ideas of extension.

Hyl. But what say you to *pure intellect?* May not abstracted ideas be framed by that faculty?

Phil. Since I cannot frame abstract ideas at all, it is plain, I cannot frame them by the help of *pure intellect*, whatsoever faculty you understand by those words. Besides—not to inquire into the nature of pure intellect and its spiritual objects, as *virtue—reason, God,* or the like, thus much seems manifest, that sensible things are only to be perceived by sense, or represented by the imagination. Figures therefore and extension, being originally perceived by sense, do not belong to pure intellect. But for your further satisfaction, try if you can frame the idea of any figure, abstracted from all particularities of size, or even from other sensible qualities.

Hyl. Let me think a little——I do not find that I can.

Phil. And can you think it possible, that should really exist in nature, which implies a repugnancy in its conception?

Hyl. By no means.

Phil. Since therefore it is impossible even for the mind to disunite the ideas of extension and motion from all other sensible qualities, doth it not follow, that where the one exist, there necessarily the other exist likewise?

Hyl. It should seem so.

Phil. Consequently the very same arguments which you admitted, as conclusive against the secondary qualities, are without any further application of force against the primary too. Besides, if you will trust your senses, is it not plain all sensible qualities co-exist, or to them appear as being in the same place? Do they ever represent a motion, or figure, as being divested of all other visible and tangible qualities?

Hyl. You need say no more on this head. I am free to own, if there be no secret error or oversight in our proceedings hitherto, that all sensible qualities are alike to be denied existence without the mind. But my fear is, that I have been too liberal in my former concessions, or overlooked some fallacy or other. In short, I did not take time to think.

Phil. For that matter, Hylas, you may take what time you please in reviewing the progress of our inquiry. You are at liberty to recover any slips you might have made, or offer whatever you have omitted, which makes for your first opinion.

Hyl. One great oversight I take to be this: that I did not sufficiently distinguish the *object* from the *sensation*. Now though this latter may not exist without the mind, yet it will not thence follow that the former cannot.

Phil. What object do you mean? The object of the senses?

Hyl. The same.

Phil. It is then immediately perceived?

Hyl. Right.

Phil. Make me to understand the difference between what is immediately perceived, and a sensation.

Hyl. The sensation I take to be an act of the mind perceiving; beside which, there is something perceived; and this I call the *object*. For example, there is red and yellow on that tulip. But then the act of perceiving those colours is in me only, and not in the tulip.

Phil. What tulip do you speak of? is it that which you see?

Hyl. The same.

Phil. And what do you see beside colour, figure, and extension?

Hyl. Nothing.

Phil. What you would say then is, that the red and yellow are co-existent with the extension; is it not?

Hyl. That is not all: I would say, they have a real existence without the mind, in some unthinking substance.

Phil. That the colours are really in the tulip which I see, is manifest. Neither can it be denied, that this tulip may exist independent of your mind or mine; but that any immediate object of the senses, that is, any idea, or combination of ideas, should exist in an unthinking substance, or exterior to all minds, is in itself an evident contradiction. Nor can I imagine how this follows from what you said just now, to wit that the red and yellow were on the tulip *you saw*, since you do not pretend to *see* that unthinking substance.

Hyl. You have an artful way, Philonous, of diverting our inquiry from the subject.

Phil. I see you have no mind to be pressed that way. To return then to your distinction between *sensation* and *object;* if I take you right, you distinguish in every perception two things, the one an action of the mind, the other not.

Hyl. True.

Phil. And this action cannot exist in, or belong to any unthinking thing; but whatever beside is implied in a perception, may.

Hyl. That is my meaning.

Phil. So that if there was a perception without any act of the mind, it were possible such a perception should exist in an unthinking substance.

Hyl. I grant it. But it is impossible there should be such a perception.

Phil. When is the mind said to be active?

Hyl. When it produces, puts an end to, or changes any thing.

Phil. Can the mind produce, discontinue, or change any thing but by an act of the will?

Hyl. It cannot.

Phil. The mind therefore is to be accounted active in its perceptions, so far forth as volition is included in them.

Hyl. It is.

Phil. In plucking this flower, I am active, because I do it by the motion of my hand, which was consequent upon my volition; so likewise in applying it to my nose. But is either of these smelling?

Hyl. No.

Phil. I act too in drawing the air through my nose; because my breathing so rather than otherwise, is the effect of my volition. But neither can this be called *smelling:* for if it were, I should smell every time I breathed in that manner.

Hyl. True.

Phil. Smelling then is somewhat consequent to all this.

Hyl. It is.

Phil. But I do not find my will concerned any further. Whatever more there is, as that I perceive such a particular smell or any smell at all, this is independent of my will, and therein I am altogether passive. Do you find it otherwise with you, Hylas?

Hyl. No, the very same.

Phil. Then as to seeing, is it not in your power to open your eyes, or keep them shut; to turn them this or that way?

Hyl. Without doubt.

Phil. But doth it in like manner depend on your will, that in looking on this flower, you perceive *white* rather than any other colour? Or directing your open eyes towards yonder part of the heaven, can you avoid seeing the sun? Or is light or darkness the effect of your volition?

Hyl. No, certainly.

Phil. You are then in these respects altogether passive.

Hyl. I am.

Phil. Tell me now, whether *seeing* consists in perceiving light and colours, or in opening and turning the eyes?

Hyl. Without doubt, in the former.

Phil. Since, therefore you are in the very perception of light and colours altogether passive, what is become of that action you were speaking of, as an ingredient in every sensation? And doth it not follow from your own concessions, that the perception of light and colours, including no action in it, may exist in an unperceiving substance? And is not this a plain contradiction?

Hyl. I know not what to think of it.

Phil. Besides, since you distinguish the *active* and *passive* in every perception, you must do it in that of pain. But how is it possible that pain, be it as little active as you please, should exist in an unperceiving substance? In short, do but consider the point, and then confess ingenuously, whether light and colours, tastes, sounds, &c., are not all equally passions or sensations in the soul. You may indeed call them *externat objects*, and give them in words what subsistence you please. But examine your own thoughts, and then tell me whether it be not as I say?

Hyl. I acknowledge, Philonous, that upon a fair observation of what passes in my mind, I can discover nothing else, but that I am a thinking being, affected with variety of sensations; neither is it possible to conceive how a sensation should exist in an unperceiving substance. But then on the other hand, when I look on sensible things in a different view, considering them as so many modes and qualities, I find it necessary to suppose a material *substratum*, without which they cannot be conceived to exist.

Phil. Material substratum call you it? Pray, by which of your senses came you acquainted with that being?

Hyl. It is not itself sensible; its modes and qualities only being perceived by the senses.

Phil. I presume then, it was by reflection and reason you obtained the idea of it.

Hyl. I do not pretend to any proper positive idea of it. However I conclude it exists, because qualities cannot be conceived to exist without a support.

Phil. It seems then you have only a relative notion of it, or that you conceive it not otherwise than by conceiving the relation it bears to sensible qualities.

Hyl. Right.

Phil. Be pleased therefore to let me know wherein that relation consists.

Hyl. Is it not sufficiently expressed in the term *substratum*, or *substance*?

Phil. If so, the word *substratum* should import, that it is spread under the sensible qualities or accidents.

Hyl. True.

Phil. And consequently under extension.

Hyl. I own it.

Phil. It is therefore somewhat in its own nature entirely distinct from extension.

Hyl. I tell you, extension is only a mode, and matter is something that supports modes. And is it not evident the thing supported is different from the thing supporting?

Phil. So that something distinct from, and exclusive of extension, is supposed to be the *substratum* of extension?

Hyl. Just so.

Phil. Answer me, Hylas. Can a thing be spread without extension? or is not the idea of extension necessarily included in *spreading?*

Hyl. It is.

Phil. Whatsoever therefore you suppose spread under any thing, must have in itself an extension distinct from the extension of that thing under which it is spread.

Hyl. It must.

Phil. Consequently every corporeal substance being the *substratum* of extension, must have in itself another extension by which it is qualified to be a *substratum:* and so on to infinity. And I ask whether this be not absurd in itself, and repugnant to what you granted just now, to wit, that the *substratum* was something distinct from, and exclusive of extension.

Hyl. Aye but Philonous, you take me wrong. I do not mean that matter is *spread* in a gross literal sense under extension. The word *substratum* is used only to express in general the same thing with *substance.*

Phil. Well then, let us examine the relation implied in the term *substance.* Is it not that it stands under accidents?

Hyl. The very same.

Phil. But that one thing may stand under or support another, must it not be extended?

Hyl. It must.

Phil. Is not therefore this supposition liable to the same absurdity with the former?

Hyl. You still take things in a strict literal sense: that is not fair, Philonous.

Phil. I am not for imposing any sense on your words : you are at liberty to explain them as you please. Only I beseech you, make me understand something by them. You tell me, matter supports or stands under accidents. How! is it as your legs support your body?

Hyl. No ; that is the literal sense.

Phil. Pray let me know any sense, literal or not literal, that you understand it in.——How long must I wait for an answer, Hylas?

Hyl. I declare I know not what to say. I once thought I understood well enough what was meant by matter's supporting accidents. But now the more I think on it, the less can I comprehend it ; in short, I find that I know nothing of it.

Phil. It seems then you have no idea at all, neither relative nor positive, of matter ; you know neither what it is in itself, nor what relation it bears to accidents.

Hyl. I acknowledge it.

Phil. And yet you asserted, that you could not conceive how qualities or accidents should really exist, without conceiving at the same time a material support of them.

Hyl. I did.

Phil. That is to say, when you conceive the real existence of qualities, you do withal conceive something which you cannot conceive.

Hyl. It was wrong, I own. But still I fear there is some fallacy or other. Pray what think you of this? It is just come into my head, that the ground of all our mistake lies in your treating of each quality by itself. Now, I grant that each quality cannot singly subsist without the mind. Colour cannot without extension, neither can figure without some other sensible quality. But as the several qualities united or blended together form entire sensible things, nothing hinders why such things may not be supposed to exist without the mind.

Phil. Either, Hylas, you are jesting, or have a very bad memory. Though indeed we went through all the qualities by name one after another; yet my arguments, or rather your concessions no where tended to prove, that the secondary qualities did not subsist each alone by itself: but that they were not *at all* without the mind. Indeed in treating of figure and motion, we concluded they could not exist without the mind, because it was impossible even in thought to separate them from all secondary qualities, so as to conceive them existing by themselves. But then this was not the only argument made use of upon that occasion. But (to pass by all that hath been hitherto said, and reckon it for nothing, if you will have it so) I am content to put the whole upon this issue. If you can conceive it possible for any mixture or combination of qualities, or any sensible object whatever, to exist without the mind, then I will grant it actually to be so.

Hyl. If it comes to that, the point will soon be decided. What more easy than to conceive a tree or house existing by itself, independent of, and unperceived by any mind whatsoever? I do at this present time conceive them existing after that manner.

Phil. How say you, Hylas, can you see a thing which is at the same time unseen?

Hyl. No, that were a contradiction.

Phil. Is it not as great a contradiction to talk of *conceiving* a thing which is *unconceived*?

Hyl. It is.

Phil. The tree or house therefore which you think of, is conceived by you.

Hyl. How should it be otherwise?

Phil. And what is conceived is surely in the mind.

Hyl. Without question, that which is conceived is in the mind.

Phil. How then came you to say, you conceived a house or tree existing independent and out of all minds whatsoever?

Hyl. That was, I own, an oversight; but stay, let me consider what led me into it.—It is a pleasant mistake enough. As I was thinking of a tree in a solitary place, where no one was present to see it, methought that was to conceive a tree as existing unperceived or unthought of, not considering that I myself conceived it all the while. But now I plainly see, that all I can do is to frame ideas in my own mind. I may indeed conceive in my own thoughts the idea of a tree, or a house, or a mountain, but that is all. And this is far from proving, that I can conceive them *existing out of the minds of all spirits*.

Phil. You acknowledge then that you cannot possibly conceive how any one corporeal sensible thing should exist otherwise than in a mind.

Hyl. I do.

Phil. And yet you will earnestly contend for the truth of that which you cannot so much as conceive.

Hyl. I profess I know not what to think, but still there are some scruples remain with me. Is it not certain I see things at a distance ? Do we not perceive the stars and moon, for example, to be a great way off? Is not this, I say, manifest to the senses ?

Phil. Do you not in a dream too perceive those or the like objects ?

Hyl. I do.

Phil. And have they not then the same appearance of being distant ?

Hyl. They have.

Phil. But you do not thence conclude the apparitions in a dream to be without the mind ?

Hyl. By no means.

Phil. You ought not therefore to conclude that sensible objects are without the mind, from their appearance or manner wherein they are perceived.

Hyl. I acknowledge it. But doth not my sense deceive me in those cases ?

Phil. By no means. The idea or thing which you immediately perceive, neither sense nor reason inform you that it actually exists without the mind. By sense you only know that you are affected with such certain sensations of light and colours, &c. And these you will not say are without the mind.

Hyl. True : but beside all that, do you not think the sight suggests something of *outness* or *distance* ?

Phil. Upon approaching a distant object, do the

visible size and figure change perpetually, or do they appear the same at all distances?

Hyl. They are in a continual change.

Phil. Sight therefore doth not suggest or in any way inform you, that the visible object you immediately perceive, exists at a distance,[1] or will be perceived when you advance further onward, there being a continued series of visible objects succeeding each other, during the whole time of your approach.

Hyl. It doth not; but still I know, upon seeing an object, what object I shall perceive after having passed over a certain distance : no matter whether it be exactly the same or no : there is still something of distance suggested in the case.

Phil. Good Hylas, do but reflect a little on the point, and then tell me whether there be any more in it than this. From the ideas you actually perceive by sight, you have by experience learned to collect what other ideas you will (according to the standing order of nature) be affected with, after such a certain succession of time and motion.

Hyl. Upon the whole, I take it to be nothing else.

Phil. Now is it not plain, that if we suppose a man born blind was on a sudden made to see, he could at first have no experience of what may be suggested by sight.

Hyl. It is.

Phil. He would not then, according to you, have any notion of distance annexed to the things he saw; but would take them for a new set of sensations existing only in his mind.

Hyl. It is undeniable.

Phil. But to make it still more plain : is not *distance* a line turned endwise to the eye?

Hyl. It is.

Phil. And can a line so situated be perceived by sight ?

Hyl. It cannot.

[1] See the Essay towards a New Theory of Vision ; and its Vindication.

Phil. Doth it not therefore follow that distance is not properly and immediately perceived by sight?

Hyl. It should seem so.

Phil. Again, is it your opinion that colours are at a distance?

Hyl. It must be acknowledged, they are only in the mind.

Phil. But do not colours appear to the eye as co-existing in the same place with extension and figures?

Hyl. They do.

Phil. How can you then conclude from sight, that figures exist without, when you acknowledge colours do not; the sensible appearance being the very same with regard to both?

Hyl. I know not what to answer.

Phil. But allowing that distance was truly and immediately perceived by the mind, yet it would not thence follow it existed out of the mind. For whatever is immediately perceived is an idea : and can any *idea* exist out of the mind?

Hyl. To suppose that were absurd : but inform me, Philonous, can we perceive or know nothing beside our ideas?

Phil. As for the rational deducing of causes from effects, that is beside our inquiry. And by the senses you can best tell, whether you perceive any thing which is not immediately perceived. And I ask you, whether the things immediately perceived, are other than your own sensations or ideas? You have indeed more than once, in the course of this conversation, declared yourself on those points; but you seem, by this last question, to have departed from what you then thought.

Hyl. To speak the truth, Philonous, I think there are two kinds of objects, the one perceived immediately, which are likewise called *ideas ;* the other are real things or external objects perceived by the mediation of ideas, which are their images and representations. Now I own, ideas do not exist without the mind ; but the latter sort of objects do. I am sorry I did not think of this distinction sooner; it would probably have cut short your discourse.

Phil. Are those external objects perceived by sense, or by some other faculty?

Hyl. They are perceived by sense.

Phil. How! is there any thing perceived by sense, which is not immediately perceived?

Hyl. Yes, Philonous, in some sort there is. For example, when I look on a picture or statue of Julius Cæsar, I may be said, after a manner, to perceive him (though not immediately) by my senses.

Phil. It seems, then, you will have our ideas, which alone are immediately perceived, to be pictures of external things: and that these also are perceived by sense, inasmuch as they have a conformity or resemblance to our ideas.

Hyl. That is my meaning.

Phil. And in the same way that Julius Cæsar, in himself invisible, is nevertheless perceived by sight; real things, in themselves imperceptible, are perceived by sense.

Hyl. In the very same.

Phil. Tell me, Hylas, when you behold the picture of Julius Cæsar, do you see with your eyes any more than some colours and figures, with a certain symmetry and composition of the whole?

Hyl. Nothing else.

Phil. And would not a man, who had never known any thing of Julius Cæsar, see as much?

Hyl. He would.

Phil. Consequently he hath his sight, and the use of it, in as perfect a degree as you.

Hyl. I agree with you.

Phil. Whence comes it then that your thoughts are directed to the Roman emperor and his are not? This cannot proceed from the sensations or ideas of sense by you then perceived; since you acknowledge you have no advantage over him in that respect. It should seem therefore to proceed from reason and memory: should it not?

Hyl. It should.

Phil. Consequently it will not follow from that instance, that any thing is perceived by sense which is not immediately perceived. Though I grant we may in one acceptation be said to perceive sensible things mediately by sense: that is, when from a frequently perceived connexion, the immediate perception of ideas by one sense suggests to the mind others perhaps belonging to another sense, which are wont to be connected with them, For instance, when I hear a coach drive along the streets, immediately I perceive only the sound; but from the experience I have had that such a sound is connected with a coach, I am said to hear the coach. It is nevertheless evident, that in truth and strictness, nothing can be *heard* but *sound:* and the coach is not then properly perceived by sense, but suggested from experience. So likewise when we are said to see a red-hot bar of iron; the solidity and heat of the iron are not the objects of sight, but suggested to the imagination by the colour and figure, which are properly perceived by that sense. In short, those things alone are actually and strictly perceived by any sense, which would have been perceived, in case that same sense had then been first conferred on us. As for other things, it is plain they are only suggested to the mind by experience grounded on former perceptions. But to return to your comparison of Cæsar's picture, it is plain, if you keep to that, you must hold the real things or archetypes of our ideas are not perceived by sense, but by some internal faculty of the soul, as reason or memory. I would therefore fain know, what arguments you can draw from reason for the existence of what you call *real things* or *material objects;* or whether you remember to have seen them formerly as they are in themselves; or if you have heard or read of any one that did.

Hyl. I see, Philonous, you are disposed to raillery; but that will never convince me.

Phil. My aim is only to learn from you the way to come at the knowledge of *material beings.* Whatever

*1483

we perceive, is perceived either immediately or mediately: by sense, or by reason and reflection. But as you have excluded sense, pray show me what reason you have to believe their existence; or what *medium* you can possibly make use of to prove it, either to mine or your own understanding.

Hyl. To deal ingenuously, Philonous, now I consider the point, I do not find I can give you any good reason for it. But thus much seems pretty plain, that it is at least possible such things may really exist; and as long as there is no absurdity in supposing them, I am resolved to believe as I did, till you bring good reasons to the contrary.

Phil. What! is it come to this, that you only believe the existence of material objects, and that your belief is founded barely on the possibility of its being true? Then you will have me bring reasons against it: though another would think it reasonable, the proof should lie on him who holds the affirmative. And after all, this very point which you are now resolved to maintain without any reason, is, in effect, what you have more than once, during this discourse, seen good reason to give up. But to pass over all this; if I understand you rightly, you say our ideas do not exist without the mind; but that they are copies, images, or representations of certain originals that do.

Hyl. You take me right.

Phil. They are then like external things.

Hyl. They are.

Phil. Have those things a stable and permanent nature independent of our senses; or are they in a perpetual change, upon our producing any motions in our bodies, suspending, exerting, or altering our faculties or organs of sense.

Hyl. Real things, it is plain, have a fixed and real nature, which remains the same, notwithstanding any change in our senses, or in the posture and motion of our bodies; which, indeed, may affect the ideas in our minds, but it were absurd to think they had the same effect on things existing without the mind.

Phil. How then is it possible, that things perpetually fleeting and variable as our ideas, should be copies or images of any thing fixed and constant? or in other words, since all sensible qualities, as size, figure, colour, &c., that is, our ideas, are continually changing upon every alteration in the distance, medium, or instruments of sensation; how can any determinate material objects be properly represented or painted forth by several distinct things, each of which is so different from and unlike the rest? Or if you say it resembles some one only of our ideas, how shall we be able to distinguish the true copy from all the false ones?

Hyl. I profess, Philonous, I am at a loss. I know not what to say to this.

Phil. But neither is this all. Which are material objects in themselves, perceptible or imperceptible?

Hyl. Properly and immediately nothing can be perceived but ideas. All material things therefore are in themselves insensible, and to be perceived only by their ideas.

Phil. Ideas then are sensible, and their archetypes or originals insensible.

Hyl. Right.

Phil. But how can that which is sensible be like that which is insensible? Can a real thing in itself *invisible* be like a *colour;* or a real thing which is not *audible,* be like a *sound?* In a word, can any thing be like a sensation or idea, but another sensation or idea?

Hyl. I must own, I think not.

Phil. Is it possible there should be any doubt in the point? Do you not perfectly know your own ideas?

Hyl. I know them perfectly; since what I do not perceive or know, can be no part of my idea.

Phil. Consider therefore, and examine them, and then tell me if there be any thing in them which can exist without the mind: or if you can conceive any thing like them existing without the mind.

Hyl. Upon inquiry, I find it is impossible for me to conceive or understand how any thing but an idea can be like an idea.   And it is most evident, that *no idea can exist without the mind.*

Phil. You are therefore by your principles forced to deny the reality of sensible things, since you made it to consist in an absolute existence exterior to the mind. That is to say, you are a downright sceptic.   So I have gained my point, which was to show your principles led to scepticism.

Hyl. For the present I am, if not entirely convinced, at least silenced.

Phil. I would fain know what more you would require in order to a perfect conviction.   Have you not had the liberty of explaining yourself all manner of ways?   Were any little slips in discourse laid hold and insisted on? Or were you not allowed to retract or reinforce any thing you had offered, as best served your purpose? Hath not every thing you could say been heard and examined with all the fairness imaginable?   In a word, have you not in every point been convinced out of your own mouth?   And if you can at present discover any flaw in any of your former concessions, or think of any remaining subterfuge, any new distinction, colour, or comment whatsoever, why do you not produce it?

Hyl. A little patience, Philonous.   I am at present so amazed to see myself ensnared, and as it were imprisoned in the labyrinths you have drawn me into, that on the sudden it cannot be expected I should find my way out.   You must give me time to look about me, and recollect myself.

Phil. Hark; is not this the college-bell?

Hyl. It rings for prayers.

Phil. We will go in then if you please, and meet here again to-morrow morning.   In the mean time you may employ your thoughts on this morning's discourse, and try if you can find any fallacy in it, or invent any new means to extricate yourself.

Hyl. Agreed.

THE SECOND DIALOGUE

Hylas. I beg your pardon, Philonous, for not meeting you sooner. All this morning my head was so filled with our late conversation, that I had not leisure to think of the time of the day, or indeed of any thing else.

Philonous. I am glad you were so intent upon it, in hopes if there were any mistakes in your concessions, or fallacies in my reasonings from them, you will now discover them to me.

Hyl. I assure you, I have done nothing ever since I saw you, but search after mistakes and fallacies, and with that view have minutely examined the whole series of yesterday's discourse: but all in vain, for the notions it led me into, upon review appear still more clear and evident; and the more I consider them, the more irresistibly do they force my assent.

Phil. And is not this, think you, a sign that they are genuine, that they proceed from nature, and are conformable to right reason? Truth and beauty are in this alike, that the strictest survey sets them both off to advantage. While the false lustre of error and disguise cannot endure being reviewed, or too nearly inspected.

Hyl. I own there is a great deal in what you say. Nor can any one be more entirely satisfied of the truth of those odd consequences, so long as I have in view the reasonings that lead to them. But when these are out of my thoughts, there seems on the other hand something so satisfactory, so natural and intelligible in the modern way of explaining things, that I profess I know not how to reject it.

Phil. I know not what way you mean.

Hyl. I mean the way of accounting for our sensations or ideas.

Phil. How is that?

Hyl. It is supposed the soul makes her residence in some part of the brain, from which the nerves take their rise, and are thence extended to all parts of the body: and that outward objects, by the different impressions they make on the organs of sense, communicate certain vibrative motions to the nerves; and these being filled with spirits, propagate them to the brain or seat of the soul, which according to the various impressions or traces thereby made in the brain, is variously affected with ideas.

Phil. And call you this an explication of the manner whereby we are affected with ideas?

Hyl. Why not, Philonous? have you any thing to object against it?

Phil. I would first know whether I rightly understand your hypothesis. You make certain traces in the brain to be the causes or occasions of our ideas. Pray tell me, whether by the *brain* you mean any sensible thing?

Hyl. What else think you I could mean?

Phil. Sensible things are all immediately perceivable; and those things which are immediately perceivable, are ideas; and these exist only in the mind. Thus much you have, if I mistake not, long since agreed to.

Hyl. I do not deny it.

Phil. The brain therefore you speak of, being a sensible thing, exists only in the mind. Now, I would fain know whether you think it reasonable to suppose, that one idea or thing existing in the mind, occasions all other ideas. And if you think so, pray how do you account for the origin of that primary idea or brain itself?

Hyl. I do not explain the origin of our ideas by that brain which is perceivable to sense, this being itself only a combination of sensible ideas, but by another which I imagine.

Phil. But are not things imagined as truly in the mind as things perceived?

Hyl. I must confess they are.

Phil. It comes therefore to the same thing; and you have been all this while accounting for ideas, by certain motions or impressions in the brain, that is, by some alterations in an idea, whether sensible or imaginable, it matters not.

Hyl. I begin to suspect my hypothesis.

Phil. Beside spirits, all that we know or conceive are

our own ideas. When therefore you say, all ideas are occasioned by impressions in the brain, do you conceive this brain or no? If you do, then you talk of ideas imprinted in an idea, causing that same idea, which is absurd. If you do not conceive it, you talk unintelligibly, instead of forming a reasonable hypothesis.

Hyl. I now clearly see it was a mere dream. There is nothing in it.

Phil. You need not be much concerned at it; for after all, this way of explaining things, as you called it, could never have satisfied any reasonable man. What connexion is there between a motion in the nerves, and the sensations of sound or colour in the mind? Or how is it possible these should be the effect of that?

Hyl. But I could never think it had so little in it, as now it seems to have.

Phil. Well then, are you at length satisfied that no sensible things have a real existence; and that you are in truth an arrant *sceptic?*

Hyl. It is too plain to be denied.

Phil. Look! are not the fields covered with a delightful verdure? Is there not something in the woods and groves, in the rivers and clear springs, that soothes, that delights, that transports the soul? At the prospect of the wide and deep ocean, or some huge mountain whose top is lost in the clouds, or of an old gloomy forest, are not our minds filled with a pleasing horror? Even in rocks and deserts, is there not an agreeable wildness? How sincere a pleasure is it to behold the natural beauties of the earth! to preserve and renew our relish for them, is not the veil of night alternately drawn over her face, and doth she not change her dress with the seasons? How aptly are the elements disposed! What variety and use in the meanest production of nature! What delicacy, what beauty, what contrivance in animal and vegetable bodies? How exquisitely are all things suited as well to their particular ends, as to constitute opposite parts of the whole! and while they mutually aid and support, do they not also set off and illustrate each other! Raise now your thoughts from this ball of earth, to all those glorious luminaries that adorn the high arch of heaven. The motion and situation of the planets, are they not admirable for use and order. Were those (miscalled *erratic*) globes ever known to stray, in their repeated journeys through the pathless void? Do they not measure areas round the sun ever proportioned to the times? So fixed, so immutable are the laws by which the unseen Author of nature actuates the universe. How vivid and radiant is the lustre of the fixed stars! how magnificent and rich that negligent profusion, with which they appear to be scattered throughout the whole azure vault! yet if you take the telescope, it brings into your sight a new host of stars that escape the naked eye. Here they seem contiguous and minute, but to a nearer view immense orbs of light at various distances, far sunk in the abyss of space. Now you must call imagination to your aid. The feeble narrow sense cannot descry innumerable worlds revolving round the central fires; and in those worlds the energy of an all-perfect mind displayed in endless forms. But neither sense nor imagination are big enough to comprehend the boundless extent with all its glittering furniture. Though the labouring mind exert and strain each power to its utmost reach, there still stands out ungrasped a surplusage immeasurable. Yet all the vast bodies that compose this mighty frame, how distant and remote soever, are by some secret mechanism, some divine art and force, linked in a mutual dependence and intercourse with each other, even with this earth, which was almost slipped from my thoughts, and lost in the crowd of worlds. Is not the whole system immense, beautiful, glorious beyond expression and beyond thought? What treatment then do those philosophers deserve, who would deprive these noble and delightful scenes of all reality? How should those principles be entertained, that lead us to think all the visible beauty of the creation a false imaginary glare? To be plain, can you expect this scepticism of yours will not be thought extravagantly absurd by all men of sense?

Hyl. Other men may think as they please: but for

your part you have nothing to reproach me with. My comfort is, you are as much a *sceptic* as I am.

Phil. There, Hylas, I must beg leave to differ from you.

Hyl. What! have you all along agreed to the premises, and do you now deny the conclusion, and leave me to maintain those paradoxes by myself which you led me into? This surely is not fair.

Phil. I deny that I agreed with you in those notions that led to scepticism. You indeed said, the reality of sensible things consisted in an *absolute existence* out of the minds of spirits, or distinct from their being perceived. And pursuant to this notion of reality, you are obliged to deny sensible things any real existence: that is, according to your own definition, you profess yourself a *sceptic*. But I neither said nor thought the reality of sensible things was to be defined after that manner. To me it is evident, for the reasons you allow of, that sensible things cannot exist otherwise than in a mind or spirit. Whence I conclude, not that they have no real existence, but that seeing they depend not on my thought, and have an existence distinct from being perceived by me, *there must be some other mind wherein they exist.* As sure therefore as the sensible world really exists, so sure is there an infinite, omnipresent Spirit who contains and supports it.

Hyl. What! this is no more than I and all Christians hold; nay, and all others too who believe there is a God, and that he knows and comprehends all things.

Phil. Ay, but here lies the difference. Men commonly believe that all things are known or perceived by God, because they believe the being of a God, whereas I, on the other side, immediately and necessarily conclude the being of a God, because all sensible things must be perceived by him.

Hyl. But so long as we all believe the same thing, what matter is it how we come by that belief?

Phil. But neither do we agree in the same opinion. For philosophers, though they acknowledge all corporeal beings to be perceived by God, yet they attribute to them an absolute subsistence distinct from their being perceived by any mind whatever, which I do not. Besides, is there no difference between saying, *there is a God, therefore he perceives all things :* and saying, *sensible things do really exist : and if they really exist, they are necessarily perceived by an infinite mind : therefore there is an infinite mind, or God.* This furnishes you with a direct and immediate demonstration, from a most evident principle, of the *being of a God.* Divines and philosophers had proved beyond all controversy, from the beauty and usefulness of the several parts of the creation, that it was the workmanship of God. But that setting aside all help of astronomy and natural philosophy, all contemplation of the contrivance, order, and adjustment of things, an infinite mind should be necessarily inferred from the bare existence of the sensible world, is an advantage peculiar to them only who have made this easy reflection : that the sensible world is that which we perceive by our several senses ; and that nothing is perceived by the senses beside ideas ; and that no idea or archetype of an idea can exist otherwise than in a mind. You may now, without any laborious search into the sciences, without any subtilty of reason, or tedious length of discourse, oppose and baffle the most strenuous advocate for atheism. Those miserable refuges, whether in an eternal succession of unthinking causes and effects, or in a fortuitous concourse of atoms ; those wild imaginations of Vanini, Hobbes, and Spinoza ; in a word, the whole system of atheism, is it not entirely overthrown by this single reflection on the repugnancy included in supposing the whole, or any part, even the most rude and shapeless of the visible world, to exist without a mind ? Let any one of those abettors of impiety but look into his own thoughts, and there try if he can conceive how so much as a rock, a desert, a chaos, or confused jumble of atoms ; how any thing at all, either sensible or imaginable, can exist independent of a mind, and he need go no further to be convinced of his folly. Can any thing be fairer than to put a dispute on such an issue, and leave it to a man himself to see if he can conceive, even in thought, what he holds to be true in fact, and from a notional to allow it a real existence?

Hyl. It cannot be denied, there is something highly serviceable to religion in what you advance. But do you not think it looks very like a notion entertained by some eminent moderns, of *seeing all things in God?*

Phil. I would gladly know that opinion ; pray explain it to me.

Hyl. They conceive that the soul being immaterial, is incapable of being united with material things, so as to perceive them in themselves, but that she perceives them by her union with the substance of God, which being spiritual is therefore purely intelligible, or capable of being the immediate object of a spirit's thought. Besides, the divine essence contains in it perfections correspondent to each created being ; and which are, for that reason, proper to exhibit or represent them to the mind.

Phil. I do not understand how our ideas, which are things altogether passive and inert, can be the essence, or any part (or like any part) of the essence or substance of God, who is an impassive, indivisible, purely active being. Many more difficulties and objections there are, which occur at first view against this hypothesis ; but I shall only add, that it is liable to all the absurdities of the common hypotheses, in making a created world exist otherwise than in the mind of a spirit. Beside all which it hath this peculiar to itself, that it makes that material world serve to no purpose. And if it pass for a good argument against other hypotheses in the sciences, that they suppose nature or the Divine Wisdom to make something in vain, or do that by tedious round-about methods, which might have been performed in a much more easy and compendious way, what shall we think of that hypothesis which supposes the whole world made in vain?

Hyl. But what say you, are not you too of opinion that we see all things in God? If I mistake not, what you advance comes near it.

Phil. Few men think, yet all will have opinions. Hence men's opinions are superficial and confused. It is nothing strange that tenets, which in themselves are ever so different, should nevertheless be confounded with each other by those who do not consider them attentively. I shall not therefore be surprised, if some men imagine that I run into the enthusiasm of Malebranche, though in truth I am very remote from it. He builds on the most abstract general ideas, which I entirely disclaim. He asserts an absolute external world, which I deny. He maintains that we are deceived by our senses, and know not the real natures, or the true forms and figures of extended beings; of all which I hold the direct contrary. So that, upon the whole, there are no principles more fundamentally opposite than his and mine. It must be owned I entirely agree with what the holy scripture saith, that "in God we live, and move, and have our being." But that we see things in his essence, after the manner above set forth, I am far from believing. Take here in brief my meaning. It is evident, that the things I perceive are my own ideas, and that no idea can exist unless it be in a mind. Nor is it less plain that these ideas, or things by me perceived, either themselves or their archetypes, exist independently of my mind, since I know myself not to be their author, it being out of my power to determine at pleasure, what particular ideas I shall be affected with upon opening my eyes or ears. They must therefore exist in some other mind, whose will it is they should be exhibited to me. The things, I say, immediately perceived, are ideas or sensations, call them which you will. But how can any idea or sensation exist in, or be produced by, any thing but a mind or spirit? This indeed is inconceivable; and to assert that which is inconceivable, is to talk nonsense: is it not?

Hyl. Without doubt.

Phil. But on the other hand, it is very conceivable that they should exist in, and be produced by, a spirit: since this is no more than I daily experience in myself, inasmuch as I perceive numberless ideas: and by an act

of my will can form a great variety of them, and raise
them up in my imagination: though it must be confessed, these creatures of the fancy are not altogether
so distinct, so strong, vivid, and permanent, as those
perceived by my senses, which latter are called *real
things*. From all which I conclude, *there is a mind
which affects me every moment with all the sensible impressions I perceive*. And from the variety, order, and
manner of these, I conclude the author of them to be
wise, powerful, and good, beyond comprehension. Mark it
well: I do not say, I see things by perceiving that which
represents them in the intelligible substance of God.
This I do not understand; but I say, the things by
me perceived are known by the understanding, and
produced by the will, of an infinite Spirit. And is not
all this most plain and evident? Is there any more
in it, than what a little observation of our own minds,
and that which passes in them, not only enableth us to
conceive, but also obligeth us to acknowledge?

Hyl. I think I understand you very clearly; and own
the proof you give of a Deity seems no less evident, than
it is surprising. But allowing that God is the supreme
and universal cause of all things, yet may not there be
still a third nature besides spirits and ideas? May we
not admit a subordinate and limited cause of our ideas?
In a word, may there not for all that be *matter?*

Phil. How often must I inculcate the same thing?
You allow the things immediately perceived by sense to
exist no where without the mind; but there is nothing
perceived by sense, which is not perceived immediately:
therefore there is nothing sensible that exists without
the mind. The matter therefore which you still insist
on, is something intelligible, I suppose; something that
may be discovered by reason, and not by sense.

Hyl. You are in the right.

Phil. Pray let me know what reasoning your belief of
matter is grounded on; and what this matter is in your
present sense of it.

Hyl. I find myself affected with various ideas, whereof
I know I am not the cause; neither are they the cause

of themselves or of one another, or capable of subsisting by themselves, as being altogether inactive, fleeting, dependent beings. They have therefore some cause distinct from me and them : of which I pretend to know no more, than that it is *the cause of my ideas.* And this thing, whatever it be, I call matter.

Phil. Tell me, Hylas, hath every one a liberty to change the current proper signification annexed to a common name in any language ? For example, suppose a traveller should tell you, that in a certain country men might pass unhurt through the fire ; and, upon explaining himself, you found he meant by the word *fire* that which others call *water:* or if he should assert there are trees which walk upon two legs, meaning men by the term *trees.* Would you think this reasonable ?

Hyl. No ; I should think it very absurd. Common custom is the standard of propriety in language. And for any man to affect speaking improperly, is to pervert the use of speech, and can never serve to a better purpose, than to protract and multiply disputes where there is no difference in opinion.

Phil. And doth not *matter*, in the common current acceptation of the word, signify an extended, solid, moveable, unthinking, inactive substance ?

Hyl. It doth.

Phil. And hath it not been made evident, that no such substance can possibly exist? And though it should be allowed to exist, yet how can that which is *inactive* be a *cause ;* or that which is *unthinking* be a *cause of thought ?* You may indeed, if you please, annex to the word *matter* a contrary meaning to what is vulgarly received ; and tell me you understand by it an unextended, thinking, active being, which is the cause of our ideas. But what else is this, than to play with words, and run into that very fault you just now condemned with so much reason ? I do by no means find fault with your reasoning, in that you collect a cause from the phenomena : but I deny that the cause deducible by reason can properly be termed *matter.*

Hyl. There is indeed something in what you say.

But I am afraid you do not thoroughly comprehend my meaning. I would by no means be thought to deny that God, or an infinite spirit, is the supreme cause of all things. All I contend for, is that subordinate to the supreme agent there is a cause of a limited and inferior nature, which concurs in the production of our ideas, not by any act of will or spiritual efficiency, but by that kind of action which belongs to matter, viz. *motion*.

Phil. I find, you are at every turn relapsing into your old exploded conceit, of a moveable and consequently an extended substance existing without the mind. What! have you already forgot you were convinced, or are you willing I should repeat what has been said on that head? In truth this is not fair dealing in you, still to suppose the being of that which you have so often acknowledged to have no being. But not to insist further on what has been so largely handled, I ask whether all your ideas are not perfectly passive and inert, including nothing of action in them?

Hyl. They are.

Phil. And are sensible qualities any thing else but ideas?

Hyl. How often have I acknowledged that they are not?

Phil. But is not motion a sensible quality?

Hyl. It is.

Phil. Consequently it is no action.

Hyl. I agree with you. And indeed it is very plain, that when I stir my finger, it remains passive; but my will which produced the motion, is active.

Phil. Now I desire to know in the first place, whether motion being allowed to be no action, you can conceive any action besides volition: and in the second place, whether to say something and conceive nothing be not to talk nonsense: and lastly, whether having considered the premises, you do not perceive that to suppose any efficient or active cause of our ideas, other than *spirit*, is highly absurd and unreasonable?

Hyl. I give up the point entirely. But though matter may not be a cause, yet what hinders it being an *instru-*

ment subservient to the supreme agent in the production
of our ideas ?

Phil. An instrument, say you ; pray what may be the
figure, springs, wheels, and motions of that instrument ?

Hyl. Those I pretend to determine nothing of, both
the substance and its qualities being entirely unknown
to me.

Phil. What ? You are then of opinion, it is made up
of unknown parts, that it hath unknown motions, and an
unknown shape.

Hyl. I do not believe it hath any figure or motion at
all, being already convinced, that no sensible qualities
can exist in an unperceiving substance.

Phil. But what notion is it possible to frame of an
instrument void of all sensible qualities, even extension
itself ?

Hyl. I do not pretend to have any notion of it.

Phil. And what reason have you to think, this unknown, this inconceivable somewhat doth exist ? Is it
that you imagine God cannot act as well without it, or
that you find by experience the use of some such thing,
when you form ideas in your own mind ?

Hyl. You are always teazing me for reasons of my
belief. Pray what reasons have you not to believe it ?

Phil. It is to me a sufficient reason not to believe the
existence of any thing, if I see no reason for believing it.
But not to insist on reasons for believing, you will not
so much as let me know what it is you would have me
believe, since you say you have no manner of notion of
it. After all, let me entreat you to consider whether it
be like a philosopher, or even like a man of common
sense, to pretend to believe you know not what and you
know not why.

Hyl. Hold, Philonous. When I tell you matter is an
instrument, I do not mean altogether nothing. It is
true, I know not the particular kind of instrument : but
however I have some notion of *instrument in general,*
which I apply to it.

Phil. But what if it should prove that there is something, even in the most general notion of *instrument,* as

taken in a distinct sense from *cause*, which makes the use of it inconsistent with the divine attributes?

Hyl. Make that appear, and I shall give up the point.

Phil. What mean you by the general nature or notion of *instrument?*

Hyl. That which is common to all particular instruments, composeth the general notion.

Phil. Is it not common to all instruments, that they are applied to the doing those things only, which cannot be performed by the mere act of our wills? Thus for instance, I never use an instrument to move my finger, because it is done by a volition. But I should use one, if I were to remove part of a rock, or tear up a tree by the roots. Are you of the same mind? Or can you show any example where an instrument is made use of in producing an effect immediately depending on the will of the agent?

Hyl. I own, I cannot.

Phil. How therefore can you suppose, that an all-perfect Spirit, on whose will all things have an absolute and immediate dependence, should need an instrument in his operations, or not needing it make use of it? Thus it seems to me that you are obliged to own the use of a lifeless inactive instrument, to be incompatible with the infinite perfection of God; that is, by your own confession to give up the point.

Hyl. It doth not readily occur what I can answer you.

Phil. But methinks you should be ready to own the truth, when it hath been fairly proved to you. We indeed, who are beings of finite powers, are forced to make use of instruments. And the use of an instrument showeth the agent to be limited by rules of another's prescription, and that he cannot obtain his end, but in such a way and by such conditions. Whence it seems a clear consequence, that the supreme unlimited agent useth no tool or instrument at all. The will of an omnipotent Spirit is no sooner exerted than executed, without the application of means, which, if they are employed by inferior agents, it is not upon account of any real efficacy that is in them, or necessary aptitude to produce any effect, but merely in compliance with the laws of nature, or those conditions prescribed to them by the first cause, who is himself above all limitation or prescription whatsoever.

Hyl. I will no longer maintain that matter is an instrument. However, I would not be understood to give up its existence neither; since, notwithstanding what hath been said, it may still be an *occasion*.

Phil. How many shapes is your matter to take? Or how often must it be proved not to exist, before you are content to part with it? But to say no more of this (though by all the laws of disputation I may justly blame you for so frequently changing the signification of the principal term) I would fain know what you mean by affirming that matter is an occasion, having already denied it to be a cause. And when you have shown in what sense you understand *occasion*, pray in the next place be pleased to show me what reason induceth you to believe there is such an occasion of our ideas.

Hyl. As to the first point: by *occasion* I mean an inactive, unthinking being, at the presence whereof God excites ideas in our minds.

Phil. And what may be the nature of that inactive, unthinking being?

Hyl. I know nothing of its nature.

Phil. Proceed then to the second point, and assign some reason why we should allow an existence to this inactive, unthinking, unknown thing.

Hyl. When we see ideas produced in our minds after an orderly and constant manner, it is natural to think they have some fixed and regular occasions, at the presence of which they are excited.

Phil. You acknowledge then God alone to be the cause of our ideas, and that he causes them at the presence of those occasions.

Hyl. That is my opinion.

Phil. Those things which you say are present to God, without doubt he perceives.

Hyl. Certainly; otherwise they could not be to him an occasion of acting.

Phil. Not to insist now on your making sense of this hypothesis, or answering all the puzzling questions and difficulties it is liable to : I only ask whether the order and regularity observable in the series of our ideas, or the course of nature, be not sufficiently accounted for by the wisdom and power of God ; and whether it doth not derogate from those attributes, to suppose he is influenced, directed, or put in mind, when and what he is to act, by any unthinking substance. And lastly, whether in case I granted all you contend for, it would make any thing to your purpose, it not being easy to conceive how the external or absolute existence of an unthinking substance, distinct from its being perceived, can be inferred from my allowing that there are certain things perceived by the mind of God, which are to him the occasion of producing ideas in us.

Hyl. I am perfectly at a loss what to think, this notion of *occasion* seeming now altogether as groundless as the rest.

Phil. Do you not at length perceive, that in all these different acceptations of *matter*, you have been only supposing you know not what, for no manner of reason, and to no kind of use ?

Hyl. I freely own myself less fond of my notions, since they have been so accurately examined. But still, methinks I have some confused perception that there is such a thing as *matter*.

Phil. Either you perceive the being of matter immediately, or mediately. If immediately, pray inform me by which of the senses you perceive it. If mediately, let me know by what reasoning it is inferred from those things which you perceive immediately. So much for the perception. Then for the matter itself, I ask whether it is object, substratum, cause, instrument, or occasion ? You have already pleaded for each of these, shifting your notions, and making matter to appear sometimes in one shape, then in another. And what you have offered hath been disapproved and rejected by yourself. If you have any thing new to advance, I would gladly hear it.

Hyl. I think I have already offered all I had to say on those heads. I am at a loss what more to urge.

Phil. And yet you are loath to part with your old prejudice. But to make you quit it more easily, I desire that, besides what has been hitherto suggested, you will further consider whether, upon supposition that matter exists, you can possibly conceive how you should be affected by it? Or supposing it did not exist, whether it be not evident you might for all that be affected with the same ideas you now are, and consequently have the very same reasons to believe its existence that you now can have?

Hyl. I acknowledge it is possible we might perceive all things just as we do now, though there was no matter in the world; neither can I conceive, if there be matter, how it should produce any idea in our minds. And I do further grant, you have entirely satisfied me, that it is impossible there should be such a thing as matter in any of the foregoing acceptations. But still I cannot help supposing that there is *matter* in some sense or other. What that is I do not indeed pretend to determine.

Phil. I do not expect you should define exactly the nature of that unknown being. Only be pleased to tell me, whether it is a substance : and if so, whether you can suppose a substance without accidents : or in case you suppose it to have accidents or qualities, I desire you will let me know what those qualities are, at least what is meant by matter's supporting them.

Hyl. We have already argued on those points. I have no more to say to them. But to prevent any further questions, let me tell you, I at present understand by *matter* neither substance nor accident, thinking nor extended being, neither cause, instrument, nor occasion, but something entirely unknown, distinct from all these.

Phil. It seems then you include in your present notion of matter, nothing but the general abstract of idea of *entity*.

Hyl. Nothing else, save only that I superadd to this general idea the negation of all those particular things, qualities, or ideas that I perceive, imagine, or in any wise apprehend.

Phil. Pray where do you suppose this unknown matter to exist?

Hyl. Oh Philonous! now you think you have entangled me; for if I say it exists in place, then you will infer that it exists in the mind, since it is agreed, that place or extension exists only in the mind: but I am not ashamed to own my ignorance. I know not where it exists; only I am sure it exists not in place. There is a negative answer for you: and you must expect no other to all the questions you put for the future about matter.

Phil. Since you will not tell me where it exists, be pleased to inform me after what manner you suppose it to exist, or what you mean by its *existence*.

Hyl. It neither thinks nor acts, neither perceives, nor is perceived.

Phil. But what is there positive in your abstracted notion of its existence?

Hyl. Upon a nice observation, I do not find I have any positive notion or meaning at all. I tell you again I am not ashamed to own my ignorance. I know not what is meant by its *existence*, or how it exists.

Phil. Continue, good Hylas, to act the same ingenuous part, and tell me sincerely whether you can frame a distinct idea of entity in general, prescinded trom and exclusive of all thinking and corporeal beings, all particular things whatsoever.

Hyl. Hold, let me think a little——I profess, Philonous, I do not find that I can. At first glance methought I had some dilute and airy notion of pure entity in abstract; but upon closer attention it hath quite vanished out of sight. The more I think on it, the more am I confirmed in my prudent resolution of giving none but negative answers, and not pretending to the least degree of any positive knowledge or conception of matter, its *where*, its *how*, its *entity*, or any thing belonging to it.

Phil. When therefore you speak of the existence ot matter, you have not any notion in your mind.

Hyl. None at all.

Phil. Pray tell me if the case stands not thus : at first, from a belief of material substance you would have it that the immediate objects existed without the mind; then that their archetypes; then causes; next instruments: then occasions: lastly, *something in general,* which being interpreted proves *nothing.* So matter comes to nothing. What think you, Hylas? is not this a fair summary of your whole proceeding?

Hyl. Be that as it will, yet I still insist upon it, that our not being able to conceive a thing, is no argument against its existence.

Phil. That from a cause, effect, operation, sign, or other circumstance, there may reasonably be inferred the existence of a thing not immediately perceived, and that it were absurd for any man to argue against the existence of that thing, from his having no direct and positive notion of it, I freely own. But where there is nothing of all this; where neither reason nor revelation induces us to believe the existence of a thing; where we have not even a relative notion of it; where an abstraction is made from perceiving and being perceived, from spirit and idea: lastly, where there is not so much as the most inadequate or faint idea pretended to: I will not indeed thence conclude against the reality of any notion or existence of any thing : but my inference shall be, that you mean nothing at all : that you imply words to no manner of purpose, without any design or signification whatsoever. And I leave it to you to consider how mere jargon should be treated.

Hyl. To deal frankly with you, Philonous, your arguments seem in themselves unanswerable, but they have not so great an effect on me as to produce that entire conviction, that hearty acquiescence which attends demonstration. I find myself still relapsing into an obscure surmise of I know not what, *matter.*

Phil. But are you not sensible, Hylas, that two things must concur to take away all scruple, and work a plenary assent in the mind? Let a visible object be set in never so clear a light, yet if there is any imperfection in the sight, or if the eye is not directed towards it, it will not be distinctly seen. And though a demonstration be never so well grounded and fairly proposed, yet if there is withal a stain of prejudice, or a wrong bias on the understanding, can it be expected on a sudden to perceive clearly and adhere firmly to the truth? No, there is need of time and pains; the attention must be awakened and detained by a frequent repetition of the same thing placed oft in the same, oft in different lights. I have said it already, and I find I must still repeat and inculcate, that it is an unaccountable license you take in pretending to maintain you know not what, for you know not what reason, to you know not what purpose. Can this be paralleled in any art or science, any sect or profession of men? Or is there any thing so barefacedly groundless and unreasonable to be met with even in the lowest of common conversation? But perhaps you will still say, matter may exist, though at the same time you neither know what is meant by *matter*, nor by its *existence*. This indeed is surprising, and the more so because it is altogether voluntary, you not being led to it by any one reason; for I challenge you to show me that thing in nature which needs matter to explain or account for it.

Hyl. The reality of things cannot be maintained without supposing the existence of matter. And is not this, think you, a good reason why I should be earnest in its defence?

Phil. The reality of things! What things, sensible or intelligible?

Hyl. Sensible things.

Phil. My glove, for example?

Hyl. That or any other thing perceived by the senses.

Phil. But to fix on some particular thing; is it not a sufficient evidence to me of the existence of this *glove*, that I see it, and feel it, and wear it? Or if this will not do, how is it possible I should be assured of the reality of this thing, which I actually see in this place, by supposing that some unknown thing, which I never did or can see, exists after an unknown manner, in an unknown place, or in no place at all? How can the supposed reality of that which is intangible, be a proof that any thing tangible really exists? Or of that which is invisible, that any visible thing, or in general of any thing which is imperceptible, that a perceptible exists? Do but explain this, and I shall think nothing too hard for you.

Hyl. Upon the whole, I am content to own the existence of matter is highly improbable; but the direct and absolute impossibility of it does not appear to me.

Phil. But granting matter to be possible, yet upon that account merely it can have no more claim to existence, than a golden mountain or a centaur.

Hyl. I acknowledge it; but still you do not deny it is possible; and that which is possible, for aught you know, may actually exist.

Phil. I deny it to be possible; and have, if I mistake not, evidently proved from your own concessions that it is not. In the common sense of the word *matter*, is there any more implied than an extended, solid, figured, moveable substance, existing without the mind? And have not you acknowledged over and over, that you have seen evident reason for denying the possibility of such a substance.

Hyl. True, but that is only one sense of the term *matter*.

Phil. But is it not the only proper genuine received sense? and if matter in such a sense be proved impossible, may it not be thought with good grounds absolutely impossible? Else how could any thing be proved impossible? Or indeed how could there be any proof at all one way or other, to a man who takes the liberty to unsettle and change the common signification of words?

Hyl. I thought philosophers might be allowed to speak more accurately than the vulgar, and were not always confined to the common acceptation of a term.

Phil. But this now mentioned is the common received sense among philosophers themselves. But not to insist on that, have you not been allowed to take matter in what sense you pleased? And have you not used this privilege in the utmost extent, sometimes entirely changing, at others leaving out or putting into the definition of it whatever for the present best served your design, contrary to all the known rules of reason and logic? And hath not this shifting, unfair method of yours spun out our dispute to an unnecessary length; matter having been particularly examined, and by your own confession refuted in each of those senses? And can any more be required to prove the absolute impossibility of a thing, than the proving it impossible in every particular sense, that either you or any one else understands it in?

Hyl. But I am not so thoroughly satisfied that you have proved the impossibility of matter in the last most obscure, abstracted and indefinite sense.

Phil. When is a thing shown to be impossible?

Hyl. When a repugnancy is demonstrated between the ideas comprehended in its definition.

Phil. But where there are no ideas, there no repugnancy can be demonstrated between ideas.

Hyl. I agree with you.

Phil. Now in that which you call the obscure, indefinite sense of the word *matter*, it is plain, by your own confession, there was included no idea at all, no sense except an unknown sense, which is the same thing as none. You are not therefore to expect I should prove a repugnancy between ideas where there are no ideas, or the impossibility of matter taken in an *unknown* sense, that is no sense at all. My business was only to show, you meant *nothing*: and this you were brought to own. So that in all your various senses, you have been shown either to mean nothing at all, or if any thing, an absurdity. And if this be not sufficient to prove the impossibility of a thing, I desire you will let me know what is.

Hyl. I acknowledge you have proved that matter is impossible; nor do I see what more can be said in defence of it. But at the same time that I give up this, I suspect all my other notions. For surely none could be more seemingly evident than this once was:

and yet it now seems as false and absurd as ever it did
true before. But I think we have discussed the point
sufficiently for the present. The remaining part of the
day I would willingly spend, in running over in my
thoughts the several heads of this morning's conversation, and to-morrow shall be glad to meet you here
again about the same time.

Phil. I will not fail to attend you.

THE THIRD DIALOGUE

Philonous. TELL me, Hylas, what are the fruits of
yesterday's meditation? Hath it confirmed you in the
same mind you were in at parting? or have you since
seen cause to change your opinion?

Hylas. Truly my opinion is, that all our opinions are
alike vain and uncertain. What we approve to-day, we
condemn to-morrow. We keep a stir about knowledge,
and spend our lives in the pursuit of it, when, alas! we
know nothing all the while: nor do I think it possible
for us ever to know any thing in this life. Our faculties
are too narrow and too few. Nature certainly never
intended us for speculation.

Phil. What! say you we can know nothing, Hylas?

Hyl. There is not that single thing in the world,
whereof we can know the real nature, or what it is in
itself.

Phil. Will you tell me I do not really know what fire
or water is?

Hyl. You may indeed know that fire appears hot, and
water fluid: but this is no more than knowing what sensations are produced in your own mind, upon the application of fire and water to your organs of sense. Their
internal constitution, their true and real nature, you are
utterly in the dark as to that.

Phil. Do I not know this to be a real stone that I
stand on, and that which I see before my eyes to be
a real tree?

Hyl. Know? No, it is impossible you or any man

alive should know it. All you know is, that you have such a certain idea or appearance in your own mind. But what is this to the real tree or stone? I tell you, that colour, figure, and hardness, which you perceive, are not the real natures of those things, or in the least like them. The same may be said of all other real things or corporeal substances which compose the world. They have none of them any thing in themselves, like those sensible qualities by us perceived. We should not therefore pretend to affirm or know any thing of them, as they are in their own nature.

Phil. But surely, Hylas, I can distinguish gold, for example, from iron: and how could this be, if I knew not what either truly was?

Hyl. Believe me, Philonous, you can only distinguish between your own ideas. That yellowness, that weight, and other sensible qualities, think you they are really in the gold? They are only relative to the senses, and have no absolute existence in nature. And in pretending to distinguish the species of real things, by the appearances in your mind, you may perhaps act as wisely as he that should conclude two men were of a different species, because their clothes were not of the same colour.

Phil. It seems then we are altogether put off with the appearances of things, and those false ones too. The very meat I eat, and the cloth I wear, have nothing in them like what I see and feel.

Hyl. Even so.

Phil. But is it not strange the whole world should be thus imposed on and so foolish as to believe their senses? And yet I know not how it is, but men eat, and drink, and sleep, and perform all the offices of life as comfortably and conveniently, as if they really knew the things they are conversant about.

Hyl. They do so: but you know ordinary practice does not require a nicety of speculative knowledge. Hence the vulgar retain their mistakes, and for all that, make a shift to bustle through the affairs of life. But philosophers know better things.

Phil. You mean, they know that they *know nothing.*

Hyl. That is the very top and perfection of human knowledge.

Phil. But are you all this while in earnest, Hylas; and are you seriously persuaded that you know nothing real in the world? Suppose you are going to write, would you not call for pen, ink, and paper, like another man; and do you not know what it is you call for?

Hyl. How often must I tell you, that I know not the real nature of any one thing in the universe? I may, indeed, upon occasion, make use of pen, ink, and paper. But what any one of them is in its own true nature, I declare positively I know not. And the same is true with regard to every other corporeal thing. And, what is more, we are not only ignorant of the true and real nature of things, but even of their existence. It cannot be denied that we perceive such certain appearances or ideas; but it cannot be concluded from thence that bodies really exist. Nay, now I think on it, I must, agreeably to my former concessions, further declare, that it is impossible any real corporeal thing should exist in nature.

Phil. You amaze me. Was ever any thing more wild and extravagant than the notions you now maintain and is it not evident you are led into all these extravagancies by the belief of *material substance?* This makes you dream of those unknown natures in every thing. It is this occasions your distinguishing between the reality and sensible appearances of things. It is to this you are indebted for being ignorant of what every body else knows perfectly well. Nor is this all: you are not only ignorant of the true nature of every thing, but you know not whether any thing really exists, or whether there are any true natures at all; forasmuch as you attribute to your material beings an absolute or external existence, wherein you suppose their reality consists. And as you are forced in the end to acknowledge such an existence means either a direct repugnancy, or nothing at all, it follows that you are obliged to pull down your own hypothesis of material substance, and positively to deny the real existence of any part of the universe. And so you are plunged into the deepest and most deplorable *scepticism* that ever man was. Tell me, Hylas, is it not as I say?

Hyl. I agree with you. *Material substance* was no more than an hypothesis, and a false and groundless one too. I will no longer spend my breath in defence of it. But whatever hypothesis you advance, or whatsoever scheme of things you introduce in its stead, I doubt not it will appear every whit as false: let me but be allowed to question you upon it. That is, suffer me to serve you in your own kind, and I warrant it shall conduct you through as many perplexities and contradictions, to the very same state of scepticism that I myself am in at present.

Phil. I assure you, Hylas, I do not pretend to frame any hypothesis at all. I am of a vulgar cast, simple enough to believe my senses, and leave things as I find them. To be plain, it is my opinion, that the real things are those very things I see and feel, and perceive by my senses. These I know, and finding they answer all the necessities and purposes of life, have no reason to be solicitous about any other unknown beings. A piece of sensible bread, for instance, would stay my stomach better than ten thousand times as much of that insensible, unintelligible, real bread you speak of. It is likewise my opinion, that colours and other sensible qualities are on the objects. I cannot for my life help thinking that snow is white, and fire hot. You indeed, who by *snow* and *fire* mean certain external, unperceived, unperceiving substances, are in the right to deny whiteness or heat to be affections inherent in them. But I, who understand by those words the things I see and feel, am obliged to think like other folks. And as I am no sceptic with regard to the nature of things, so neither am I as to their existence. That a thing should be really perceived by my senses, and at the same time not really exist, is to me a plain contradiction; since I cannot prescind or abstract, even in thought, the existence of a sensible thing from its being perceived. Wood,

stones, fire, water, flesh, iron, and the like things, which
I name and discourse of, are things that I know.   And
I should not have known them, but that I perceived
them by my senses, and things perceived by the senses
are immediately perceived; and things immediately perceived are ideas; and ideas cannot exist without the
mind; their existence therefore consists in being perceived; when therefore they are actually perceived, there
can be no doubt of their existence.   Away then with
all that scepticism, all those ridiculous philosophical
doubts.   What a jest is it for a philosopher to question
the existence of sensible things, till he hath it proved
to him from the veracity of God: or to pretend our
knowledge in this point falls short of intuition or
demonstration!   I might as well doubt of my own
being, as of the being of those things I actually see
and feel.

Hyl. Not so fast, Philonous: you say you cannot
conceive how sensible things should exist without the
mind.   Do you not?

Phil. I do.

Hyl. Supposing you were annihilated, cannot you
conceive it possible that things perceivable by sense
may still exist?

Phil. I can; but then it must be in another mind.
When I deny sensible things an existence out of the
mind, I do not mean my mind in particular, but all
minds.   Now it is plain they have an existence exterior
to my mind, since I find them by experience to be
independent of it.   There is therefore some other mind
wherein they exist, during the intervals between the
times of my perceiving them: as likewise they did before
my birth, and would do after my supposed annihilation.
And as the same is true with regard to all other finite
created spirits, it necessarily follows, there is an *omnipresent, eternal Mind*, which knows and comprehends
all things, and exhibits them to our view in such a
manner, and according to such rules as he himself hath
ordained, and are by us termed the *laws of nature*.

Hyl. Answer me, Philonous.   Are all our ideas perfectly inert beings? Or have they any agency included in them?

Phil. They are altogether passive and inert.

Hyl. And is not God an agent, a being purely active?

Phil. I acknowledge it.

Hyl. No idea therefore can be like unto, or represent the nature of God.

Phil. It cannot.

Hyl. Since therefore you have no idea of the mind of God, how can you conceive it possible, that things should exist in his mind? Or, if you can conceive the mind of God without having an idea of it, why may not I be allowed to conceive the existence of matter, notwithstanding that I have no idea of it?

Phil. As to your first question: I own I have properly no idea, either of God or any other spirit; for these being active, cannot be represented by things perfectly inert, as our ideas are. I do nevertheless know, that I, who am a spirit or thinking substance, exist as certainly, as I know my ideas exist. Further, I know what I mean by the terms *I* and *myself;* and I know this immediately, or intuitively, though I do not perceive it as I perceive a triangle, a colour, or a sound. The mind, spirit, or soul, is that indivisible, unextended thing, which thinks, acts, and perceives. I say *indivisible*, because unextended, and *unextended*, because extended, figured, moveable things, are ideas; and that which perceives ideas, which thinks and wills, is plainly itself no idea, nor like an idea. Ideas are things inactive, and perceived: and spirits a sort of beings altogether different from them. I do not therefore say my soul is an idea, or like an idea. However, taking the word *idea* in a large sense, my soul may be said to furnish me with an idea, that is, an image, or likeness of God, though indeed extremely inadequate. For all the notion I have of God, is obtained by reflecting on my own soul, heightening its powers, and removing its imperfections. I have therefore, though not an inactive idea, yet in myself some sort of an active thinking image of the Deity. And though I perceive him not by sense, yet I have a notion of him, or know him by reflection and reasoning. My own mind and my own ideas I have an immediate knowledge of; and by the help of these, do mediately apprehend the possibility of the existence of other spirits and ideas. Further, from my own being, and from the dependency I find in myself and my ideas, I do by an act of reason necessarily infer the existence of a God, and of all created things in the mind of God. So much for your first question. For the second: I suppose by this time you can answer it yourself. For you neither perceive matter objectively, as you do an inactive being or idea, nor know it, as you do yourself, by a reflex act: neither do you mediately apprehend it by similitude of the one or the other: nor yet collect it by reasoning from that which you know immediately. All which makes the case of *matter* widely different from that of the *Deity*.

Hyl. You say your own soul supplies you with some sort of an idea or image of God. But at the same time you acknowledge you have, properly speaking, no idea of your own soul. You even affirm that spirits are a sort of beings altogether different from ideas. Consequently that no idea can be like a spirit. We have therefore no idea of any spirit. You admit nevertheless that there is spiritual substance, although you have no idea of it; while you deny there can be such a thing as material substance, because you have no notion or idea of it. Is this fair dealing? To act consistently, you must either admit matter or reject spirit. What say you to this?

Phil. I say in the first place, that I do not deny the existence of material substance merely because I have no notion of it, but because the notion of it is inconsistent, or in other words, because it is repugnant that there should be a notion of it. Many things, for aught I know, may exist, whereof neither I nor any other man hath or can have any idea or notion whatsoever. But then those things must be possible, that is, nothing inconsistent must be included in their definition. I say secondly, that although we believe things to exist which we do not perceive; yet we may not believe that any particular thing exists, without some reason for such belief: but I have no reason for believing the existence of matter. I have no immediate intuition thereof: neither can I mediately from my sensations, ideas, notions, actions, or passions, infer an unthinking, unperceiving, inactive substance, either by probable deduction, or necessary consequence. Whereas the being of myself, that is, my own soul, mind, or thinking principle, I evidently know by reflection. You will forgive me if I repeat the same things in answer to the same objections. In the very notion or definition of material substance, there is included a manifest repugnance and inconsistency. But this cannot be said of the notion of spirit. That ideas should exist in what doth not perceive, or be produced by what doth not act, is repugnant. But it is no repugnancy to say, that a perceiving thing should be the subject of ideas, or an active thing the cause of them. It is granted we have neither an immediate evidence nor a demonstrative knowledge of the existence of other finite spirits; but it will not thence follow that such spirits are on a foot with material substances: if to suppose the one be inconsistent, and it be not inconsistent to suppose the other; if the one can be inferred by no argument, and there is a probability for the other; if we see signs and effects indicating distinct finite agents like ourselves, and see no sign or symptom whatever that leads to a rational belief of matter. I say lastly, that I have a notion of spirit, though I have not, strictly speaking, an idea of it. I do not perceive it as an idea or by means of an idea, but know it by reflection.

Hyl. Notwithstanding all you have said, to me it seems, that according to your own way of thinking, and in consequence of your own principles, it should follow that you are only a system of floating ideas, without any substance to support them. Words are not to be used without a meaning. And as there is no more meaning in spiritual substance than in material substance, the one is to be exploded as well as the other.

Phil. How often must I repeat, that I know or am conscious of my own being ; and that I myself am not my ideas, but somewhat else, a thinking, active principle that perceives, knows, wills, and operates about ideas ? I know that I, one and the same self, perceive both colours and sounds : that a colour cannot perceive a sound, nor a sound a colour : that I am therefore one individual principle, distinct from colour and sound ; and, for the same reason, from all other sensible things and inert ideas. But I am not in like manner conscious either of the existence or essence of matter. On the contrary, I know that nothing inconsistent can exist, and that the existence of matter implies an inconsistency. Further, I know what I mean, when I affirm that there is a spiritual substance or support of ideas, that is, that a spirit knows and perceives ideas. But I do not know what is meant, when it is said, that an unperceiving substance hath inherent in it and supports either ideas or the archetypes of ideas. There is therefore upon the whole no parity of case between spirit and matter.

Hyl. I own myself satisfied in this point. But do you in earnest think, the real existence of sensible things consists in their being actually perceived ? If so, how comes it that all mankind distinguish between them ? Ask the first man you meet, and he shall tell you, *to be perceived* is one thing, and *to exist* is another.

Phil. I am content, Hylas, to appeal to the common sense of the world for the truth of my notion. Ask the gardener, why he thinks yonder cherry-tree exists in the garden, and he shall tell you, because he sees and feels it ; in a word, because he perceives it by his senses. Ask him, why he thinks an orange-tree not to be there, and he shall tell you, because he does not perceive it. What he perceives by sense, that he terms a real being, and saith it *is*, or *exists ;* but that which is not perceivable, the same, he saith, hath no being.

Hyl. Yes, Philonous, I grant the existence of a sensible thing consists in being perceivable, but not in being actually perceived.

Phil. And what is perceivable but an idea? And can an idea exist without being actually perceived? These are points long since agreed between us.

Hyl. But be your opinion never so true, yet surely you will not deny it is shocking, and contrary to the common sense of men. Ask the fellow, whether yonder tree hath an existence out of his mind: what answer, think you, he would make?

Phil. The same that I should myself, to wit, that it doth exist out of his mind. But then to a Christian it cannot surely be shocking to say, the real tree existing without his mind is truly known and comprehended by (that is, *exists in*) the infinite mind of God. Probably he may not at first glance be aware of the direct and immediate proof there is of this, inasmuch as the very being of a tree, or any other sensible thing, implies a mind wherein it is. But the point itself he cannot deny. The question between the materialists and me is not, whether things have a real existence out of the mind of this or that person, but whether they have an absolute existence, distinct from being perceived by God, and exterior to all minds. This indeed some heathens and philosophers have affirmed, but whoever entertains notions of the Deity suitable to the holy scriptures, will be of another opinion.

Hyl. But according to your notions, what difference is there between real things, and chimeras formed by the imagination, or the visions of a dream, since they are all equally in the mind?

Phil. The ideas formed by the imagination are faint and indistinct; they have besides an entire dependence on the will. But the ideas perceived by sense, that is, real things, are more vivid and clear, and being imprinted on the mind by a spirit distinct from us, have not a like dependence on our will. There is therefore no danger of confounding these with the foregoing: and there is as little of confounding them with the visions of a dream, which are dim, irregular, and confused. And though they should happen to be never so lively and natural, yet by their not being connected, and of a piece with the preceding and subsequent transactions of our lives, they might easily be distinguished from realities. In short, by whatever method you distinguish *things* from *chimeras* on your own scheme, the same, it is evident, will hold also upon mine. For it must be, I presume, by some perceived difference, and I am not for depriving you of any one thing that you perceive.

Hyl. But still, Philonous, you hold, there is nothing in the world but spirits and ideas. And this, you must needs acknowledge, sounds very oddly.

Phil. I own the word *idea*, not being commonly used for *thing*, sounds something out of the way. My reason for using it was, because a necessary relation to the mind is understood to be implied by that term; and it is now commonly used by philosophers, to denote the immediate objects of the understanding. But however oddly the proposition may sound in words, yet it includes nothing so very strange or shocking in its sense, which in effect amounts to no more than this, to wit, that there are only things perceiving, and things perceived; or that every unthinking being is necessarily, and from the very nature of its existence, perceived by some mind; if not by any finite created mind, yet certainly by the infinite mind of God, in whom " we live, and move, and have our being." Is this as strange as to say, the sensible qualities are not on the objects: or, that we cannot be sure of the existence of things, or know any thing of their real natures, though we both see and feel them, and perceive them by all our senses?

Hyl. And in consequence of this, must we not think there are no such things as physical or corporeal causes; but that a spirit is the immediate cause of all the phenomena in nature? Can there be any thing more extravagant than this?

Phil. Yes, it is infinitely more extravagant to say, a thing which is inert, operates on the mind, and which is unperceiving, is the cause of our perceptions. Besides, that which to you, I know not for what reason, seems so extravagant, is no more than the holy scriptures assert in a hundred places. In them God is represented as the sole and immediate author of all those effects, which some heathens and philosophers are wont to ascribe to nature, matter, fate, or the like unthinking principle. This is so much the constant language of scripture, that it were needless to confirm it by citations.

Hyl. You are not aware, Philonous, that in making God the immediate author of all the motions in nature, you make him the author of murder, sacrilege, adultery, and the like heinous sins.

Phil. In answer to that, I observe first, that the imputation of guilt is the same, whether a person commits an action with or without an instrument.   In case therefore you suppose God to act by the mediation of an instrument, or occasion, called *matter*, you as truly make him the author of sin as I, who think him the immediate agent in all those operations vulgarly ascribed to nature. I further observe, that sin or moral turpitude doth not consist in the outward physical action or motion, but in the internal deviation of the will from the laws of reason and religion.   This is plain, in that the killing an enemy in a battle, or putting a criminal legally to death, is not thought sinful, though the outward act be the very same with that in the case of murder.   Since therefore sin doth not consist in the physical action, the making God an immediate cause of all such actions, is not making him the author of sin.   Lastly, I have no where said that God is the only agent who produces all the motions in bodies.   It is true, I have denied there are any other agents beside spirits : but this is very consistent with allowing to thinking, rational beings, in the production of motions, the use of limited powers, ultimately indeed derived from God, but immediately under the direction of their own wills, which is sufficient to entitle them to all the guilt of their actions.

Hyl. But the denying matter, Philonous, or corporeal substance ; there is the point.   You can never persuade me that this is not repugnant to the universal sense of mankind.   Were our dispute to be determined by most voices, I am confident you would give up the point, without gathering the votes.

Phil. I wish both our opinions were fairly stated and submitted to the judgment of men who had plain common sense, without the prejudices of a learned education. Let me be represented as one who trusts his senses, who thinks he knows the things he sees and feels, and entertains no doubts of their existence ; and you fairly set forth with all your doubts, your paradoxes, and your scepticism about you, and I shall willingly acquiesce in the determination of any indifferent person. That there is no substance wherein ideas can exist beside spirit, is to me evident. And that the objects immediately perceived are ideas, is on all hands agreed. And that sensible qualities are objects immediately perceived, no one can deny. It is therefore evident there can be no *substratum* of those qualities but spirit, in which they exist, not by way of mode or property, but as a thing perceived in that which perceives it. I deny therefore that there is any unthinking *substratum* of the objects of sense, and in that acceptation that there is any material substance. But if by *material substance* is meant only sensible body, that which is seen and felt (and the un-philosophical part of the world, I dare say, mean no more), then I am more certain of matter's existence than you, or any other philosopher, pretend to be. If there be any thing which makes the generality of mankind averse from the notions I espouse, it is a misapprehension that I deny the reality of sensible things : but as it is you who are guilty of that and not I, it follows that in truth their aversion is against your notions, and not mine. I do therefore assert that I am as certain as of my own being, that there are bodies or corporeal substances (meaning the things I perceive by my senses) ; and that granting this, the bulk of mankind will take no thought about, nor think themselves at all concerned in the fate of those unknown natures, and philosophical quiddities, which some men are so fond of.

Hyl. What say you to this ? Since, according to you, men judge of the reality of things by their senses, how can a man be mistaken in thinking the moon a plain lucid surface, about a foot in diameter; or a square tower, seen at a distance, round; or an oar, with one end in the water, crooked?

Phil. He is not mistaken with regard to the ideas he actually perceives; but in the inferences he makes from his present perceptions. Thus in the case of the oar, what he immediately perceives by sight is certainly crooked; and so far he is in the right. But if he thence conclude, that upon taking the oar out of the water he shall perceive the same crookedness, or that it would affect his touch as crooked things are wont to do, in that he is mistaken. In like manner, if he should conclude from what he perceives in one station, that in case he advances toward the moon or tower, he should still be affected with the like ideas, he is mistaken. But his mistake lies not in what he perceives immediately and at present (it being a manifest contradiction to suppose he should err in respect of that), but in the wrong judgment he makes concerning the ideas he apprehends to be connected with those immediately perceived: or concerning the ideas that, from what he perceives at present, he imagines would be perceived in other circumstances. The case is the same with regard to the Copernican system. We do not here perceive any motion of the earth: but it were erroneous thence to conclude, that in case we were placed at as great a distance from that, as we are now from the other planets, we should not then perceive its motion.

Hyl. I understand you; and must needs own you say things plausible enough: but give me leave to put you in mind of one thing. Pray, Philonous, were you not formerly as positive that matter existed, as you are now that it does not?

Phil. I was. But here lies the difference. Before, my positiveness was founded without examination, upon prejudice; but now, after inquiry, upon evidence.

Hyl. After all, it seems our dispute is rather about words than things. We agree in the thing, but differ in the name. That we are affected with ideas from without is evident; and it is no less evident, that there must be (I will not say archetypes, but) powers without the mind, corresponding to those ideas. And as these powers cannot subsist by themselves, there is some subject of them necessarily to be admitted, which I call *matter*, and you call *spirit*. This is all the difference.

Phil. Pray, Hylas, is that powerful being, or subject of powers, extended?

Hyl. It hath not extension; but it hath the power to raise in you the idea of extension.

Phil. It is therefore itself unextended.

Hyl. I grant it.

Phil. Is it not also active?

Hyl. Without doubt: otherwise, how could we attribute powers to it?

Phil. Now let me ask you two questions: first, whether it be agreeable to the usage either of philosophers or others, to give the name *matter* to an unextended active being? And secondly, whether it be not ridiculously absurd to misapply names contrary to the common use of language?

Hyl. Well then, let it not be called matter, since you will have it so, but some *third nature* distinct from matter and spirit. For, what reason is there why you should call it spirit? Does not the notion of spirit imply, that it is thinking as well as active and unextended?

Phil. My reason is this: because I have a mind to have some notion or meaning in what I say; but I have no notion of any action distinct from volition, neither can I conceive volition to be any where but in a spirit: therefore when I speak of an active being, I am obliged to mean a spirit. Beside, what can be plainer than that a thing which hath no ideas in itself, cannot impart them to me; and if it hath ideas, surely it must be a spirit. To make you comprehend the point still more clearly, if it be possible: I assert as well as you, that since we are affected from without, we must allow powers to be without in a being distinct from ourselves. So far we are agreed. But then we differ as to the kind of this powerful being. I will have it to be spirit, you matter, or I know not what (I may add too, you know not what) third nature. Thus I prove it to be spirit. From the effects I see produced, I conclude there are actions; and because actions, volitions; and because there are volitions, there must be a will. Again, the things I perceive must have an existence, they or their archetypes, out of my mind : but being ideas, neither they nor their archetypes can exist otherwise than in an understanding : there is therefore an understanding. But will and understanding constitute in the strictest sense a mind or spirit. The powerful cause therefore of my ideas, is in strict propriety of speech a *spirit*.

Hyl. And now I warrant you think you have made the point very clear, little suspecting that what you advance leads directly to a contradiction. Is it not an absurdity to imagine any imperfection in God ?

Phil. Without doubt.

Hyl. To suffer pain is an imperfection.

Phil. It is.

Hyl. Are we not sometimes affected with pain and uneasiness by some other being ?

Phil. We are.

Hyl. And have you not said that being is a spirit, and is not that spirit God ?

Phil. I grant it.

Hyl. But you have asserted, that whatever ideas we perceive from without, are in the mind which affects us. The ideas therefore of pain and uneasiness are in God ; or in other words, God suffers pain : that is to say, there is an imperfection in the divine nature, which you acknowledged was absurd. So you are caught in a plain contradiction.

Phil. That God knows or understands all things, and that he knows among other things what pain is, even every sort of painful sensation, and what it is for his creatures to suffer pain, I make no question. But that God, though he knows and sometimes causes painful sensations in us, can himself suffer pain, I positively deny. We who are limited and dependent spirits, are liable to impressions of sense, the effects of an external agent, which being produced against our wills, are sometimes painful and uneasy. But God, whom no external being can affect, who perceives nothing by sense as we do, whose will is absolute and independent, causing all things, and liable to be thwarted or resisted by nothing ; it is evident, such a being as this can suffer nothing, nor be affected with any painful sensation, or indeed any sensation at all. We are chained to a body, that is to say, our perceptions are connected with corporeal motions. By the law of our nature we are affected upon every alteration in the nervous parts of our sensible body : which sensible body rightly considered, is nothing but a complexion of such qualities or ideas, as have no existence distinct from being perceived by a mind; so that this connexion of sensations with corporeal motions, means no more than a correspondence in the order of nature between two sets of ideas, or things immediately perceivable. But God is a pure spirit, disengaged from all such sympathy or natural ties. No corporeal motions are attended with the sensations of pain or pleasure in his mind. To know every thing knowable is certainly a perfection ; but to endure, or suffer, or feel any thing by sense, is an imperfection. The former, I say, agrees to God, but not the latter. God knows or hath ideas : but his ideas are not conveyed to him by sense, as ours are. Your not distinguishing where there is so manifest a difference, makes you fancy you see an absurdity where there is none.

Hyl. But all this while you have not considered, that the quantity of matter hath been demonstrated to be proportioned to the gravity of bodies. And what can withstand demonstration ?

Phil. Let me see how you demonstrate that point ?

Hyl. I lay it down for a principle, that the moments or quantities of motion in bodies, are in a direct compounded reason of the velocities and quantities of matter contained in them. Hence, where the velocities are equal, it follows, the moments are directly as the quantity of matter in each. But it is found by experience, that all bodies (bating the small inequalities arising from the resistance of the air) descend with an equal velocity ;

the motion therefore of descending bodies, and consequently their gravity, which is the cause or principle of that motion, is proportional to the quantity of matter : which was to be demonstrated.

Phil. You lay it down as a self-evident principle, that the quantity of motion in any body is proportional to the velocity and *matter* taken together : and this is made use of to prove a proposition, from whence the existence of *matter* is inferred. Pray is not this arguing in a circle ?

Hyl. In the premise I only mean, that the motion is proportional to the velocity, jointly with the extension and solidity.

Phil. But allowing this to be true, yet it will not thence follow, that gravity is proportional to *matter*, in your philosophic sense of the word ; except you take it for granted, that unknown *substratum*, or whatever else you call it, is proportional to those sensible qualities ; which to suppose is plainly begging the question. That there is magnitude, and solidity, or resistance, perceived by sense, I readily grant ; as likewise that gravity may be proportional to those qualities, I will not dispute. But that either these qualities as perceived by us, or the powers producing them, do exist in a *material substratum ;* this is what I deny, and you indeed affirm, but notwithstanding your demonstration, have not yet proved.

Hyl. I shall insist no longer on that point. Do you think, however, you shall persuade me that natural philosophers have been dreaming all this while? pray what becomes of all their hypotheses and explications of the phenomena, which suppose the existence of matter?

Phil. What mean you, Hylas, by the phenomena ?

Hyl. I mean the appearances which I perceive by my senses.

Phil. And the appearances perceived by sense, are they not ideas?

Hyl. I have told you so a hundred times.

Phil. Therefore, to explain the phenomena, is to show

how we come to be affected with ideas, in that manner and order wherein they are imprinted on our senses. Is it not?

Hyl. It is.

Phil. Now if you can prove, that any philosopher hath explained the production of any one idea in our minds by the help of *matter*, I shall for ever acquiesce, and look on all that hath been said against it as nothing: but if you cannot, it is in vain to urge the explication of phenomena. That a being endowed with knowledge and will, should produce or exhibit ideas, is easily understood. But that a being which is utterly destitute of these faculties should be able to produce ideas, or in any sort to affect an intelligence, this I can never understand. This I say, though we had some positive conception of matter, though we knew its qualities, and could comprehend its existence, would yet be so far from explaining things, that it is itself the most inexplicable thing in the world. And yet for all this, it will not follow, that philosophers have been doing nothing; for by observing and reasoning upon the connexion of ideas, they discover the laws and methods of nature, which is a part of knowledge both useful and entertaining.

Hyl. After all, can it be supposed God would deceive all mankind? Do you imagine, he would have induced the whole world to believe the being of matter, if there was no such thing?

Phil. That every epidemical opinion arising from prejudice, or passion, or thoughtlessness, may be imputed to God, as the author of it, I believe you will not affirm. Whatsoever opinion we father on him, it must be either because he has discovered it to us by supernatural revelation, or because it is so evident to our natural faculties, which were framed and given us by God, that it is impossible we should withhold our assent from it. But where is the revelation, or where is the evidence that extorts the belief of matter? Nay, how does it appear that matter, taken for something distinct from what we perceive by our senses, is thought to exist by all mankind, or indeed by any except a few philosophers, who

do not know what they would be at? Your question
supposes these points are clear; and when you have
cleared them, I shall think myself obliged to give you
another answer. In the mean time let it suffice that
I tell you, I do not suppose God has deceived mankind at all.

Hyl. But the novelty, Philonous, the novelty! There
lies the danger. New notions should always be discountenanced; they unsettle men's minds, and nobody
knows where they will end.

Phil. Why the rejecting a notion that hath no foundation either in sense, or in reason, or in divine authority,
should be thought to unsettle the belief of such opinions
as are grounded on all or any of these, I cannot imagine.
That innovations in government and religion are dangerous, and ought to be discountenanced, I freely own. But
is there the like reason why they should be discouraged
in philosophy? The making any thing known which
was unknown before, is an innovation in knowledge:
and if all such innovations had been forbidden, men
would have made a notable progress in the arts and
sciences. But it is none of my business to plead for
novelties and paradoxes. That the qualities we perceive
are not on the objects: that we must not believe our
senses: that we know nothing of the real nature of
things, and can never be assured even of their existence:
that real colours and sounds are nothing but certain unknown figures and motions: that motions are in themselves neither swift nor slow: that there are in bodies
absolute extensions, without any particular magnitude
or figure: that a thing stupid, thoughtless, and inactive,
operates on a spirit: that the least particle of a body
contains innumerable extended parts. These are the
novelties, these are the strange notions which shock the
genuine uncorrupted judgment of all mankind; and being
once admitted, embarrass the mind with endless doubts
and difficulties. And it is against these and the like
innovations, I endeavour to vindicate common sense.
It is true, in doing this, I may perhaps be obliged to use
some *ambages*, and ways of speech not common. But

if my notions are once thoroughly understood, that which is most singular in them will in effect be found to amount to no more than this : that it is absolutely impossible, and a plain contradiction to suppose, any unthinking being should exist without being perceived by a mind. And if this notion be singular, it is a shame it should be so at this time of day, and in a Christian country.

Hyl. As for the difficulties other opinions may be liable to, those are out of the question. It is your business to defend your own opinion. Can any thing be plainer, than that you are for changing all things into ideas? You, I say, who are not ashamed to charge me with *scepticism*. This is so plain, there is no denying it.

Phil. You mistake me. I am not for changing things into ideas, but rather ideas into things; since those immediate objects of perception, which, according to you, are only appearances of things, I take to be the real things themselves.

Hyl. Things! you may pretend what you please; but it is certain, you leave us nothing but the empty forms of things, the outside only which strikes the senses.

Phil. What you call the empty forms and outside of things, seems to me the very things themselves. Nor are they empty or incomplete otherwise, than upon your supposition, that matter is an essential part of all corporeal things. We both therefore agree in this, that we perceive only sensible forms : but herein we differ, you will have them to be empty appearances, I real beings. In short you do not trust your senses, I do.

Hyl. You say you believe your senses; and seem to applaud yourself that in this you agree with the vulgar. According to you therefore, the true nature of a thing is discovered by the senses. If so, whence comes that disagreement? Why is not the same figure, and other sensible qualities, perceived all manner of ways? and why should we use a microscope, the better to discover the true nature of a body, if it were discoverable to the naked eye?

Phil. Strictly speaking, Hylas, we do not see the same object that we feel; neither is the same object perceived by the microscope, which was by the naked eye. But in case every variation was thought sufficient to constitute a new kind or individual, the endless number or confusion of names would render language impracticable. Therefore to avoid this as well as other inconveniences which are obvious upon a little thought, men combine together several ideas, apprehended by divers senses, or by the same sense at different times, or in different circumstances, but observed however to have some connexion in nature, either with respect to co-existence or succession; all which they refer to one name, and consider as one thing. Hence it follows that when I examine by my other senses a thing I have seen, it is not in order to understand better the same object which I had perceived by sight, the object of one sense not being perceived by the other senses. And when I look through a microscope, it is not that I may perceive more clearly what I perceived already with my bare eyes, the object perceived by the glass being quite different from the former. But in both cases my aim is only to know what ideas are connected together; and the more a man knows of the connexion of ideas, the more he is said to know of the nature of things. What therefore if our ideas are variable? What if our senses are not in all circumstances affected with the same appearances? It will not thence follow, they are not to be trusted, or that they are inconsistent either with themselves or any thing else, except it be with your preconceived notion of (I know not what) one single, unchanged, unperceivable, real nature, marked by each name: which prejudice seems to have taken its rise from not rightly understanding the common language of men speaking of several distinct ideas, as united into one thing by the mind. And indeed there is cause to suspect several erroneous conceits of the philosophers are owing to the same original: while they began to build their schemes, not so much on notions as words, which were framed by the vulgar, merely for conveniency and despatch in the common actions of life, without any regard to speculation.

Hyl. Methinks I apprehend your meaning.

Phil. It is your opinion, the ideas we perceive by our senses are not real things, but images, or copies of them. Our knowledge therefore is no further real, than as our ideas are the true representations of those originals. But as these supposed originals are in themselves unknown, it is impossible to know how far our ideas resemble them; or whether they resemble them at all. We cannot therefore be sure we have any real knowledge. Further, as our ideas are perpetually varied, without any change in the supposed real things, it necessarily follows they cannot all be true copies of them; or if some are, and others are not, it is impossible to distinguish the former from the latter. And this plunges us yet deeper in uncertainty. Again, when we consider the point, we cannot conceive how any idea, or any thing like an idea, should have an absolute existence out of a mind; nor consequently, according to you, how there should be any real thing in nature. The result of all which is, that we are thrown into the most hopeless and abandoned *scepticism*. Now give me leave to ask you, first, whether your referring ideas to certain absolutely existing unperceived substances, as their originals, be not the source of all this *scepticism?* Secondly, whether you are informed, either by sense or reason, of the existence of those unknown originals? And in case you are not, whether it be not absurd to suppose them? Thirdly, whether upon inquiry, you find there is any thing distinctly conceived or meant by the *absolute or external existence of unperceiving substances?* Lastly, whether, the premises considered, it be not the wisest way to follow nature, trust your senses, and laying aside all anxious thought about unknown natures or substances, admit with the vulgar those for real things, which are perceived by the senses?

Hyl. For the present, I have no inclination to the answering part. I would much rather see how you can get over what follows. Pray are not the objects perceived by the senses of one, likewise perceivable to others present? If there were a hundred more here,

they would all see the garden, the trees, and flowers as I
see them. But they are not in the same manner affected
with the ideas I frame in my imagination. Does not
this make a difference between the former sort of objects
and the latter?

Phil. I grant it does. Nor have I ever denied a
difference between the objects of sense and those of
imagination. But what would you infer from thence?
You cannot say that sensible objects exist unperceived,
because they are perceived by many.

Hyl. I own, I can make nothing of that objection:
but it hath led me into another. Is it not your opinion
that by our senses we perceive only the ideas existing in
our minds?

Phil. It is.

Hyl. But the same idea which is in my mind, cannot
be in yours, or in any other mind. Doth it not therefore follow from your principles, that no two can see
the same thing? And is not this highly absurd?

Phil. If the term *same* be taken in the vulgar acceptation, it is certain (and not at all repugnant to the
principles I maintain) that different persons may perceive
the same thing; or the same thing or idea exist in different minds. Words are of arbitrary imposition; and
since men are used to apply the word *same* where no
distinction or variety is perceived, and I do not pretend
to alter their perceptions, it follows, that as men have
said before, *several saw the same thing*, so they may upon
like occasions still continue to use the same phrase,
without any deviation either from propriety of language,
or the truth of things. But if the term *same* be used in
the acceptation of philosophers, who pretend to an abstracted notion of identity, then, according to their
sundry definitions of this notion (for it is not yet agreed
wherein that philosophic identity consists), it may or
may not be possible for divers persons to perceive the
same thing. But whether philosophers shall think fit to
call a thing the *same* or no, is, I conceive, of small importance. Let us suppose several men together, all
endued with the same faculties, and consequently

*L 483

affected in like sort by their senses, and who had yet never known the use of language; they would without question agree in their perceptions. Though perhaps, when they came to the use of speech, some regarding the uniformness of what was perceived, might call it the *same* thing: others especially regarding the diversity of persons who perceived, might choose the denomination of different things. But who sees not that all the dispute is about a word; to wit, whether what is perceived by different persons, may yet have the term *same* applied to it? Or suppose a house, whose walls or outward shell remaining unaltered, the chambers are all pulled down, and new ones built in their place; and that you should call this the *same*, and I should say it was not the *same* house: would we not for all this perfectly agree in our thoughts of the house, considered in itself? And would not all the difference consist in a sound? If you should say, we differ in our notions; for that you superadded to your idea of the house the simple abstracted idea of identity, whereas I did not; I would tell you I know not what you mean by that *abstracted idea of identity;* and should desire you to look into your own thoughts, and be sure you understood yourself.——Why so silent, Hylas? Are you not yet satisfied, men may dispute about identity and diversity, without any real difference in their thoughts and opinions, abstracted from names? Take this further reflection with you: that whether matter be allowed to exist or no, the case is exactly the same as to the point in hand. For the materialists themselves acknowledge what we immediately perceive by our senses to be our own ideas. Your difficulty therefore, that no two see the same thing, makes equally against the materialists and me.

Hyl. But they suppose an external archetype, to which referring their several ideas, they may truly be said to perceive the same thing.

Phil. And (not to mention your having discovered those archetypes) so may you suppose an external archetype on my principles: *external,* I mean, to your own mind; though indeed it must be supposed to exist in that mind which comprehends all things; but then this serves all the ends of identity, as well as if it existed out of a mind. And I am sure you yourself will not say, it is less intelligible.

Hyl. You have indeed clearly satisfied me, either that there is no difficulty at bottom in this point; or if there be, that it makes equally against both opinions.

Phil. But that which makes equally against two contradictory opinions, can be a proof against neither.

Hyl. I acknowledge it. But after all, Philonous, when I consider the substance of what you advance against scepticism, it amounts to no more than this. We are sure that we really see, hear, feel; in a word, that we are affected with sensible impressions.

Phil. And how are we concerned any further? I see this *cherry*, I feel it, I taste it: and I am sure *nothing* cannot be seen, or felt, or tasted: it is therefore *real*. Take away the sensations of softness, moisture, redness, tartness, and you take away the *cherry*. Since it is not a being distinct from sensations; a *cherry*, I say, is nothing but a congeries of sensible impressions, or ideas perceived by various senses; which ideas are united into one thing (or have one name given them) by the mind; because they are observed to attend each other. Thus when the palate is affected with such a particular taste, the sight is affected with a red colour, the touch with roundness, softness, &c. Hence, when I see, and feel, and taste, in sundry certain manners, I am sure the *cherry* exists, or is real; its reality being in my opinion nothing abstracted from those sensations. But if by the word *cherry* you mean an unknown nature distinct from all those sensible qualities, and by its existence something distinct from its being perceived; then indeed I own, neither you, nor I, nor any one else can be sure it exists.

Hyl. But what would you say, Philonous, if I should bring the very same reasons against the existence of sensible things in a mind, which you have offered against their existing in a material *substratum?*

Phil. When I see your reasons, you shall hear what I have to say to them.

Hyl. Is the mind extended or unextended?

Phil. Unextended, without doubt.

Hyl. Do you say the things you perceive are in your mind?

Phil. They are.

Hyl. Again, have I not heard you speak of sensible impressions?

Phil. I believe you may.

Hyl. Explain to me now, O Philonous! how it is possible there should be room for all those trees and houses to exist in your mind. Can extended things be contained in that which is unextended? or are we to imagine impressions made on a thing void of all solidity? You cannot say objects are in your mind, as books in your study: or that things are imprinted on it, as the figure of a seal upon wax. In what sense therefore are we to understand those expressions? Explain me this if you can: and I shall then be able to answer all those queries you formerly put to me about my substratum.

Phil. Look you, Hylas, when I speak of objects as existing in the mind or imprinted on the senses, I would not be understood in the gross literal sense, as when bodies are said to exist in a place, or a seal to make an impression upon wax. My meaning is only that the mind comprehends or perceives them; and that it is affected from without, or by some being distinct from itself. This is my explication of your difficulty; and how it can serve to make your tenet of an unperceiving material substratum intelligible, I would fain know.

Hyl. Nay, if that be all, I confess I do not see what use can be made of it. But are you not guilty of some abuse of language in this?

Phil. None at all: it is no more than common custom, which you know is the rule of language, hath authorized: nothing being more usual, than for philosophers to speak of the immediate objects of the understanding as things existing in the mind. Nor is there any thing in this, but what is conformable to the general analogy of language; most part of the mental operations being signi-

fied by words borrowed from sensible things; as is plain
in the terms *comprehend, reflect, discourse,* &c., which
being applied to the mind, must not be taken in their
gross original sense.

Hyl. You have, I own, satisfied me in this point; but
there still remains one great difficulty, which I know not
how you will get over. And, indeed, it is of such importance, that if you could solve all others, without
being able to find a solution for this, you must never
expect to make me a proselyte to your principles.

Phil. Let me know this mighty difficulty.

Hyl. The scripture account of the creation is what
appears to me utterly irreconcilable with your notions.
Moses tells us of a creation: a creation of what? of
ideas? No, certainly, but of things, of real things, solid
corporeal substances. Bring your principles to agree
with this, and I shall perhaps agree with you.

Phil. Moses mentions the sun, moon, and stars, earth
and sea, plants and animals: that all these do really
exist, and were in the beginning created by God, I make
no question. If by *ideas* you mean fictions and fancies
of the mind, then these are no ideas. If by *ideas* you
mean immediate objects of the understanding, or sensible things which cannot exist unperceived, or out of a
mind, then these things are ideas. But whether you do
or do not call them *ideas*, it matters little. The difference is only about a name. And whether that name be
retained or rejected, the sense, the truth, and reality of
things continues the same. In common talk, the objects
of our senses are not termed *ideas*, but *things.* Call
them so still; provided you do not attribute to them
any absolute external existence, and I shall never quarrel
with you for a word. The creation, therefore, I allow
to have been a creation of things, of *real* things.
Neither is this in the least inconsistent with my principles, as is evident from what I have now said; and
would have been evident to you without this, if you had
not forgotten what had been so often said before. But
as for solid corporeal substances, I desire you to show
where Moses makes any mention of them; and if they

should be mentioned by him, or any other inspired writer, it would still be incumbent on you to show those words were not taken in the vulgar acceptation, for things falling under our senses, but in the philosophic acceptation, for matter, or an unknown quiddity, with an absolute existence. When you have proved these points, then (and not till then) may you bring the authority of Moses into our dispute.

Hyl. It is in vain to dispute about a point so clear. I am content to refer it to your own conscience. Are you not satisfied there is some peculiar repugnancy between the Mosaic account of the creation and your notions?

Phil. If all possible sense, which can be put on the first chapter of Genesis, may be conceived as consistently with my principles as any other, then it has no peculiar repugnancy with them. But there is no sense you may not as well conceive, believing as I do. Since, beside spirits, all you conceive are ideas, and the existence of these I do not deny. Neither do you pretend they exist without the mind.

Hyl. Pray let me see any sense you can understand it in.

Phil. Why I imagine that if I had been present at the creation, I should have seen things produced into being; that is, become perceptible, in the order described by the sacred historian. I ever before believed the Mosaic account of the creation, and now find no alteration in my manner of believing it. When things are said to begin or end their existence, we do not mean this with regard to God, but his creatures. All objects are eternally known by God, or, which is the same thing, have an eternal existence in his mind: but when things before imperceptible to creatures, are by a decree of God, made perceptible to them; then are they said to begin a relative existence with respect to created minds. Upon reading therefore the Mosaic account of the creation, I understand that the several parts of the world became gradually perceivable to finite spirits, endowed with proper faculties; so that, whoever such were present, they were in truth per-

ceived by them. This is the literal, obvious sense
suggested to me by the words of the holy scripture:
in which is included no mention or no thought, either
of substratum, instrument, occasion, or absolute existence.
And upon inquiry, I doubt not it will be found, that most
plain, honest men, who believe the creation, never think
of those things any more than I. What metaphysical
sense you may understand it in, you only can tell.

Hyl. But, Philonous, you do not seem to be aware,
that you allow created things in the beginning only a
relative, and, consequently, hypothetical being; that is
to say, upon supposition there were men to perceive
them, without which they have no actuality of absolute existence, wherein creation might terminate. Is
it not, therefore, according to you plainly impossible,
the creation of any inanimate creatures should precede
that of man? And is not this directly contrary to the
Mosaic account?

Phil. In answer to that I say, first, created beings
might begin to exist in the mind of other created intelligences, beside men. You will not therefore be
able to prove any contradiction between Moses and
my notions, unless you first show, there was no other
order of finite created spirits in being before man. I
say further, in case we conceive the creation, as we
should at this time a parcel of plants or vegetables
of all sorts, produced by an invisible power, in a
desert where nobody was present: that this way of
explaining or conceiving it, is consistent with my principles, since they deprive you of nothing, either sensible
or imaginable: that it exactly suits with the common,
natural, undebauched notions of mankind: that it mani-
fests the dependence of all things on God; and consequently hath all the good effect or influence, which it
is possible that important article of our faith should
have in making men humble, thankful, and resigned
to their Creator. I say moreover, that in this naked
conception of things, divested of words, there will not
be found any notion of what you call the *actuality of
absolute existence.* You may indeed raise a dust with

those terms, and so lengthen our dispute to no purpose. But I entreat you calmly to look into your own thoughts, and then tell me if they are not a useless and unintelligible jargon.

Hyl. I own I have no very clear notion annexed to them. But what say you to this? Do you not make the existence of sensible things consist in their being in a mind? and were not all things eternally in the mind of God? Did they not therefore exist from all eternity, according to you? And how could that which was eternal be created in time? Can any thing be clearer or better connected than this?

Phil. And are not you too of opinion, that God knew all things from eternity?

Hyl. I am.

Phil. Consequently they always had a being in the divine intellect.

Hyl. This I acknowledge.

Phil. By your own confession therefore, nothing is new, or begins to be, in respect of the mind of God. So we are agreed in that point.

Hyl. What shall we make then of the creation?

Phil. May we not understand it to have been entirely in respect of finite spirits; so that things, with regard to us, may properly be said to begin their existence, or be created, when God decreed they should become perceptible to intelligent creatures, in that order and manner which he then established, and we now call the laws of nature? You may call this a *relative*, or *hypothetical existence* if you please. But so long as it supplies us with the most natural, obvious, and literal sense of the Mosaic history of the creation; so long as it answers all the religious ends of that great article; in a word, so long as you can assign no other sense or meaning in its stead; why should we reject this? Is it to comply with a ridiculous sceptical humour of making every thing nonsense and unintelligible? I am sure you cannot say it is for the glory of God. For allowing it to be a thing possible and conceivable, that the corporeal world should have an absolute sub-

sistence extrinsical to the mind of God, as well as to
the minds of all created spirits: yet how could this
set forth either the immensity or omniscience of the
Deity, or the necessary and immediate dependence of
all things on him? Nay, would it not rather seem to
derogate from those attributes?

Hyl. Well, but as to this decree of God's, for making
things perceptible: what say you, Philonous, is it not
plain, God did either execute that decree from all
eternity, or at some certain time began to will what
he had not actually willed before, but only designed
to will? If the former, then there could be no creation or beginning of existence in finite things. If the
latter, then we must acknowledge something new to
befall the Deity; which implies a sort of change; and
all change argues imperfection.

Phil. Pray consider what you are doing. Is it not
evident, this objection concludes equally against a creation in any sense; nay, against every other act of the
Deity, discoverable by the light of nature? None of
which can we conceive, otherwise than as performed
in time, and having a beginning. God is a being of
transcendent and unlimited perfections: his nature
therefore is incomprehensible to finite spirits. It is not
therefore to be expected, that any man, whether *mate-
rialist* or *immaterialist*, should have exactly just notions
of the Deity, his attributes, and ways of operation. If
then you would infer any thing against me, your difficulty must not be drawn from the inadequateness of our
conceptions of the divine nature, which is unavoidable
on any scheme: but from the denial of matter, of which
there is not one word, directly or indirectly, in what you
have now objected.

Hyl. I must acknowledge the difficulties you are
concerned to clear, are such only as arise from the
non-existence of matter, and are peculiar to that notion.
So far you are in the right. But I cannot by any means
bring myself to think there is no such peculiar repugnancy between the creation and your opinion; though
indeed where to fix it, I do not distinctly know.

Phil. What would you have? Do I not acknowledge a twofold state of things, the one ectypal or natural, the other archetypal and eternal? The former was created in time; the latter existed from everlasting in the mind of God. Is not this agreeable to the common notions of divines? or is any more than this necessary in order to conceive the creation? But you suspect some peculiar repugnancy, though you know not where it lies. To take away all possibility of scruple in the case, do but consider this one point. Either you are not able to conceive the creation on any hypothesis whatsoever; and if so, there is no ground for dislike or complaint against my particular opinion on that score: or you are able to conceive it; and if so, why not on my principles, since thereby nothing conceivable is taken away? You have all along been allowed the full scope of sense, imagination, and reason. Whatever therefore you could before apprehend, either immediately or mediately by your senses, or by ratiocination from your senses; whatever you could perceive, imagine, or understand, remains still with you. If therefore the notion you have of the creation by other principles be intelligible, you have it still upon mine; if it be not intelligible, I conceive it to be no notion at all; and so there is no loss of it. And indeed it seems to me very plain, that the supposition of matter, that is, a thing perfectly unknown and inconceivable, cannot serve to make us conceive any thing. And I hope, it need not be proved to you, that if the existence of matter doth not make the creation conceivable, the creation's being without it inconceivable, can be no objection against its non-existence.

Hyl. I confess, Philonous, you have almost satisfied me in this point of the creation.

Phil. I would fain know why you are not quite satisfied. You tell me indeed of a repugnancy between the Mosaic history and immaterialism: but you know not where it lies. Is this reasonable, Hylas? Can you expect I should solve a difficulty without knowing what it is? But to pass by all that, would not a man think

you were assured there is no repugnancy between the
received notions of materialists and the inspired writings?

Hyl. And so I am.

Phil. Ought the historical part of scripture to be understood in a plain, obvious sense, or in a sense which is
metaphysical and out of the way?

Hyl. In the plain sense, doubtless.

Phil. When Moses speaks of herbs, earth, water, &c.,
as having been created by God; think you not the sensible things, commonly signified by those words, are suggested to every unphilosophical reader?

Hyl. I cannot help thinking so.

Phil. And are not all ideas, or things perceived by
sense, to be denied a real existence by the doctrine of
the materialists?

Hyl. This I have already acknowledged.

Phil. The creation therefore, according to them, was
not the creation of things sensible, which have only a
relative being, but of certain unknown natures, which
have an absolute being, wherein creation might terminate.

Hyl. True.

Phil. Is it not therefore evident, the asserters of
matter destroy the plain obvious sense of Moses, with
which their notions are utterly inconsistent; and instead
of it obtrude on us I know not what, something equally
unintelligible to themselves and me.

Hyl. I cannot contradict you.

Phil. Moses tells us of a creation. A creation of
what? of unknown quiddities, of occasions, or sub-
stratums? No, certainly; but of things obvious to the
senses. You must first reconcile this with your notions,
if you expect I should be reconciled to them.

Hyl. I see you can assault me with my own weapons.

Phil. Then as to *absolute existence;* was there ever
known a more jejune notion than that? Something
it is, so abstracted and unintelligible, that you have
frankly owned you could not conceive it, much less
explain any thing by it. But allowing matter to exist,
and the notion of absolute existence to be as clear as

light, yet was this ever known to make the creation more credible? Nay, hath it not furnished the atheists and infidels of all ages with the most plausible argument against a creation? That a corporeal substance, which hath an absolute existence without the minds of spirits, should be produced out of nothing by the mere will of a spirit, hath been looked upon as a thing so contrary to all reason, so impossible and absurd, that not only the most celebrated among the ancients, but even divers modern and Christian philosophers, have thought matter co-eternal with the Deity. Lay these things together, and then judge you whether materialism disposes men to believe the creation of things.

Hyl. I own, Philonous, I think it does not. This of the *creation* is the last objection I can think of; and I must needs own it hath been sufficiently answered as well as the rest. Nothing now remains to be overcome, but a sort of unaccountable backwardness that I find in myself toward your notions.

Phil. When a man is swayed, he knows not why, to one side of a question, can this, think you, be any thing else but the effect of prejudice, which never fails to attend old and rooted notions? And indeed in this respect I cannot deny the belief of matter to have very much the advantage over the contrary opinion, with men of a learned education.

Hyl. I confess it seems to be as you say.

Phil. As a balance therefore to this weight of prejudice, let us throw into the scale the great advantages that arise from the belief of immaterialism, both in regard to religion and human learning. The being of a God, and incorruptibility of the soul, those great articles of religion, are they not proved with the clearest and most immediate evidence? When I say the being of a *God*, I do not mean an obscure, general cause of things, whereof we have no conception, but *God*, in the strict and proper sense of the word. A being whose spirituality, omnipresence, providence, omniscience, infinite power, and goodness, are as conspicuous as the existence of sensible things, of which (notwithstanding the fallacious pretences and affected scruples of sceptics) there is no more reason to doubt than of our own being. Then with relation to human sciences; in natural philosophy, what intricacies, what obscurities, what contradictions, hath the belief of matter led men into ! To say nothing of the numberless disputes about its extent, continuity, homogeneity, gravity, divisibility, &c., do they not pretend to explain all things by bodies operating on bodies, according to the laws of motion? and yet, are they able to comprehend how any one body should move another? Nay, admitting there was no difficulty in reconciling the notion of an inert being with a cause; or in conceiving how an accident might pass from one body to another; yet by all their strained thoughts and extravagant suppositions, have they been able to reach the mechanical production of any one animal or vegetable body? Can they account by the laws of motion, for sounds, tastes, smells, or colours, or for the regular course of things? Have they accounted by physical principles for the aptitude and contrivance, even of the most inconsiderable parts of the universe? But laying aside matter and corporeal causes, and admitting only the efficiency of an all-perfect mind, are not all the effects of nature easy and intelligible? If the phenomena are nothing else but *ideas;* God is a *spirit,* but matter an unintelligent, unperceiving being. If they demonstrate an unlimited power in their cause; God is active and omnipotent, but matter an inert mass. If the order, regularity, and usefulness of them can never be sufficiently admired; God is infinitely wise and provident, but matter destitute of all contrivance and design. These surely are great advantages in *physics.* Not to mention that the apprehension of a distant Deity naturally disposes men to a negligence in their *moral* actions, which they would be more cautious of in case they thought him immediately present, and acting on their minds without the interposition of matter, or unthinking second causes. Then in *metaphysics;* what difficulties concerning entity in abstract, substantial forms, hylarchic principles, plastic natures, substance and accident, principle of individuation, possibility of matter's thinking, origin of ideas, the manner how two independent substances, so widely different as *spirit* and *matter*, should mutually operate on each other! what difficulties, I say, and endless disquisitions concerning these and innumerable other the like points, do we escape by supposing only spirits and ideas? Even the *mathematics* themselves, if we take away the absolute existence of extended things, become much more clear and easy; the most shocking paradoxes and intricate speculations in those sciences, depending on the infinite divisibility of finite extension, which depends on that supposition. But what need is there to insist on the particular sciences? Is not that opposition to all science whatsoever, that frenzy of the ancient and modern sceptics, built on the same foundation? Or can you produce so much as one argument against the reality of corporeal things, or in behalf of that avowed utter ignorance of their natures, which doth not suppose their reality to consist in an external absolute existence. Upon this supposition indeed, the objections from the change of colours in a pigeon's neck, or the appearances of a broken oar in the water, must be allowed to have weight. But those and the like objections vanish, if we do not maintain the being of absolute external originals, but place the reality of things in ideas, fleeting indeed, and changeable; however not changed at random, but according to the fixed order of nature. For herein consists that constancy and truth of things, which secures all the concerns of life, and distinguishes that which is *real* from the irregular visions of the fancy.

Hyl. I agree to all you have now said, and must own that nothing can incline me to embrace your opinion, more than the advantages I see it is attended with. I am by nature lazy, and this would be a mighty abridgment in knowledge. What doubts, what hypotheses, what labyrinths of amusement, what fields of disputation, what an ocean of false learning, may be avoided by that single notion of *immaterialism* !

Phil. After all, is there any thing further remaining

to be done? You may remember you promised to embrace that opinion which upon examination should appear most agreeable to common sense, and remote from scepticism. This, by your own confession, is that which denies matter, or the absolute existence of corporeal things. Nor is this all; the same notion has been proved several ways, viewed in different lights, pursued in its consequences, and all objections against it cleared. Can there be a greater evidence of its truth? or is it possible it should have all the marks of a true opinion, and yet be false?

Hyl. I own myself entirely satisfied for the present in all respects. But what security can I have that I shall still continue the same full assent to your opinion, and that no unthought-of objection or difficulty will occur hereafter?

Phil. Pray, Hylas, do you in other cases, when a point is once evidently proved, withhold your assent on account of objections or difficulties it may be liable to? Are the difficulties that attend the doctrine of incommensurable quantities, of the angle of contact, of the asymptotes to curves, or the like, sufficient to make you hold out against mathematical demonstration? Or will you disbelieve the providence of God, because there may be some particular things which you know not how to reconcile with it? If there are difficulties attending immaterialism, there are at the same time direct and evident proofs for it. But for the existence of matter there is not one proof, and far more numerous and insurmountable objections lie against it. But where are those mighty difficulties you insist on? Alas! you know not where or what they are; something which may possibly occur hereafter. If this be a sufficient pretence for withholding your full assent, you should never yield it to any proposition, how free soever from exceptions, how clearly and solidly soever demonstrated.

Hyl. You have satisfied me, Philonous.

Phil. But to arm you against all future objections, do but consider, that which bears equally hard on two contradictory opinions, can be a proof against neither.

Whenever therefore any difficulty occurs, try if you can
find a solution for it on the hypothesis of the *materialists*. Be not deceived by words; but sound your
own thoughts. And in case you cannot conceive it
easier by the help of *materialism*, it is plain it can be
no objection against *immaterialism*. Had you proceeded all along by this rule, you would probably have
spared yourself abundance of trouble in objecting; since
of all your difficulties I challenge you to show one that
is explained by matter; nay, which is not more unintelligible with, than without that supposition, and consequently makes rather *against* than *for* it. You should
consider in each particular, whether the difficulty arises
from the *non-existence of matter*. If it doth not, you
might as well argue from the infinite divisibility of
extension against the divine prescience, as from such
a difficulty against *immaterialism*. And yet upon recol-
lection I believe you will find this to have been often,
if not always the case. You should likewise take heed
not to argue on a *petitio principii*. One is apt to say,
the unknown substances ought to be esteemed real
things, rather than the ideas in our minds : and who
can tell but the unthinking external substance may
concur as a cause or instrument in the production of
our ideas? But is not this proceeding on a supposition that there are such external substances? And to
suppose this, is it not begging the question? But above
all things you should beware of imposing on yourself
by that vulgar sophism, which is called *ignoratio elenchi*.
You talked often as if you thought I maintained the
non-existence of sensible things : whereas in truth no
one can be more thoroughly assured of their existence
than I am, and it is you who doubt; I should have
said, positively deny it. Every thing that is seen, felt,
heard, or any way perceived by the senses, is, on the
principles I embrace, a real being, but not on yours.
Remember the matter you contend for is an unknown
somewhat (if indeed it may be termed *somewhat*), which
is quite stripped of all sensible qualities, and can neither
be perceived by sense, nor apprehended by the mind.

Remember, I say, that it is not any object which is hard or soft, hot or cold, blue or white, round or square, &c. For all these things I affirm do exist. Though indeed I deny they have any existence distinct from being perceived; or that they exist out of all minds whatsoever. Think on these points; let them be attentively considered and still kept in view. Otherwise you will not comprehend the state of the question; without which your objections will always be wide of the mark, and instead of mine, may possibly be directed (as more than once they have been) against your own notions.

Hyl. I must needs own, Philonous, nothing seems to have kept me from agreeing with you more than this same *mistaking the question.* In denying matter, at first glimpse I am tempted to imagine you deny the things we see and feel; but upon reflection find there is no ground for it. What think you therefore of retaining the name *matter*, and applying it to sensible things? This may be done without any change in your sentiments: and believe me it would be a means of reconciling them to some persons, who may be more shocked at an innovation in words than in opinion.

Phil. With all my heart: retain the word *matter*, and apply it to the objects of sense, if you please, provided you do not attribute to them any subsistence distinct from their being perceived. I shall never quarrel with you for an expression. *Matter*, or *material substance*, are terms introduced by philosophers; and as used by them, imply a sort of independency, or a subsistence distinct from being perceived by a mind: but are never used by common people; or if ever, it is to signify the immediate objects of sense. One would think therefore, so long as the names of all particular things, with the terms *sensible*, *substance*, *body*, *stuff*, and the like, are retained, the word *matter* should be never missed in common talk. And in philosophical discourses it seems the best way to leave it quite out; since there is not perhaps any one thing that hath more favoured and strengthened the depraved bent of the mind toward *atheism*, than the use of that general confused term.

Hyl. Well but, Philonous, since I am content to give up the notion of an unthinking substance exterior to the mind, I think you ought not to deny me the privilege of using the word *matter* as I please, and annexing it to a collection of sensible qualities subsisting only in the mind. I freely own there is no other substance in a strict sense, than *spirit*. But I have been so long accustomed to the term *matter*, that I know not how to part with it. To say, there is no *matter* in the world, is still shocking to me. Whereas to say, there is no *matter*, if by that term be meant an unthinking substance exist- ing without the mind; but if by matter is meant some sen- sible thing, whose existence consists in being perceived, then there is *matter :* this distinction gives it quite another turn : and men will come into your notions with small difficulty, when they are proposed in that manner. For after all, the controversy about matter, in the strict acceptation of it, lies altogether between you and the philosophers, whose principles, I acknowledge, are not near so natural, or so agreeable to the common sense of mankind, and holy scripture, as yours. There is nothing we either desire or shun, but as it makes, or is appre- hended to make some part of our happiness or misery. But what hath happiness or misery, joy or grief, pleasure or pain, to do with absolute existence, or with unknown entities, abstracted from all relation to us? It is evident, things regard us only as they are pleasing or displeasing : and they can please or displease only so far forth as they are perceived. Further therefore we are not concerned ; and thus far you leave things as you found them. Yet still there is something new in this doctrine. It is plain, I do not now think with the philosophers, nor yet altogether with the vulgar. I would know how the case stands in that respect : precisely, what you have added to, or altered in my former notions.

Phil. I do not pretend to be a setter-up of *new notions*. My endeavours tend only to unite and place in a clearer light that truth, which was before shared between the vulgar and the philosophers : the former being of opinion, that *those things they immediately per-ceive are the real things:* and the latter, that *the things immediately perceived are ideas which exist only in the mind.* Which two notions put together, do in effect constitute the substance of what I advance.

Hyl. I have been a long time distrusting my senses; methought I saw things by a dim light, and through false glasses. Now the glasses are removed, and a new light breaks in upon my understanding. I am clearly convinced that I see things in their native forms; and am no longer in pain about their unknown natures or absolute existence. This is the state I find myself in at present: though indeed the course that brought me to it I do not yet thoroughly comprehend. You set out upon the same principles that Academics, Cartesians, and the like sects, usually do; and for a long time it looked as if you were advancing their philosophical scepticism; but in the end your conclusions are directly opposite to theirs.

Phil. You see, Hylas, the water of yonder fountain, how it is forced upwards, in a round column, to a certain height; at which it breaks and falls back into the basin from whence it rose: its ascent, as well as descent, proceeding from the same uniform law or prin-ciple of *gravitation.* Just so, the same principles which at first view lead to scepticism, pursued to a certain point, bring men back to common sense.

EVERYMAN'S LIBRARY: A Selected List

BIOGRAPHY

HISTORY

POETRY AND DRAMA